CAMPUS CRIME: LEGAL, SOCIAL, AND POLICY PERSPECTIVES

CAMPUS CRIME: LEGAL, SOCIAL, AND POLICY PERSPECTIVES

By

BONNIE S. FISHER
University of Cincinnati

and

JOHN J. SLOAN, III
University of Alabama—Birmingham

CHARLES C THOMAS · PUBLISHER
Springfield • Illinois • U.S.A.

Published and Distributed Throughout the World by

CHARLES C THOMAS • PUBLISHER
2600 South First Street
Springfield, Illinois 62794-9265

© *1995 by* CHARLES C THOMAS • PUBLISHER

ISBN 0-398-05939-X (cloth)
ISBN 0-398-05956-X (paper)

Library of Congress Catalog Card Number: 94-36429

Printed in the United States of America
SC-R-3

Library of Congress Cataloging-in-Publication Data

Fisher, Bonnie, 1959–
    Campus crime : legal, social, and policy perspectives / by Bonnie
S. Fisher and John J. Sloan, III.
        p.   cm.
    Includes bibliographical references and index.
    ISBN 0-398-05939-X
    1. College students—Crimes against—United States.
    2. Universities and colleges—Security measures—United States.
    3. Campus police—Legal status, laws, etc.—United States.
    I. Sloan, John J.   II. Title.
HV6250.4.S78F57   1995
378.1'88—dc20   94-36429
                                                                              CIP

To Caroline, my parents and my family, and to JoAnn
with thanks for the training

J.J.S.

To Nick and my family

B.S.F.

ABOUT THE CONTRIBUTORS

Joanne Belknap is an Associate Professor at the University of Cincinnati and received her Ph.D. in Criminal Justice from Michigan State University. Her research examines women as victims, offenders, and workers in the criminal processing system. Dr. Belknap is currently finishing work on her book, *The Invisible Woman: Gender, Crime, and Justice,* to be published by Wadsworth.

Patricia L. Brantingham is Professor of Criminology at Simon Fraser University. She holds a B.A. and M.A. in theoretical mathematics and the M.S.P. and Ph.D. in Urban Planning. From 1985 to 1988 she was Director of Programme Evaluation at the Department of Justice Canada. She is one of the founders of the modern field of environmental criminology. Dr. Brantingham is the author or editor of two dozen books and scientific monographs and more than 100 scientific articles and papers.

Paul J. Brantingham is Professor of Criminology at Simon Fraser University. A lawyer and criminologist by training, he is a member of the California Bar. From 1985 through 1987 he was Director of Special Reviews at the Public Service Commission of Canada. His books include *Patterns in Crime, Environmental Criminology,* and *Juvenile Justice Philosophy.*

Max L. Bromley, Ed.D., is currently Associate Director of University Police and Adjunct Instructor of Criminology at the University of South Florida. In 1986, he was recognized by the International Association of Campus Law Enforcement Administrators for his publication *Departmental Self-Study: A Guide for Campus Law Enforcement Administrators* which has been used at over 1,000 post-secondary institutions. He is coauthor of *Hospital and College Security Liability, College Crime Prevention and Personal Safety Awareness,* and *Crime and Justice in America.*

Francis T. Cullen is a Distinguished Research Professor of Criminal Justice and Sociology at the University of Cincinnati. He is author of

Rethinking Crime and Deviance Theory and coauthor of *Reaffirming Rehabilitation, Corporate Crime Under Attack, Criminological Theory,* and *Criminology.* He is a past President of the Academy of Criminal Justice Sciences.

Edna Erez is Professor of Criminal Justice Studies at Kent State University. She holds a law degree from Hebrew University of Jerusalem and Ph.D. in Sociology from the University of Pennsylvania. Dr. Erez has many publications in the areas of victimology, women in crime and justice, law and society and comparative criminology. She is currently the editor of *Justice Quarterly.*

Adriana Fernandez is currently a doctoral student in the School of Criminal Justice at the University of Albany. She is also a Research Associate for the Consortium for Higher Education Campus Crime Research (CHECCR). Her primary interests are the study of crime on campus, victimization, and the relationship between race/ethnicity and crime as they relate to campus and community crime. Her dissertation will study factors that contribute to crime on campus.

Bonnie Fisher is an Assistant Professor of Political Science and a Research Fellow at the Behavioral Sciences Laboratory at the University of Cincinnati. Currently, she is analyzing victimization data from a national sample of students at four-year post-secondary institutions. Her current research focuses on crime and fear of victimization on campuses, and the evaluation of the effectiveness of campus crime prevention and fear reduction programs. Her recent work has appeared in *Crime and Delinquency,* the *Journal of Criminal Justice,* and the *Journal of Security Administration.*

Michael C. Griffaton is currently a Staff Attorney with the Ohio Legislative Service Commission, Columbus, Ohio. He received his J.D. (*magna cum laude*) from Case Western Reserve University in Cleveland, Ohio. His research interests include Criminal and Constitutional Law, particularly the First Amendment. His recent work has appeared in the *Case Western Reserve Law Review.*

Mark M. Lanier is currently an Assistant Professor at the University of Central Florida. He received his Ph.D. from the School of Criminal Justice at Michigan State University. His primary research interests are AIDS/HIV and proactive policing activities. His work has been published in *The American Journal of Public Health, Criminal Justice and Behavior,*

Journal of Criminal Justice, and *Women and Criminal Justice.* Currently, he is evaluating the effects of community policing on officers working in Chicago Public Housing projects.

Edward J. Latessa is Professor and Head of the Criminal Justice Department at the University of Cincinnati. He received his Ph.D. in 1979 from Ohio State University. He has written extensively on correctional policy and treatment and on evaluation research. He is coauthor of *Probation and Parole in America, Introduction to Criminal Justice Research Methods,* and *Statistical Applications in Criminal Justice,* and is a past President of the Academy of Criminal Justice Sciences.

Alan J. Lizotte is a Professor in the School of Criminal Justice and is Director of the Consortium of Higher Education Campus Crime Research (CHECCR) at the University at Albany. His research interests include patterns of firearm ownership and use, campus crime and victimization, and juvenile delinquency. Professor Lizotte is coprincipal investigator of the Rochester Youth Development Study, a multiwave panel study designed to examine the development of delinquent behavior and drug use among adolescents.

Kenneth J. Peak is currently Professor of Criminal Justice at the University of Nevada-Reno, where he was Acting Director of Public Safety. He has published more than 30 book chapters and journal articles and two books, *Policing America: Methods, Issues, and Challenges* and *Justice Administration: Police Courts, and Corrections Management.* Dr. Peak has extensive experience with law enforcement and criminal justice planning, having been Director of University Police at Pittsburg State and Director of a four-state Technical Assistance Institute (for LEAA). He also worked as a municipal police officer.

Jayne Seagrave is a Ph.D. candidate at Simon Fraser University. She has worked as a principal researcher in the Home Office Research Unit in England and as Director of Research for the Manchester Police. Her current research interests include patterns of crime on university campuses and the application of modern organization theory to the study of police operations.

Magnus J. Seng is an Associate Professor in the Department of Criminal Justice at Loyola University of Chicago. He received his doctorate from the University of Chicago in 1970 and worked for county and state criminal justice agencies before joining the Loyola faculty in 1981. He has published many articles on crime and evaluation issues and most recently has written a series of articles and papers relating to campus crime.

John J. Sloan III is currently an Associate Professor of Criminal Justice and Sociology at the University of Alabama-Birmingham. He received his Ph.D. in Sociology in 1987 from Purdue University. His recent work explores campus crime, campus law enforcement, and fear of crime. His articles have been published in *Crime and Delinquency, Social Forces,* and the *Journal of Criminal Justice.*

Deborah L. Wilkins is currently pursuing a Master's Degree in Criminal Justice at the University of Alabama-Birmingham. Her research interests include crime and fear of crime on college campuses, and campus policing. Her thesis research involves a time-series analysis of "hot spots" of crime on a university campus.

John D. Wooldredge is an Associate Professor of Criminal Justice and Director of Graduate Studies at the University of Cincinnati. His current research involves an analysis of individual-level and aggregate-level influences on victimization likelihoods of correctional facility inmates in Ohio. His recent work has appeared in the *Journal of Quantitative Criminology, Justice Quarterly, Crime and Delinquency,* and the *Journal of Criminal Justice.*

PREFACE

*C*ampus Crime: Legal, Social and Policy Perspectives examines the legal, social and policy contexts of crime and security issues on college and university campuses. Each of the book's chapters addresses a specific issue, presents original research bearing on the issue, and discusses the policy implications of this research. Instead of compiling a collection of "journal-type" articles which might have limited appeal, we have targeted the book to a general audience of students, academicians, practitioners, and college administrators. We have compiled chapters from criminologists, political scientists, sociologists, planners, lawyers, security experts, and practitioners.

Each of the chapters introduces the reader to issues about specific campus crime topics. Second, each chapter introduces the reader to research findings on these issues. Finally, each chapter presents the policy implications of the research. Thus, we designed the volume to be a collection of essays on campus crime issues, research, and the policy implications of this research.

The first section, Part I, presents a collection of three essays addressing the legal context of campus crime and security. The three chapters acquaint the reader with (1) the major areas of liability confronting colleges and universities whose students have been crime victims, (2) the strengths and the weaknesses of the Student Right-to-Know and Campus Security Act of 1990, and (3) recent state-level legislation designed to require colleges and universities to report their campus crime statistics, security policies, and related information.

Part II examines the social context of campus crime. The five chapters in this section examine (1) the relationship between campus crime and community crime, (2) the relationship between university faculty victimization, individual demographics and routine activities, (3) fear of crime and actual crime at a Canadian university, (4) the victimization of women on college campuses, and (5) perceived risk and fear of victimization among students, faculty, and staff at an urban university.

Part III examines security issues on campus. The chapters examine (1) the complex web of forces affecting the ways college administrators address security issues on campus and uses a case study of one school in Florida to illustrate these forces, (2) the professionalization of campus law enforcement, and (3) the application of community-based policing on college and university campuses.

In the Postscript, we suggest future directions for campus crime research. Here, we review some of the major questions about campus crime still in need of answers and relate these to policymaking decisions by administrators.

This book could be used as a supplementary text in advanced undergraduate and graduate courses in criminology, criminal justice, or higher education. More importantly, the book should provide useful and timely information on a variety of campus crime topics to both academic researchers and campus officials.

B.S.F.
J.J.S.

ACKNOWLEDGMENTS

We thank our editor, Michael Payne Thomas, for his help and guidance in putting together this volume. We also thank our contributors for producing high-quality chapters and for adhering to our deadlines. Their enthusiasm for the project and dedicated efforts give us hope for the future of research in this important area.

John Sloan thanks Caroline for her unending support and patience. He also thanks Dr. Charles A. Lindquist, Chair of the Department of Criminal Justice at UAB, for his encouragement, his colleagues for their understanding and support, and Jennifer Chamblee for her word processing assistance.

Bonnie S. Fisher thanks Nick for his limitless patience and encouragement, and her colleagues for their guidance and support. Many thanks to her students who provided ideas and insight into campus crime.

Both editors contributed equally to the completion of this volume. Ordering of their names was randomly selected.

CONTENTS

CAMPUS CRIME: LEGAL, SOCIAL, AND POLICY PERSPECTIVES

Chapter 1

CAMPUS CRIME: LEGAL, SOCIAL, AND POLICY CONTEXTS

JOHN J. SLOAN, III AND BONNIE S. FISHER

INTRODUCTION

The tranquil and serene campus, the place set aside for intellectual pursuits, seems an unlikely setting for fear and crime (Smith, 1988). Perceived risk of victimization, fear of victimization, campus crime and security, however, have become matters of growing concern among college students, their parents, faculty, staff, administrators, and elected officials in the United States and Canada. For many years, the reality of campus crime was hidden, passed off as youthful pranks, or held up as idiosyncratic events. More recently, however, celebrated cases have caused the media to cast a spotlight on campuses in the United States and to portray the campus as a dangerous environment: professors slain at Stanford University and the University of Iowa, a professor kidnapped at the University of Cincinnati, and students killed in shooting, hazing, and stalking incidents. Canadian colleges and universities have also experienced similar sensational criminal incidents: an office shooting spree that wounded and killed administrators, faculty, and staff at Concordia University in Montreal, and mass killings of students at the University of Montreal (Brantingham, Brantingham and Seagrave, 1995).

These violent cases are rare events. However, "official campus crimes" —crimes known to the campus police—in the U.S. reveal that property crimes, particularly thefts and larcenies, are quite prevalent on campuses (Fernandez & Lizotte, 1995; Sloan, 1994). Sex offenses, forcible and nonforcible, although not the most prevalent crime on campus according to official crime statistics, are among the utmost concern to colleges and universities given the nature of these crimes and their devastating effects on the victim (Belknap & Erez, 1995).

These growing crime concerns coupled with lawsuits by campus crime victims against colleges and universities stimulated statutory interven-

3

tions by some state legislatures and the U.S. Congress. In 1990, after grassroots campaigns spearheaded by the parents of Jeanne Cleary, who was murdered in 1986 while she slept in her dorm room at Lehigh University in Pennsylvania, and congressional hearings where witnesses recounted the problems of crime and security at college and university campuses, congress passed the "Student-Right-To-Know and Campus Security Act" (20 USC 1092), hereafter referred to as the "Campus Security Act." The Campus Security Act authorized the U.S. Department of Education to oversee the administration of the legislation.

The Campus Security Act was aimed at getting colleges and universities to finally "break the wall of silence" surrounding campus crime. This legislation requires post-secondary institutions receiving federal financial aid funds to annually publish and distribute statistics on the number of murders, sex offenses, robberies, aggravated assaults, burglaries and motor vehicle thefts when the crimes were committed on campus property and reported to campus police or security. These institutions must also report the number of on-campus arrests for liquor law and drug abuse violations, and weapons possessions. Finally, they must also disseminate information on crime prevention policies (Seng, 1995).

Fourteen state legislatures have also passed legislation that imposes stricter campus crime reporting mandates on post-secondary institutions than the mandates found in the Campus Security Act; these state-level initiatives include civil and criminal penalties as well as the loss of state financial aid for institutional failure to comply with the legislation (Griffaton, 1995). Brantingham, Brantingham and Seagrave (1995) note that there is presently no systematic collection of information about campus crime in Canada like the federal and state mandates in the United States.

Before federal and state legislation mandated otherwise, some post-secondary institutions voluntarily reported their crime statistics known to the police to the FBI's *Uniform Crime Reports.* However, less than 20% of *all* post-secondary institutions reported their statistics, and fewer have done so each year since reporting began in 1972. Further, some scholars argue that the FBI's campus crime data are incomplete, inconsistent, and inaccurate (Fisher & Sloan, 1993; Seng & Koehler, 1993).

Although the passage of the Campus Security Act and state-level campus crime reporting legislation has partially improved the *availability* of some campus crime statistics in the U.S., concern about campus crime and security remain newsworthy. For example, *The Chronicle of Higher*

Education, devoted two cover stories during 1994 to reporting campus crime statistics and to disclosing the disturbing possibility that people on campus are not only carrying books but packing guns. The *Chronicle* has followed up with reports in virtually every issue on campus crimes across the nation. The *Chronicle* has also published stories about the concerns of faculty, students, and parents about crime and lax securing on campuses, and stories about administrators faced with increased lawsuits and legal liability for criminal victimization and their attempts to enhance campus security (see Lederman, 1993, 1994a, 1994b). As Smith (1988) describes it, many people no longer view college campuses as ivy-covered, tree-lined islands of tranquility but as dangerous places.

Besides the newsworthy appeal of campus crime and the growing concerns voiced by various interest groups, little is understood about campus crime and fear, especially their prevalence and causes. This situation is partly because of a lack of good data on campus crime. The available campus crime data are drawn largely from official sources—crimes reported to the police—and do not (necessarily) reflect crimes unreported to officials (i.e., campus police or security). While not without value, this statistical information is mostly descriptive and tells little about crimes not officially known by the police. It is commonly thought, for example, that many cases of sexual assault and date rape are not reported on college campuses (Belknap & Erez, 1995). But nonreporting of criminal victimizations extends to virtually every form of crime that occurs on campuses. In fact, studies in society generally indicate that as many as two-thirds of all victimizations are not reported to the police (Biderman & Lynch, 1991).

These official mandated data leave many salient legal and research questions unanswered and, therefore, many policy issues have not been fully addressed. Only in the last few years have legal experts, criminologists, sociologists, political scientists, and planners begun to rigorously examine issues like campus victimization, perceived risk and fear of victimization on campus, campus security, and crime prevention. As a result, research on crime and fear of victimization on U.S. or Canadian campuses is very limited.

In this chapter, we present a picture of the current landscape of the legal, social, and policy issues surrounding campus crime and security. We preview some of the major issues covered by the chapters to follow, the important questions raised and answered by each chapter, and what we see as possible future trends in campus crime research.

THE LEGAL CONTEXT OF CAMPUS CRIME

Recent court rulings, as well as congressional and state legislative action, have caused the legal context of campus crime and security to continue to develop and expand. Generally, this context involves separate, but related, arenas: the judicial and the legislative. In the former, campus crime policy is shaped by precedent-setting court decisions holding institutions liable for foreseeable victimizations on their campuses. In the latter area, federal and state legislative mandates are requiring colleges and universities to report and disseminate information about crime on their campuses. In the following discussion, we review developments in these areas.

The Judicial Arena: Institutional Liability

Only recently have campus crime victims begun to sue their institutions for injuries received during criminal victimization incidents. Smith (1995) describes that the late 1970s saw the first of these lawsuits, but their impact was not felt until the early 1980s. By the end of the 1980s, litigation of this type became increasingly frequent, partly because plaintiffs were winning their suits against colleges and universities. By 1990, college and universities across the country were responding to these lawsuits, or to the threats posed by them, by upgrading security and warning students, faculty members and staff about crimes occurring on campus.

As Smith (1988, 1992, 1995) has reported, two general areas of claims by student victims have emerged. The first claim involves the institution owing them a legal *duty to warn* of known risks of victimization. The second claim involves students arguing that colleges and universities have a *duty to provide them with reasonable security protection.* Recent court decisions have established both duties; however, the decisions have been narrow in focus. The courts have *NOT* ruled institutions owe these legal duties to the public or others with whom the institution does not have a "special relationship." Thus, the courts have limited institutional duties to warn and to provide reasonable security to individuals or groups with whom the institution has a special relationship, specifically, employees, students, and those on campus at the behest of the institution (i.e., invitees).

Two legal theories appear to have guided the courts in these decisions.

The first is a theory of negligence, and the second is a theory of contract. Under a negligence theory, for an institution to be held liable the plaintiff must prove the crime was "foreseeable," and if the crime was foreseeable, the institution failed to provide reasonable security procedures to protect potential victims. Plaintiffs' cases have proved "foreseeability" by providing evidence either of previous crimes in the area (e.g., a "history of crime") or of the existence of other dangerous factors (e.g., college policies allowing male guests to stay overnight in female students' dorm rooms). Establishing reasonable security protection is more difficult; generally, this determination is decided, in part, once the foreseeability issue is settled. In other words, given the foreseeability of the crime, what steps (if any) were taken by the university to reduce the likelihood of victimization?

A more interesting situation arises when, though no duty is imposed under a negligence theory, an institution *creates a duty* by "promising" students (or others) to protect them from victimization. Pledges of this type may be found in college catalogs or campus housing contracts (e.g., where a university says its residence halls are locked at night). Given these circumstances, in effect, the courts may construe a promise of security to be a *contract* between the institution (the seller) and the individual (the buyer) and a failure to provide the protection may constitute a breach of contract.

Because post-secondary liability for campus victimization is an emerging area of the law, campus administrators and policymakers must keep abreast of developments in the area. Administrators wishing to avoid liability, negative publicity, and the risk of institutional assets and reputations have much to lose by failing to closely monitor the legal context of campus crime.

The Legislative Arena: Campus Security Acts

The *legislative* component of the legal context of campus crime involves federal- and state-level initiatives, some of which supplement court rulings on institutional liability, while others require colleges and universities to "come clean" on how much crime occurs on campus and what they are doing about it. Griffaton (1995) notes that while there is variation in the specifics of state and federal legislation, there is a common goal of the legislation: to increase awareness about, and discussion of, crime on campus. As post-secondary institutions are required by state and federal legislation to prepare, publish, and distribute reports about crime and security, students and other interested parties may finally gain some insight into what is going on around them. Additionally, armed with this information, members of the campus community can begin to take steps to help prevent criminal victimizations from occurring on campus. Thus, on the positive side, the legislation should encourage campus discussion about crime and violence and what to do about it.

However, these laws are not panaceas, and Seng (1995) and Griffaton (1995) argue that several problems exist with them, especially the Campus Security Act. They argue one problem with the laws is their requirement to disseminate information only on crimes *reported* to the campus police or security authorities. Obviously, these figures will be affected by the extent people are willing to report their on-campus victimizations to the police. Additionally, some of the laws do not require reporting a comprehensive list of property offenses, which research shows is the predominant form of crime on campus (see Fernandez & Lizotte, 1995; Sloan, 1993, 1994; Bromely, 1993; Mansour & Sloan, 1992). By failing to require the reporting of common property offenses like larceny/theft and auto burglary, incomplete information is distributed. Even more importantly, the information that is distributed is skewed because it includes only the most serious (yet rare) forms of violent and property crimes.

Additionally, few pieces of legislation require the reporting of crime *rates,* that is, the number of offenses per some population figure (e.g., the number of full-time students, or total faculty members, staff and students at the institution). Reporting raw numbers of offenses creates misperceptions since there is no baseline for comparison with other institutions. These numbers might be used inappropriately to describe one school as "rife" with crime, while another school would be described as "safe" in terms of its crime figures (see Brantingham, Brantingham & Seagrave, 1995).

In summary, the legislative arena is somewhat broader in scope than the judicial. Campus crime and security legislation attempts to address two major areas of concern: securing and publishing campus crime statistics and informing the public about university and college crime prevention policies. There are, however, problems with the legislation. For example, federal legislation fails to require the reporting of crime figures for common offenses like theft. Additionally, it does not require colleges and universities to evaluate crime prevention programs, merely report their existence. State-level initiatives suffer similar flaws. As a result of these problems, the impact of this legislation on both campus crime and campus crime policy may be seriously hampered.

THE SOCIAL CONTEXT

For our purposes, the social context of campus crime refers to social scientific research which attempts to describe or to explain the phenomenon. However, the volume of research in the area is not as large as one might think. Despite recent interest with campus crime, perceived risk and fear of victimization, and related topics, few published studies have examined these phenomena (see Fisher, 1992, 1993).

Generally, the published research literature on campus crime can be divided into two categories: studies which *describe* the extent and nature of campus crime and perceived risk and fear of victimization, and studies which *explain* the correlates and causes of campus crime, or perceived risk and fear of victimization.

Descriptive studies *describe* the amount of crime on a campus, victimization rates, or the extent of perceived risk and fear among students, faculty members and staff. Using statistics gathered from a variety of sources (e.g., victims, official records, or the FBI's *Uniform Crime Reports*), research in this area typically describes (1) the extent of victimization among a sample of students at one or more campuses (e.g., the proportion of women who were victims of date rape), (2) the extent and nature of official levels of crime on one or more campuses (i.e., how much violent crime or property crime there is), (3) how institutional-level characteristics or characteristics of the students may be related to rates of campus crime, or (4) the levels of fear and perceived risk and the correlates of risk and fear. Because these studies are purely descriptive, they cannot answer questions about the possible *causal* forces at work resulting in campus crime or high levels of risk or fear of victimization.

Explanatory studies attempt to *model* (using sophisticated multivariate analyses) the possible of campus crime, perceived risk and fear. Using existing criminological theories (e.g., ecological theory or routine activities theory), these studies model the causal ordering of theoretically appropriate variables to explain campus crime. This research, because it is theoretically driven, uses theoretically relevant constructs and measures, involves sophisticated multivariate analyses, and clarifies relationships among sets of causally related variables.

Both types of studies are found in the present volume. For example, some of the studies describe, while others explain or model, (1) the relationship between community crime rates and campus crime rates, (2) victimization patterns among faculty members at an urban university, (3) crime and fear of crime at a suburban university campus in Canada, and (4) perceived risk and fear of victimization among faculty members, staff, and students at an urban university in the Southeast.

Each of these chapters emphasizes the *social* context of the college campus as an important component of campus crime research. Each of the studies uses existing theory and research developed in other contexts and applies them to the campus context. Each of the studies is an example of current campus crime research. Most important, each lays a foundation for *future* theoretically and empirically driven research on campus crime.

THE SECURITY CONTEXT

The final context involves controlling campus crime, what we call the "security and police context." This context includes examining the role and the function of campus police (and campus security), as well as security issues on campus (e.g., crime prevention programs and services).

In considering security issues, campus administrators confront the problem of providing a safe campus while, at the same time, allowing public access to it. As Bromley (1995) describes it, administrators face the challenge of *simultaneously* allowing the freedom of movement required in the pursuit of academic endeavors, yet providing reasonably safe grounds and facilities.

As part of this dilemma, administrators confront the problems associated with the scheduling of classes, permitting access to campus buildings, and establishing security standards for campus grounds and the physical design of buildings. Also important is the decision whether to use a campus police department or to contract out for services from a private security agency. Finally, administrators must make decisions about which crime prevention services and programs to offer on their campuses, if for no other reason than to satisfy legislative mandates like those found in the Student Right-to-Know and Campus Security Act of 1990.

General Security Issues

Campus security is a major issue that confronts campus administrators and policymakers. Security decisions affect campus life, including class scheduling, building construction or renovation, building access, and even access to the campus itself. According to Bromley (1995), many national-level higher education organizations have developed security guidelines for campus policymakers. In 1984, for example, in Massachusetts, the Association of Independent Colleges and Universities (AICU) published a set of "reasonable" security standards for all post-secondary institutions in the state. A year later, the American Council on Education (ACE) also published a report outlining guidelines for achieving reasonable campus security. Other organizations (e.g., the National Association of College and University Business Officers, the National Association of Student Personal Administrators) have followed suit.

Several security issues confront administrators at post-secondary institutions (see Bromley, 1995; Fisher & Sloan, 1993). First, providing security for students attending at night is an important consideration. Assuming most campuses have night classes, the administrator confronts the following questions: Where should most classes be scheduled? Is it possible to provide additional security during the evening hours? Should there be an escort service available to those attending classes at night? If so, during what hours should the service be available? Should the service include escorts to off-campus locations?

Second, access to campus facilities is a major security issue. Campus policymakers must balance the need to protect students, staff, and faculty with the need for the campus to be accessible (including odd hours of day and night). Additionally, because the courts have held institutions liable for campus victimizations, some of which involved activities by people who were campus "outsiders," access to campus buildings is extremely important. As Bromley (1995) describes it, administrators must strike a balance between allowing open access to campus and its facilities (dormitories, laboratories, and offices), and prohibiting individuals from interfering with the normal educational process and routines occurring on campus.

Campus administrators must also consider the impact on security of new building construction, or the renovation of existing structures. Establishing a "crime impact" plan for proposed facilities or major renovation projects is one approach some administrators have taken.

This type of review is similar to that done for fire safety reviews and can be accomplished through cooperation between security experts, architects and engineers, and campus planners.

In a related vein, campus planners can benefit from an understanding of the relationship between crime and physical design (Brantingham, Brantingham & Seagrave, 1995). Campus areas with overgrown foliage or trees, poor lighting, or limited escape routes for potential victims should be carefully reviewed and changes made to reduce the likelihood of "targeting" these areas by prospective offenders.

Finally, campus policymakers need to address the issue of crime prevention programs (e.g., rape awareness education) or services (e.g., "blue light" emergency phones strategically placed around the campus) available at their campuses.

These are but some of the areas of concern when it comes to making security policy. These policies must reflect the interests of not only the administrator but also the community being served. Additionally, as Bromley (1995) points out, these decisions are influenced by both political (e.g., legislative) and economic (e.g., costs and benefits) factors. Campus administrators responsible for these decisions must bear in mind that campus security is a *comprehensive* issue that touches all parts of campus life. Approaching campus security as a collective effort that involves campus police/security forces, student groups, and representatives from faculty and staff groups, brings together the campus community to address its concerns and allows multiple resources to be brought to bear on the problem.

Policing Issues

Since the 1960s, police departments have become fundamental parts of campus security at many colleges and universities in this country. During this time, there has been a fundamental shift in both the characteristics of the officers and in the police organizations found on campus. These shifts have strong implications for the security context of campus crime.

As Peak (1995) argues, one of the key problems confronting campus police agencies in this country is a basic issue of identity. Campus officers may often feel they are "second-rate cops" because they must wear three hats: police officer, security guard, and "door-shaker." Wearing "three hats," in turn, creates a possible image problem for campus officers. Are they real police officers in the minds of members of the campus community?

An apparent response to the "image" problem has been for many campus police departments to try and "professionalize" their image. This response is accomplished by requiring training of campus officers which parallels that received by municipal police officers, by equipping officers with all manner of accoutrements (e.g., side arm, walkie-talkie, Mace, handcuffs, baton), and by enhancing the minimum standards for the job. There is also the fact that, recently, some campus departments have sought and been awarded national accreditation by the same agency that awards accreditation to municipal police departments.

Further, the organization and administration of campus law enforcement agencies parallels that found in municipal police departments. Many campus police agencies are organized hierarchically using a paramilitary rank structure. Additionally, a high degree of specialization is also found in many departments (e.g., use of detectives, K-9 squad, mounted or bike patrol officers, and community service officers). Additionally, a recent and significant trend has been the experimentation by various campus police departments with different "models" of policing involving "community-based or problem-oriented policing" (Lanier, 1995).

Finally, although not the norm, officers at some campus police agencies have jurisdiction on *and* off campus. For example, Sloan (1992a) found that officers at the University of Kentucky had statewide jurisdiction on any property owned by the university. He also found officers at a number of institutions in the South and Midwest could respond to calls involving crimes occurring off campus (e.g., a robbery in progress or an assist-officer call). This indicates that in many departments, officers are deputized and have jurisdiction that extends beyond campus boundaries.

Thus, there is mounting evidence that many campus law enforcement agencies are transforming themselves into mirror images of local police departments. In doing so, these departments have sought to transform the image of their officers from "door-shakers" to "professional law enforcers."

However, campus administrators must be mindful of some potential problems with this transformation. For example, it is simply not clear that campus police *need* to transform themselves into "traditional" police agencies. The mandate for campus officers is NOT necessarily the same as the mandate for municipal police officers. For example, as Jackson (1992) has argued, the mandate for municipal law enforcement is *solely* the control of crime (through response, deterrence, and apprehension). On the other hand, the mandate for campus police is varied and includes law enforcement, disciplinary action, ensuring campus order, preventing crime and reactive policing.

Perhaps even more important than a different mandate is the relationship between the community and the police. In a municipal setting, that relationship has traditionally been one in which the police (more often than not) are passive: they simply *respond* to calls for service. On a college campus, however, the relationship between the community and the campus police is different. Here, the police are more active, are involved in policymaking, and share with the community the responsibility for reducing crime and maintaining order.

As campus administrators, directors of campus security, and chiefs of campus police departments consider the specific role and function of campus law enforcement agencies, they should be aware of the differences between the role and the function of local police departments and the role and function of campus police. To ignore these differences could invite some of the same problems involving police-community relations that many local police departments confront.

THE POLICY CONTEXT

Finally, many college and university administrators have begun to respond to the court decisions, legal mandates and concerns voiced by various interest groups. Several contributors to this volume note different types of crime prevention and rape education programs or security procedures have been established and note that some campuses are developing and instituting new strategies, or making changes in existing crime or security policies.

The many-faceted nature of campus crime, perceived risk and fear of victimization, combined with variety in campus settings, has led campus administrators to develop different responses. Many campuses have taken prevention measures including upgrading lighting around buildings and parking lots and offering escort services or frequent shuttles between the campus and satellite parking lots. Some campuses have also addressed safety and security in terms of the physical landscape by minimizing shrubbery. Some campuses have incorporated standards for the interior and exterior of design buildings. For example, some campuses require crime-impact statements for existing buildings when changes are proposed for an existing building or when new building construction is considered.

Campuses have also responded to crime and safety concerns by sponsoring educational and awareness programs. Many campuses now require students, especially freshman and transfer students, to attend a crime-awareness seminar that focuses on issues such as sexual assault, burglary, crime prevention and self-defense classes. Others offer crime prevention programs for faculty and staff.

Bromley (1995), Lanier (1995) and Peak (1995) point out that some universities and colleges have made procedural changes in their public safety departments. Some have hired more officers; others have changed how officers handle crime and related problems on campus. Still others have initiated foot patrols or the use of police dogs (Lederman, 1993). Some campuses have picked more high-tech responses; they have enhanced security by installing target-hardening devices (e.g., computerized card-entry systems) in dormitories, class and office buildings.

Despite the implementation of new programs or procedures or changes to current ones, there are several issues within the policy context that need to be addressed. First, the nature and prevalence of crime, perceived risk and fear of victimization need to be more fully understood before *any* programs or procedures should be developed or established. This means campus policymakers must *understand* the problem of crime, risk and fear by using multiple data sources. As noted in this chapter and in other chapters in this volume, official crime statistics have limitations and caution should be exercised when using official data. They should not be used as the sole source of information when making policy and procedure decisions. Some of the research presented in this volume used an alternative method to gather their data: victizmization surveys. As these authors show, surveys can be used to obtain information from faculty, staff and students about victimization and reporting history, perceptions of risk and fear, fear spots (exact locations where individuals perceive danger though criminal incidents may not have been recorded by the police), and perceptions and attitudes about the police and effectiveness of crime prevention and safety programs and security procedures. This information can be used to better understand crime and perceptions about crime on campus and in the development of institutional-level responses.

The development and implementation of policies and procedures are only two parts in the policy context. If we are to understand "what works" in terms of reducing risk, fear and crime on campuses, evaluation of changes or new programs or procedures should also be done and be done properly. By properly, we mean at minimum designing an evaluation that documents the process of implementing change or creating new programs by collecting data before and after the changes are instituted (Cook & Campbell, 1979). Both process and impact need to be examined as well as the use of a rigorous evaluation design. Campuses may vary in size and location, but they are settings where evaluation of process and impact are quite manageable. The use of a rigorous evaluation design is imperative to understanding "what works" (Rosenbaum, 1986). Without rigorous evaluations, there is no way of accurately identifying safety problems or security needs, developing programs of policies or making changes to address problems and needs, or determining the success of the respective program or policies. Campus administrators may never know "what works" and, as a result, are held liable by the courts or receive negative feedback from students and their parents.

As an example of taking a multifaceted approach to campus crime policy, we are involved with a university in the Southeast which is conducting a large-scale research project to help campus administrators make rational policy decisions about campus crime. The two-year project involves a quasi-experimental design. During the first year of the project, data were collected from a sample of faculty, staff, and students on their victimization patterns, fear and perceived risk of victimization, and attitudes about crime and security policy. Additionally, lighting and physical design features of the campus were reviewed. Data on police calls for service were also collected and "hot spots" of crime identified.

At the end of the first year, lighting was upgraded, shrubbery and trees were trimmed (to reduce hiding places), "fear spots" on campus were identified, and new programs created to reduce fear and perceived risk of victimization, as well as "opening the books" on campus crime. For example, a "campus watch" was developed (similar to a neighborhood watch program), a campus escort service was created, campus officers began using bicycles to patrol the campus, and the student newspaper began publishing crime reports.

The second year of the project involves evaluating the results of the changes. Data from the same sample of faculty, staff, and students were collected (although additional information was collected) and the results will be used to adjust the programs as necessary.

The approach taken by administrators at this university illustrates interdepartmental cooperation in designing, implementing, and evaluating campus crime policy. Multiple departments on campus (e.g., campus police, planning, vice-president for administration, and maintenance) are involved in the project. Each department can make a valuable contribution to administrations as part of the policymaking process.

CONCLUSION

Campus crime may be explored from any number of perspectives because it exists in many contexts. The legal context of campus crime is shaped by judicial precedent and legislative action. Its social context is shaped by the results of social scientific research designed to describe or to explain the "reality" of campus crime. The security context of campus crime involves decisions as simple as whether to allow students open access to dormitories after midnight, to complex decisions about the potential crime impact of a new building. Finally, the policy context involves those stages of a process whereby officials first recognize campus crime as a problem, develop plans to address the problem, and implement the plans. At the same time, campus administrators ultimately are responsible for policy success for failure, for it is they who are responsible for creating the policy.

For many years, crime and violence on college campuses were the "dirty little secret" of higher education. There would be occasional whispers about the tragedy of a campus rape or an assault, but no real effort was made to find out how much of it was going on, to understand the mechanisms at work generating it, or to do something about it. Members of post-secondary institutions have only recently begun to focus on campus crime. This shift has been brought about by mandates from state and federal courts and legislatures, by media pressures, and by the concerns of students and their parents.

Because so little research has been done in the area, many questions remain, some of which are basic: How much crime is there on campus? What is the nature of campus crime? What policies and procedures are "reasonable" efforts to address crime on campus? What is unique about crime in campus setting?

As campus policymakers struggle to address the concerns of students, staff, and faculty, they must keep in mind that the policies they make should be based on reasonable information. This volume offers a starting place.

REFERENCES

Biderman, A.B. and J.P. Lynch (1991) *Understanding Crime Incidence Statistics.* New York: Springer-Verlag.

Belknap, J. and E. Erez (1995) "The Victimization of Women on College Campuses: Courtship Violence, Date Rape, and Sexual Harassment." In B.S. Fisher and J.J. Sloan, III (eds.) *Campus Crime: Legal, Social and Policy Perspectives.* Springfield, IL: Charles C Thomas.

Bromley, M. (1995) "Securing the Campus: Political and Economic Factors Affecting Decision Makers." In B.S. Fisher and J.J. Sloan, III (eds.) *Campus Crime: Legal, Social and Policy Perspectives.* Springfield, IL: Charles C Thomas.

—— (1993) "Campus and Community Crime Rate Comparisons." *Journal of Security Administration 15*(2):49–64.

Brantingham, P., P. Brantingham and J. Seagrave (1995) "Crime and Fear of Crime at a Canadian University." In B.S. Fisher and J.J. Sloan, III (eds.) *Campus Crime: Legal, Social and Policy Perspectives.* Springfield, IL: Charles C Thomas.

Cook, T. and D.T. Campbell (1989) *Quasi-Experimentation: Design and Analysis Issues for Field Settings.* Chicago: Rand McNally.

Fernandez, A. and A.J. Lizotte (1995) "An Analysis of the Relationship Between Community Crime and Campus Crime: Reciprocal Effects?" In B.S. Fisher and J.J. Sloan, III (eds.) *Campus Crime: Legal, Social and Policy Perspectives.* Springfield, IL: Charles C Thomas.

Fisher, B. (1993) "Editorial." *Journal of Security Administration 16*(1): 1–4.

—— (1992) "Editorial". *Journal of Security Administration 15*(2): 1–4.

Fisher, B.S. and J.J. Sloan (1993) "University Responses to the Campus Security Act of 1990: Evaluating Programs Designed to Reduce Campus Crime." *Journal of Security Administration, 16*(1):67–79.

Griffaton, M.C. (1995) "State-Level Initiatives and Campus Crime." In B.S. Fisher and J.J. Sloan, III (eds.) *Campus Crime: Legal, Social and Policy Perspectives.* Springfield, IL: Charles C Thomas.

Jackson, E. (1992) "Campus Police Embrace Community-Based Approach." *The Police Chief 59*(12):63–64.

Lanier, M.M. (1995) "Community Policing on University Campuses: Tradition, Practice, and Outlook." In B.S. Fisher and J.J. Sloan, III (eds.) *Campus Crime: Legal, Social and Policy Perspectives.* Springfield, IL: Charles C Thomas.

Lederman, D. (1994b) "Weapons on Campus?: Officials Warn That Colleges Are Not Immune From the Scourge of Handguns." *The Chronicle of Higher Education,* March 9, pp. A33–A35.

—— (1994a) "Crime on the Campuses: Increases Reported in Robberies and Assaults; Colleges Remain Confused Over Federal Law." *The Chronicle of Higher Education,* February 2, pp. A31–A41.

—— (1993) "Colleges Report 7,500 Violent Crimes on Their Campuses in First Annual Statements Required Under Federal Law." *The Chronicle of Higher Education,* January 20, pp. A32–A42.

Mansour, N. and J.J. Sloan (1992) "Campus Crime and Campus Communities:

Theoretical and Empirical Linkages." Paper Presented at the 1992 Annual Meetings of the Academy of Criminal Justice Sciences, Pittsburgh.

Peak, K.J. (1995) "The Professionalization of Campus Law Enforcement: Comparing Campus and Municipal Police Agencies." In B.S. Fisher and J.J. Sloan, III (eds.), *Campus Crime: Legal, Social and Policy Perspectives.* Springfield, IL: Charles C Thomas.

Rosenbaum, D.R. (ed.) (1986) *Community Crime Prevention: Does It Work?* Beverly Hills, CA: Sage.

Seng, M.J. (1995) "The Crime Awareness and Campus Security Act: Some Observations, Critical Comments, and Suggestions." In B.S. Fisher and J.J. Sloan, III (eds.) *Campus Crime: Legal, Social and Policy Perspectives.* Springfield, IL: Charles C Thomas.

Seng, M.J. and N.S. Koehler (1993) "The Crime Awareness and Campus Security Act: A Critical Analysis." *Journal of Crime and Justice 16*(1):97–110.

Sloan, J.J. (1994) "The Correlates of Campus Crime: An Analysis of Crimes Known to Campus Police." *Journal of Criminal Justice 22*(1):51–62.

—— (1992b) "Campus Crime and Campus Communities: An Analysis of Crimes Known to Campus Police and Security." *Journal of Security Administration 15*(2):31–45.

—— (1992a) "The Modern Campus Police: An Analysis of Their Evolution, Structure, and Function." *American Journal of Police 11*(2):85–104.

Smith, M.C. (1995) "Vexatious Victims of Campus Crime." In B.S. Fisher and J.J. Sloan, III (eds.) *Campus Crime: Legal, Social and Policy Perspectives.* Springfield, IL: Charles C Thomas.

—— (1993) "Vexatious Victims of Campus Crime: Student Lawsuits as Impetus for Risk Management." *Journal of Security Administration 15*(2):5–18.

—— (1988) *Coping with Crime on Campus.* New York: MacMillan.

PART I
THE LEGAL CONTEXT OF CAMPUS CRIME

INTRODUCTION TO PART I
THE LEGAL CONTEXT OF CAMPUS CRIME

In 1990, Congress passed the Student Right-to-Know and Campus Security Act in response to concerns about campus crime from students, their parents, victims, and others. State legislatures have passed similar legislation which, generally, asks post-secondary institutions to "open their books" on campus crime by forcing them to publish and disseminate their crime statistics. Further, in recent years, the courts have begun to hold post-secondary institutions liable for victimizations occurring on college campuses. Thus, both the legislative and judicial branches of government have slowly begun to respond to campus crime and to develop policies to address the problem.

In this first part of the book, we present three chapters that address the *legal context* of campus crime. This context involves both judicial and legislative responses to campus crime. Each of the chapters explores these judicial and legislative responses.

Chapter 2, "Vexatious Victims of Campus Crime" by Michael Clay Smith, reviews current law on post-secondary institutional liability for victimizations occurring on campus. The chapter explores the case law in the area and describes various legal theories the courts have used to hold colleges and universities liable for crime victimizations occurring on their campuses.

Chapter 3, "The Crime Awareness and Campus Security Act: Some Observations, Critical Comments, and Suggestions," by Magnus Seng, takes a hard look at the Student Right-to-Know and Campus Security Act. The chapter examines the strengths and the weaknesses of the legislation and offers suggestions for its modification.

We conclude this first section of the book with Michael Griffaton's chapter, "State-Level Initiatives on Campus Crime," which extends the analysis of legislative responses to campus by examining state-level legislation. Griffaton describes the similarities and differences among these statutes and critiques them.

In summary, the first section of the book presents an overview of the major judicial and legislative actions taken in response to campus crime concerns. The chapters also make reasonable suggestions for enhancing the quality of judicial and legislative responses to campus crime.

Chapter 2

VEXATIOUS VICTIMS OF CAMPUS CRIME

MICHAEL CLAY SMITH[1]

INTRODUCTION

Crime has transformed the legal landscape on America's campuses enormously. While violent crime frequently occurs on the campuses of America's institutions of higher education, it is a phenomenon of only the past three decades; campus crime was almost unknown before the 1960s (Smith, 1988). Damage suits brought against their colleges by student crime victims are an even newer phenomena. The first such suits were litigated in the late 1970s, the first to be won by students were decided in the early and mid-1980s, and such litigation became routine only in the late 1980s (Smith, 1989). By 1990, colleges and universities across the country were upgrading security and improving their crime warnings to students (Kalette, 1990). This sequence suggests that such lawsuits—or, more accurately, the threats posed by them—are a force behind today's campus crime control efforts.

It is widely recognized by legal scholars that damage suits serve as quality control devices within industry. The threat of tort liability can turn businesses away from myopic concern with dollar costs, toward normative values of social responsibility (Malloy, 1990). As a result, suits by injured customers or consumers have led to changes in products, services, and practices. This may be particularly true with industries that do not effectively regulate themselves and are not subject to real external policing—factors often present with industries that have grown exponentially and quickly. The areas of medical malpractice and consumer product safety offer examples; it is claimed that both health care delivery practices (Cartwright, 1975) and the production and marketing of consumer products (Galanter, 1986) have been made safer because of the adoption of risk-management strategies. There may be a corollary in campus security.

The higher education industry has undergone enormous growth in recent years. Between 1960 and 1990, the number of students pursuing higher education in the United States more than tripled, increasing from 4 million to about 14 million people, and the number of institutions increased from about 2,000 to more than 3,500 (Digest of Education Statistics, 1991). With this dramatic growth, all the problems of the parent society—including crime and violence—found their way onto the nation's campuses. Until the recent intervention of some state legislatures and the federal Congress—in 1989 and 1990—to compel colleges to publish their campus crime statistics, most institutions handled campus crime problems with no outside regulation or oversight.

Until 1979, American jurisprudence was devoid of any reported appellate case in which the courts held a college or university liable for damages to a student injured by crime on campus. But times have changed. During the 1980s, many campus crime victims around the country sued their institutions, and precedents imposing liability on colleges and universities, under various circumstances, are now well settled.

THEORIES OF LIABILITY

A look at the theories of liability advanced by the student-victim litigants may be useful. An examination of the duties students have claimed their institutions owed them, but failed to meet, and the treatment of these claims by the courts, should be especially helpful to institutions as they develop risk-management strategies.

The student victim suits can be lumped into four general types of claimed duty. These are (1) a duty to warn about known risks, (2) a duty to provide adequate security protection, (3) a duty to screen other students and employees for dangers, and (4) a duty to control student conduct. Both legislative actions and court decisions now firmly impose a strong duty on colleges and universities regarding the first category. The courts have established some duty in regard to the second category, but limited in circumstances and extent. On the other hand, to date no duty has been connected with the latter two categories.

It must also be noted that, where such a duty may be owed, the duty is not owed to everyone; it is owed only to those persons with whom an institution has what the law calls a "special relationship." For a college or university, this relationship clearly exists regarding its students and others who come onto the campus at the institution's behest, as its business "invitees." Thus, where a college operated a day-care center and a woman was abducted from a college parking lot when she went there to leave her child, the court held the college owed her no duty of security protection because she was not a student at the institution and was merely using the parking lot out of convenience (*Figueroa v. Evangelical Covenant Church,* 1989).

DUTY TO WARN OF KNOWN RISKS

On-Campus Risks

The seminal case in the campus crime liability field was *Duarte v. State,* a 1979 decision by a California appellate court which held that campus administrators must be honest when inquiries are made about campus safety. The suit was brought by the mother of a female student who was raped and murdered in her dormitory room at California State University in San Diego. The mother alleged that, before enrolling her daughter, she had inquired of university personnel about crime and safety on the campus and was not told of known prior crimes. The California Court of Appeals held that the university's action, if proven, would support a suit against the school for misrepresentation and deceit.

That case was followed five years later by *Peterson v. San Francisco Community College District,* a 1984 decision of the California Supreme Court which held that a college was liable to a student injured in a rape attempt because the college had failed to give her a timely warning of known risks. The facts were these: the student was assaulted by an assailant who jumped from behind thick foliage along a parking lot stairway. It turned out that the college had known of recent, prior attacks at the same location. Although the college had stepped up security patrols after the earlier attacks, the incidents had not been publicized.

While the *Duarte* case had established the duty of college officials to be forthcoming when asked about known risks, the *Peterson* case went beyond that to impose a positive duty on the institution to warn potential victims of foreseeable risks, though nobody had asked. Still, there was a widespread perception that some college officials were, at worst, covering up crimes and, at best, being lukewarm about efforts to warn. Howard and Constance Clery, whose 19-year-old daughter, Jeanne, was raped, sodomized, slashed and strangled in her dormitory room at Lehigh University in 1986, launched a relentless crusade to publicize campus crimes and pressed a $25 million lawsuit against Lehigh (Hanchette, 1988). In 1989, *USA TODAY* editorialized that colleges should be required to "open the books" on campus crime. The publication charged that "most" colleges conceal crime information to "protect their images" and the "privacy" of the students involved ("Open the Books," 1989).

By 1990, the legislatures of eight states had passed statutes requiring colleges to make crime statistics available, and in November, 1990, Congress superseded the state legislation and passed the Student Right-to-Know and Campus Security Act (see Seng, 1995; Griffaton, 1995). This far-reaching law requires every college and university receiving federal funds to report, annually, their crime statistics and other data about security operations to all current and prospective students and employees.

Warning of Off-Campus Risks

The federal and state disclosure laws, as well as the *Duarte* and *Peterson* cases, deal only with risks within the geographical boundaries of institutional campuses. What of known risks off campus? The law is not clear in this regard, but liability may inure in some future situations, and prudent administrators should consider the possibilities.

The recent case of *Hartman v. Bethany College* addressed this question. Heather Hartman, a 17-year-old female freshman at Bethany, went to a bar near the college, Bubba's Bison Inn, where she illegally drank alcoholic beverages with two men—not students—whom she met there. Later, she went with the men to the home of one of them, where both sexually assaulted her. She sued the college, alleging she should have been warned of the dangers of going to the bar. Noting that there was no evidence that Bethany was aware of any prior incidents similar to the assault on Heather Hartman, District Judge Stamp ruled that the college had no obligation to warn students of dangers in their non-curricular activities when the school neither supported nor condoned such activities.

In other cases, however, the circumstances could be quite different and a different holding could result. What of possible cases in which a college might be aware of a history of prior untoward incidents at a particular place or location and be aware that students—especially young freshman, away from home for the first time—frequent the place? An additional aggravating circumstance might be found if the college in question does not have adequate facilities to house or provide social activities for all its students and must rely on the area or facility in question to accommodate student needs. Several campus legal experts have predicted that courts may yet impose liability in some such circumstances (Kalette, 1990). A news service recently reported that a jury had awarded $1.6 million to a student raped at an off-campus dormitory operated in Los Angeles by the University of Southern California. The suit was based, at least in part, on a claim that the university had concealed information about crime in the neighborhood ("Rape Victim," 1992).

DUTY TO PROVIDE ADEQUATE SECURITY PROTECTION

The law imputes to colleges and universities not only a duty to warn but a duty to provide reasonably adequate security protection. This duty may arise in two ways: either under a "negligence" theory based upon tort law or upon a breach of contract theory based upon some assurance that the institution has given as to protection or safety.

Security protection, of course, takes many forms. Locks, lights, fences, police officers and security guards, the trim or elimination of shrubbery and other hiding places, and monitoring systems are among the first level of consideration. But of equal importance, in some circumstances, are modifications to programs and architecture so classes, research and other regular activities are not required in remote or lonely places and that residence halls, cafeterias, libraries, and parking lots are safely accessible and constantly watched.

Negligence Theories

Once a school is on notice of the "foreseeability" of criminal harm because of a history of criminal incidents at a location, the institution has not only a duty to warn but also a duty to use due care to provide reasonably adequate security protection. How much is reasonably adequate? The answer must be determined by the facts and circumstances of each individual case, given the history and location of the place, and other pertinent risk data. If it comes to a lawsuit, the ultimate answer to whether particular efforts were sufficient will lie with the decision of the jury.

The leading case illustrating the need for adequate security measures is *Miller v. State of New York* (1984), a decision of New York's highest court. The case involved a 19-year-old junior at the State University of

New York at Stony Brook confronted in the laundry room of her residence hall at 6 o'clock one morning by an intruder armed with a large butcher knife. He blindfolded her and marched her, at knife point, through an unlocked outer door of the dormitory basement, back into another unlocked door of the building, and then upstairs to a third-floor room where she was raped twice under threat of mutilation or death if she made noise. The man then led her back downstairs and outside to a parking lot. He fled and was never identified.

In court the victim showed that before her attack, strangers had been common in dormitory hallways, and there had been reports to campus security of men being in the women's bathroom. The student herself had twice complained to dormitory supervisors about nonresidents loitering in the building. The campus newspaper had published accounts of many crimes in the dormitories at the school, including armed robbery, burglaries, trespass, and another rape. Even so, all 10 dormitory doors were admittedly kept unlocked.

The court held that the college was in essence a landlord and owed the same duty any landlord owed a tenant: the premises must be kept in a "reasonably safe condition," which included a duty to maintain "minimal security measures" against foreseeable dangers. Failure to lock the doors breached that duty, the court ruled. An award of $400,000 to the student was upheld.

Foreseeability need not be based upon a history of campus crimes. Other sorts of dangers may suffice. In *Mullins v. Pine Manor College* (1983), the highest court of Massachusetts addressed a crime much like that in *Miller*, but took a different posture as to the foreseeability issue. Lisa Mullins was awakened in her dormitory room in the early morning hours by a male intruder who placed a pillowcase over her head and, with threats, marched her out of her dormitory, across the campus to the refectory, back outside, then back into the refectory where he raped her. He, too, fled and was never identified. The whole episode lasted from 60 to 90 minutes, and the pair was outside for at least 20 minutes.

Prior known criminal offenses on the Pine Manor campus were minimal. However, the court held that the jury was justified in finding foreseeability based upon, among others, the proximity of the campus to transportation lines leading to downtown Boston and on college policies allowing men to stay overnight in women's dormitories. The court noted that the college had itself acknowledged the danger of crime in its orientation program for new students. The evidence presented at trial showed the dormitory locks could readily be opened with credit cards or knives, that fences around the campus were inadequate and gates were left unlocked, and although two guards were on night duty, there was no system to ensure they were actually patrolling—a critical point because the attack had lasted so long without detection. The court left standing the jury's award of $175,000 against the college's vice-president for operations— whose duty it was to oversee security operations—though the $175,000 verdict against the college was reduced to $20,000 because of a Massachusetts law which limits liability of charitable, nonprofit institutions.

Adequacy of police protection has been the central issue in several cases. Recognizing the Pandora's box that could be opened, the courts have been hesitant to impose any duty to guarantee, through policing, that crime does not occur. The tone was set several years ago by the U.S. Supreme Court, in the landmark case of *DeShaney v. Winnebago County Dept. of Social Servs.* (1989), which held that the due process clause does not impose an affirmative obligation upon government to ensure that citizens are not harmed through the wrongful acts of other private citizens. Campus police cases have, generally, taken the same tack. In *Klobuchar v. Purdue University* (1990), the Indiana Court of Appeals reiterated that the police duty is one owed to the public and does not give an individual grounds to sue based on failure to protect from crime. Likewise, the Appeals Court of Massachusetts, in the recent case of *Robinson v. Commonwealth* (1992), cited *Winnebago* in holding that a failure of police protection will not generally constitute a deprivation of the civil rights of someone injured by a criminal.

On the other hand, if the threat is individualized enough and a concrete security action evident, a duty may arise. In *Jesik v. Maricopa Community College* (1980), the Arizona Supreme Court indicated that, under an Arizona statute imposing upon colleges a duty to use reasonable care to protect students, a duty to provide police protection could arise in some circumstances. The case involved a campus argument that led to a shooting. The victim, Peter Jesik, had become involved in a violent argument with another student during college registration, and after the other student threatened to go home to get a gun to kill Jesik, Jesik reported the threat to a college security guard and received assurances of help and protection. The other student did later return with a briefcase. The guard talked to the student but did not look into the briefcase. After the guard departed, the student pulled a gun out of the case and shot Jesik to death. The Arizona high court ruled that an issue of fact was presented and remanded the case for trial.

Contractual Theories

Though tort law may impart no duty to provide adequate protection in a given situation, it is possible that a college or university could create its own duty if it were to give assurance to its students—in catalogs, brochures, housing contracts or the like—that it will protect them. In a recent case the Supreme Court of Georgia was cautious about such a claim. The court said that if a college is to be held liable in that way, the assurance would have to be clearly expressed in the document in question and not just implied. The court declined to find any such implied duty just because a college's housing policy agreement contained rules which said they were intended to protect the security of dormitory residents (*Savannah College of Art and Design, Inc. v. Roe*, 1991).

One federal case has, however, indicated that assurances about security practices given in university publications might constitute a valid breach of contract claim if they could be proven. The case is *Nieswand v. Cornell University* (1988), brought by the parents of a female first-year student who was fatally shot, along with her roommate, in their residence hall room by the roommate's disgruntled suitor. The parents argued that leaflets and brochures sent to prospective students by Cornell gave assurances of security. Specifically, they alleged, two publications stated that residence halls were kept locked at night. This allegation was pertinent, because the killer—armed with a rifle—had gained entrance to the residence hall when it was supposed to be locked. The university had responded in the suit alleging that the victim herself had propped open the dormitory doors. After the federal district court ruled that the matter should be decided by a jury, the university settled the claim for $200,000 (Parents of Slain Student, 1989).

Duty to Protect Off-Campus

Does the duty of protection extend off-campus? Apparently not, at least under existing law. The sole appellate case to thus far address the issue of college duty is *Donnell v. California Western School of Law* (1988), in which a California Court of Appeals declined to extend a college's duty of protection to off-campus property, even though it immediately adjoined the campus and was necessarily used by students. The case arose when an unidentified robber stabbed a law student as he walked back to his car after studying late in the law library. The law school occupied one city block in San Diego, and the attack occurred on the public sidewalk which ran along the side of the building. The school provided no parking, and students had to park on adjacent city streets. Though there had been previous criminal attacks in the area, the school provided neither lighting nor security patrols on the sidewalk. The court held that because the school did not own the sidewalk, it could not control it and concomitantly owed no duty to protect its students on it.

Donnell may not be the last word on this issue, however. A contrary holding was made by a federal appeals court in New Orleans in an almost identical case that involved a hotel guest and not a college student. In that case, a man was slain by a street robber as he stood on a city sidewalk, outside the hotel's doors but under an overhang that was actually part of the hotel. The court said the hotel owed the man, its invitee, a duty of protection from foreseeable criminal assault in that location (*Banks v. Hyatt Corp.*, 1984). Important to the holding was the implication that the hotel could easily have extended some protection to the location; although the hotel did not hold actual title to the real estate, the site was integral to its operations.

DUTY TO SCREEN STUDENTS AND EMPLOYEES

Do colleges have a duty to screen those coming onto campus to discover dangerous persons? The only case to date addressing the question, *Eiseman v. State of New York* (1987), grew out of an experimental program at the State University College at Buffalo that was designed to provide college opportunities for disadvantaged persons. One such applicant was a convict in the state penitentiary. After being admitted, he was invited to an off-campus party by unsuspecting students. At the party, the parolee went on a bloody spree of murder and rape which left two other students dead and one maimed. In the aftermath, it was learned that the parolee had a long and ugly history of heroin abuse, violent attacks on others, and two penitentiary sentences. Though they had known he was incarcerated when he applied for admission, college officials had made no effort to learn whether he might pose a risk to the college community.

The trial jury awarded more than $360,000 to the family of one of the slain students, and the award was upheld by the intermediate courts.

New York's highest court ultimately overturned the verdict, however, declaring that because the parole board—the "experts"—had decided the man was ready for society, the college could not be expected to do better. While this decision has left colleges, at least in New York, with no duty to screen admittees, it cannot be certain that other courts will reach the same conclusion in later cases, particularly when colleges are knowingly dealing with criminals.

Similar issues surround campus employees—particularly those who will have master keys or access to dormitories or other places where students may be especially vulnerable. No such campus cases have yet reached the appellate courts, but liability has been imposed in cases involving other sorts of commercial landlords. Under the doctrine of *respondent superior,* an employer is generally liable for the acts of his employee incidental to the class of acts the person was hired to perform, and an employer might also be liable for negligence in hiring, retaining, or assigning a dangerous employee.

Cases involving security guards—whose roles are analogous to many campus security and housing employees—illustrate the principle of negligent hiring. Several courts have held that an employer of security personnel has a duty to use reasonable care in hiring to discover the unfitness of such employees. In a case where an apartment tenant was raped by the apartment complex's security guard, the Illinois Court of Appeals held that the landlord was negligent in failing to conduct a reasonable and adequate investigation before hiring the man (*Easley v. Apollo Detective Agency,* 1979). In a similar case, the Illinois Supreme Court held that a failure to properly control the distribution of master keys, and failure to take reasonable precautions to prevent unauthorized entries by persons possessing those keys, could result in landlord liability (*Rowe v. State Bank,* 1988).

Accordingly, the prudent institutional employer will take steps to screen potential hirees for criminal backgrounds, and colleges should, within parameters of local law, ask potential students whether they have felony records. If they do, further inquiry could be made into the safety issue and, if indicated, in consultation with campus counsel, steps could be taken to keep the person from the campus community.

DUTY TO CONTROL STUDENT CONDUCT

Students commit most campus crime (Smith & Smith, 1990). The control of student conduct, then, is pertinent to campus crime liability issues. Must a college or university control its students? Happily for most administrators, the answer is no.

The sole case raising the theory that colleges must control crime by their students, or pay the bill, is *Smith v. Day* (1987). The case grew out of off-campus actions of Kenneth Day, a student at Norwich University, a military school. Day fired a rifle into a passing railroad train, wounding two members of the train crew. Day was sent to jail for one year as a result of the shooting, and the wounded men, looking for a pocket deeper than Day's, sued the university. They alleged that because Day was a member of the Corps of Cadets and his actions violated university rules, the university should pay the bill for his actions. The Vermont Supreme Court held that the university owed no duty of care running to the wounded men, who were not connected with the university, and opined that it is "unrealistic to expect the Modern American College to control the actions of its students."

CONCLUSION

Crime has altered much on the face of America in recent years. It has changed the way people live, work, play, and even study. It has given birth to a new category of concerns for college and university students, their parents, and institutional administrators.

Clearly, American courts are receptive to the plight of students injured by crime and are willing to till new legal ground to find remedies for victims and encourage campus crime control. This chapter's purpose has been to provide an exposition of representative leading cases in the field and explore their role as incentives for risk management.

Clearly, campus administrators must be aware of their duty to be forthcoming about foreseeable crime risks and must take steps to assure that security protection is adequate, measured against those risks. In addition, they must be cautious about the assurances they give relating to security protection; promises not delivered upon may well increase institutional liability beyond that imputed by general law.

The new federal statute requiring disclosure of campus crime statistics—the Student Right-to-Know and Campus Security Act—may be expected to increase student awareness of crime problems. It will surely increase the awareness of campus administrators, because it elevates campus crime to a marketing issue; an institution's image is all important in the sometimes fierce competition for students and dollars. In the short term, the act may increase the numbers of student suits; over time, however, it will surely ameliorate campus crime risks as more and better resources are directed toward the problem.

In a closing note, it is important to remember that many—and perhaps most—crime liability claims asserted against colleges and universities are won by the institutions. The numbers are uncertain because there is no way to tabulate how many claims are settled before going to court or the number of cases that end at the trial court level, whether by judgment or settlement. In any event, the reported appellate opinions reveal that colleges win many such cases because the court found (1) the risk was not foreseeable, or (2) the risk was foreseeable, but the institution took adequate steps to warn and protect, or (3) regardless of liability issues, the institution or defendant was immune from suit because of sovereign or charitable immunity principles, which vary greatly from state to state.

NOTES

(1) Portions of this chapter were originally published in the *Journal of Security Administration, 16*(1):5–18 (June, 1993). We thank Norman Bottom, Editor, for permission to reprint excerpts from the original article.

REFERENCES

Cartwright, R.E. (1975) "The Cure and the Prevention." *Trial 11*(3):2.
Galanter, M. (1986) "The Day After the Litigation Explosion." *Maryland Law Review 46:*1–39.
Griffaton, M. (1995) "State-Level Initiatives and Campus Crime." In B.S. Fisher and J.J. Sloan, III (eds.) *Campus Crime: Legal, Social and Policy Perspectives.* Springfield, IL: Charles C Thomas.
Hanchette, J. (1988) *Hattiesburg American,* October 6, p. 1.
Kalette, D. (1990a) "Colleges Confront Liability." *USA TODAY,* September 14, p. 6A.
—— (1990b) "Violent Crime No Stranger on Campuses." *USA TODAY,* November 29, pp. 1A–2A.
Malloy, R.P. (1990) *Law and Economics.* St. Paul, MN: West Publishing Co.
"Open the Books on Campus Crime." (1989) *USA TODAY,* November 13, p. 10A.

"Parents of Slain Student Settle Suit Against Cornell." (1989) *The Chronicle of Higher Education,* September 28, p.A2.

"Rape Victim Awarded $1.6 million, USC to Pay." (1992) *The Sun-Herald,* March 27, p.A4.

Seng, M.J. (1995) "The Crime Awareness and Campus Security Act: Some Observations, Critical Comments and Recommendations." In B.S. Fisher and J.J. Sloan, III (eds.) *Campus Crime: Legal, Social and Policy Perspectives.* Springfield, IL: Charles C Thomas.

Smith, M.C. and M.D. Smith (1990) *Wide Awake: A Guide to Safe Campus Living in the 90s.* Princeton, NJ: Peterson's Guides.

Smith, M.C. (1989) "Institutional Liability Resulting from Campus Crime: An Analysis of Theories of Recovery." *Education Law Reporter 55:*361–368.

—— (1988) *Coping With Crime on Campus.* New York: Macmillan.

United States Department of Education (1991) *Digest of Education Statistics.* Washington, DC: U.S. Department of Education.

Cases and Statutes Cited

Banks v. Hyatt Corp. 722 F.2d 214 (1984).

DeShaney v. Winnebago County Dept. of Social Servs., 489 U.S. 189 (1989)

Donnell v. California Western School of Law, 200 Cal. App. 3d 715, 246 Cal. Rptr. 199 (4 Dist. 1988).

Duarte v. State, 88 Cal. App. 3d 473, 151 Cal. Rptr. 727 (Cal. App. 1979).

Easley v. Apollo Detective Agency, Inc., 387 N.E.2d 1241 (Ill. App. 1979).

Eiseman v. State of New York, 70 N.Y.2d 175, 518 N.Y.S.2d 608, 511 N.E.2d 1128 (1987).

Figueroa v. Evangelical Covenant Church d/b/a North Park College, 879 F.2d 1427 (7th Cir. 1989).

Hartman v. Bethany College, 778 F.Supp. 286 (N.D.W.Va. 1991).

Jesik v. Maricopa Community College, 125 Ariz. 543, 611 P.2d 547 (1980).

Klobuchar v. Purdue University, 553 N.E.2d 169 (Ind. App. 4 Dist. 1990).

Miller v. State of New York, 62 N.Y.2d 506, 478 N.Y.S.2d 829, 467 N.E.2d 493 (1984); as to damages see 110 A.D.2d 627, 487 N.Y.S.2d 115 (1985).

Mullins v. Pine Manor College, 389 Mass. 47, 449 N.E.2d 331 (1983).

Nieswand v. Cornell University, 692 F. Supp. 1464 (N.D.N.Y. 1988).

Peterson v. San Francisco Community College District, 685 P.2d 1193 (Cal. 1984).

Robinson v. Commonwealth, 584 N.E.2d 636 (Mass. App. Ct. 1992).

Rowe v. State Bank, 531 N.E.2d 1358 (Ill. 1988).

Savannah College of Art and Design, Inc. v. Roe, 409 S.E.2d 848 (Ga. 1990).

Smith v. Day, 148 Vt. 595, 538 A.2d 157 (1987).

Student Right-to-Know and Campus Security Act, Public Law No. 101-542 (1990); amended by Public Law No. 102-26, Sec. 10(e) (1991); 20 U.S.C. 1092(f).

Chapter 3

THE CRIME AWARENESS AND CAMPUS SECURITY ACT: SOME OBSERVATIONS, CRITICAL COMMENTS, AND SUGGESTIONS

MAGNUS J. SENG

INTRODUCTION

In November, 1990, President Bush signed the Crime Awareness and Campus Security Act. Its primary objective was to require post-secondary educational institutions which receive federal funds to report crime statistics and security procedures annually to the Department of Education. Such reports were also to receive wide distribution to the campus community and to prospective employees, students and their parents. The Crime Awareness and Campus Security Act (hereafter, the Act) had its genesis in the increased public concern about crime on college and university campuses following extensive media coverage of rape-related homicides at universities in Pennsylvania and Florida. The Act was heralded as a significant step toward addressing the problem of crime on our nation's college and university campuses. It took effect September 1, 1991, and the first reports were due a year later in September, 1992. Published commentaries (e.g., Seng & Koehler, 1993) on this legislation observe that the Act is useful because it encourages colleges and universities to openly address the campus crime problem. Major criticism of the legislation points to serious deficiencies in the crime-reporting requirements of the law (see Seng & Koehler, 1993; Lederman, 1993; Burd, 1992). This chapter critiques the major provisions of the Act and expands critical observations I have made elsewhere (Seng & Koehler, 1993). My observations are supplemented by data from a convenience sample of first-year security reports from four colleges and universities. These data lend support to my view that current crime-reporting requirements of the Act create a misleading picture of the extent of crime on campus. As a result, the Act has the potential to further confuse the issue of how much crime occurs on college campuses. I conclude my discussion by offering recommendations for improving the Act, including recommending the abandonment of the crime and violation reporting requirements of the Act.

BASIC PROVISIONS OF THE ACT

The Crime Awareness and Campus Security Act is part of the General Education Provisions Act (20 USC 1092 b) and is found in Title II of the Student Right-to-Know and Campus Security Act. Responsibility for its administration rests with the U.S. Department of Education. Basic provisions of the Act are summarized here; details of the Act's requirements are found in the appendix to the chapter.

The Act requires post-secondary educational institutions which receive federal funds to prepare, publish and distribute an annual report on campus security policies. This report must include a statement of the procedures used by students and others for reporting crimes or other emergencies; a statement about access to campus facilities and student residences; a statement addressing the enforcement authority of security personnel; a description of crime prevention and crime awareness programs; statistics on the number of on-campus murders, sexual offenses, robberies, aggravated assaults, burglaries, and motor vehicle thefts reported to local police and institution officials; and arrest statistics for on-campus alcohol, drug, and weapons violations. In addition, the report must include a statement of policies for monitoring criminal activities at selected off-campus student organizations.

These primary sections of the Act define the nature and scope of the report which must be prepared. Additional sections ask for policy statements about the handling of sexual offense charges, use of alcohol, and enforcement of underage drinking and drug laws. In addition, according to the Act, no special policies, procedures, or practices involving campus crime or campus security are required by the Secretary of Education. The only requirement is preparation of the report.[1]

Finally, the Act defines the term "campus" as including "any building or property owned or controlled by the institution in the same or contiguous geographic area and used by the institution in direct support of . . . educational purposes." "Campus" also includes any building or property owned or controlled by student organizations recognized by the institution. Schools with branch campuses not in a reasonable contiguous geographic area must regard each of them as separate campuses for reporting purposes.

OBSERVATIONS AND CRITIQUE OF THE ACT

A compelling feature of the Act is the likelihood it will live up to its title and increases awareness of crime and security procedures on campus. The annual report required by the Act is to be distributed to students, faculty members, and other employees of the institution; in the short term, at least, the report will no doubt heighten awareness. In the past, crime and campus security issues were usually discussed by the department of student life or similar entities at orientation for first-year students. Additionally, some reference to crime, security precautions and procedures was usually found in the student handbook. At Loyola University of Chicago, for example, for many years crime and security issues were discussed this way. However, with passage of the Act, this information is now presented in a *Safety Bulletin* given to each student at admission. In addition, copies of the *Bulletin* are placed at strategic locations throughout the campus (e.g., dorms, lecture halls, student lounges, and libraries). The *Bulletin* is printed in bright, attractive colors and is thoughtfully laid out so important information is easily found.

In an earlier analysis, I collected similar documents from 10 other colleges and universities as part of a study examining implementation of the Act.[2] While the documents' format varied considerably, all contained a frank recognition of the realities of crime and security at their institution. Recognizing this should make it easier for students to confront these realities. In addition, the Act and the security documents I reviewed emphasized crime prevention.

Besides increased awareness, the Act will lend legitimacy to the open discussion of crime and security on campus. Most colleges and universities located in urban areas have had a well-developed crime awareness program in place for years. Educational institutions located in or near inner-city areas have had to address this issue. The subject was reluctantly addressed, however, because crime and security are not popular public relations issues. Now, because of the Act, campus crime and security may now be openly discussed. As a result, more creative and effective approaches may be developed. Reluctance to address campus crime issues is analogous to society's handling of AIDS and other sexually transmitted diseases. Because we pretended they did not occur or gave only quiet recognition to their existence, preventive measures were given low priority. Once they came to the forefront, addressing these problems became legitimate and was even encouraged. The Crime Awareness and Campus Security Act does the same for crime on campus.

The Act is also likely to contribute to an increased awareness and openness about crime on nonurban campuses. Many colleges and universities are located in peaceful, picturesque small-town settings where crime is a rare occurrence. These institutions are required to prepare the same type of report as their urban counterparts. Even if the number of crimes reported is small, distribution of security reports in these settings can heighten student awareness that crime can occur anywhere and may counteract the false sense of security created by the pristine setting of many educational institutions.

Another possible benefit of the Act is that it calls attention to the institution's security department. This could result in the improvement of the personnel and their level of training. A review of security procedures, a necessary step in the development of the report required by the Act, may highlight the need for revision in security procedures or identify the need to increase the number of security personnel and upgrade their training.

The positive side of the Crime Awareness and Campus Security Act results from requiring educational institutions to prepare, publish and distribute a document describing the institution's security policies and procedures. This should contribute to increased awareness by faculty members, students, and staff of the potential for crime on their campus, the importance of security policies and procedures, and the department on campus charged with instituting the policies.

The most serious deficiency of the Act and the source of most of its criticism centers on section (a)(6) which requires that educational institutions collect and report:

> [S]tatistics concerning the occurrence *on campus* of the following criminal offenses reported to local police agencies and to any official of the institution who has significant responsibility for student and campus activities: (A) murder, (B) sexual offenses, forcible or non-forcible, (C) robbery, (D) aggravated assault, (E) burglary, (F) motor vehicle theft (emphasis added).[3]

The Act's preamble indicates one of the primary goals of the legislation is to provide uniformity and consistency in the reporting of campus crimes. If that goal is to be achieved, the manner in which college crime statistics are gathered and reported must be improved. The most frequently consulted source for these data, the *Uniform Crime Reports,* is incomplete, inconsistent, and inaccurate. These problems arise because few post-secondary institutions regularly report their crime statistics to the FBI. Further, among those reporting, some do so irregularly, reporting in some years but not in others. Finally, data from some of the institutions is clearly inaccurate (see Seng & Koehler, 1993).

On learning of the Act, some observers naively expected that the *Uniform Crime Reports* based campus crime data would be greatly improved.[4] However, improving the caliber of *UCR* campus crime data is unlikely because there is no requirement in the Act that the data be reported to the FBI or to *any* "official" agency outside the university community. The Act only mandates that crime reports should filed at the institution. In section (b)(4), the Act says that "[*At*] *the request of the Secretary,* an institution must submit to the Secretary the statistics required. . . . " (emphasis added). To date, the Secretary of Education has yet to request the data. If the Secretary were to do so, the Act requires him or her only to report the statistics to the House Committee on Education and Labor and the Senate Committee on Labor and Human Resources, not to the Judiciary Committees of the House or the Senate, the Justice Department, or the FBI.

The first report to these Congressional committees is due in 1995. The Policy Section of the Pell Grant Branch of the U.S. Department of Education is responsible for collecting these data; however, a formal procedure to do so has yet to be developed (personal communication with Paula M. Husselmann, U.S. Department of Education).

The lack of improvement in *UCR* campus crime data is further demonstrated by a count of post-secondary educational institutions reporting their crime statistics to the FBI in 1990 (the year before the Act took effect) and 1992 (the year after it took effect). In 1990, 403 universities, colleges, and post-secondary institutions reported their crime statistics in the *UCR.* In 1992, the *UCR* contained reports from 455 institutions, a 13% increase. However, over one-third of the increase (19 schools) came from post-secondary schools in Georgia. Though the number of reporting institutions increased, the number of institutions reporting their crime statistics to the FBI is small compared to the number of institutions listed in the *Higher Education Directory* (Rodenhouse, 1992).

The absence of an "official" report on campus crime, based solely on the requirements of the Act, is a blessing since this report would be incomplete and misleading. The reason is the Act requires statistics be collected on crimes of "most concern" (murder, sexual offenses, robbery, assault, and burglary) but does *not* require that statistics be collected on crimes which occur most frequently and best reflect the legitimate campus crime situation. Although it might be argued that the primary intent of the Act is to only focus on crimes of "high concern," the reports will likely be interpreted as a report on *all* crimes. For example, a recent article in Loyola of Chicago's student newspaper commented on how comparatively few crimes were disclosed in the security bulletin (Gottis, 1993).

Two of the security reports I examined (from Cincinnati and Georgetown) for this chapter clearly indicated their statistics were incomplete. Most notable among the excluded crimes was theft. There is ample evidence, both from the *Uniform Crime Reports* and the campus crime literature, that theft is the most frequently occurring crime on college campuses (Sloan, 1994, 1992; FBI, 1993; Sigler & Koehler, 1993; Bromley, 1992; Bromley & Territo, 1990; Smith, 1988). The absence of theft statistics in the reports renders them useless for gauging the extent of crime on an individual campus. These points are clearly illustrated in Table I, which I developed from data from four universities providing statistics for the Act and other crimes. A completely different picture of crime at these campuses emerges when theft statistics are included.

In reviewing Table I, one is tempted to make comparisons across the universities. However, without data on student, campus, and community variables, these comparisons are meaningless (Wooldredge, Cullen & Latassa, 1992). Too often, we make them anyway. This illustrates another serious problem with the statistical requirements of the Act: it does not require reporting of data on comparative variables. Instead of requiring the reporting of crime *rates* per some population (e.g., the number of reported offenses per 1,000 students), the Act requires the reporting of crime *totals* for each institution. As a result, large institutions (e.g., The Ohio State University) should have more crime than smaller institutions (e.g., Oberlin College) solely because they have more potential victims. Reporting the number of crimes without reference to the number of students (let alone the number of faculty members and staff) is misleading and of little use. Finally, other frequently occurring campus crimes excluded from the Act include criminal damage to property, vandalism, and disorderly conduct.

The absence of complete crime data in the security reports (especially the absence of theft) is a matter of concern to the security personnel with

TABLE I
COMPARISON OF CAMPUS CRIME REPORTS
(WITH AND WITHOUT THEFT)

	Universities			
	Loyola[a] *Chicago*	*Illinois*[b] *Chicago*	*Cincinnati*[c]	*Georgetown*[d]
Security Act Crimes				
Murder	0	0	0	0
Sexual Assault	0	0	0	2
Robbery	0	12	2	2
Aggravated Assault	0	3	34	1
Burglary	1	29	85	14
Motor Vehicle Theft	2	47	5	1
Totals w/o theft:	3	91	126	19
Thefts	199	1057	375	216
Totals w/ theft:	202	1148	501	235

Sources: Loyola and Illinois data provided in separate reports. Cincinnati and Georgetown data contained in Security Act Reports. All data is for 1992 calendar year.
a. Loyola University of Chicago, main and downtown campus data only.
b. University of Illinois at Chicago.
c. East and West campus data, January to July only.
d. Main campus data only.
Universities reported in Table I are those for whom theft data were available.

whom I have communicated. This omission contributed to a belief among the security personnel the reports were of little value for describing campus crime. Although there was a distinct level of pride taken in the production of the security procedures section of the reports, there was a corresponding absence of pride in the statistical data provided.[5]

The disparity between what *should* be reported and what is *required* to be reported has led some institutions to incorporate theft into their data on burglaries or robberies. Lederman (1993), writing in *The Chronicle of Higher Education,* published crime data supplied to The *Chronicle* by over 2,400 colleges (Lederman, 1993). Examination of these data revealed 17 institutions included thefts in their burglary data and 2 institutions included theft as part of their robbery data. The comparatively large count of burglaries reported at other institutions suggests they also may be including thefts with their burglary data. It should be noted, however, that if theft can be counted as burglary, then burglary could be counted as theft and *not* reported. Either way, the exclusion of theft from the list of required offenses dramatically distorts the campus crime picture.

As it is currently written, the Act discourages complete reporting of campus crimes. Because of this problem, institutions which have been open about reporting their crimes could be placed at a disadvantage if they continue this practice; as a result, they could become less open. Institutions which have been *less* open about their crime statistics can continue to do so, confident in the realization they are in compliance with the law.

If observers agreed the Act should focus *only* on serious crimes as it is now written, the Act is not likely to create reliable data on these crimes because it only requires reporting of crimes committed *on campus* and because it is ambiguous in key areas. To limit reporting of crimes only to the areas defined in the Act as part of the campus ignores the realities of campus life, because many students either live or are victimized off campus (Bromley & Territo, 1990). When they are complete, campus crime statistics may reflect the fact that the campus is safer than the surrounding community. In 1992, for example, the University of Illinois at Chicago had an on-campus index crime rate of 5,889 offenses per 100,000 population, while the area surrounding this campus had a rate of 10,832 index offenses per 100,000 population (FBI, 1993; Chicago Police Department, 1993). Although the greater danger lies off campus, on-campus crime rates are affected by crime rates in the surrounding community (Fernandez & Lizotte, 1995; Fox & Hellman, 1985). It is misguided for the Act to emphasize where the crime occurred and not who was victimized. Understanding the dynamics of campus crime comes from studying victims and victimizations and not reported crimes.

Even if there is wisdom in limiting the Act's focus to on-campus crime, it is far from clear about what should and should not be included by the term "campus." One key area of ambiguity is whether fraternities and sororities are included. Section (a)(7) of the Act requires security policies about "monitoring and recording through local police agencies of criminal activity in which students engage at off-campus locations of student organizations recognized by the institution." This quotation is apparently referencing fraternities and sororities, but it is ambiguous. The section requires campus security to monitor the occurrence of criminal activity at these locations but they are not required to include the crimes in their annual report. The ambiguity arises because the Act, in defining the term "campus," includes "any building or property owned or controlled by student organizations recognized by the institution." This suggests the Act considers fraternities and sororities "on campus" and that criminal activity occurring at them should be included in the annual report.

The issue of what constitutes "on campus" was explored by the International Campus Law Enforcement Association (IACLEA) (1992) in a newsletter to its members. It noted the Act was unclear whether public streets in a campus location were included in the definition of "campus." The letter advised its members that the Department of Education's interpretations of the Act indicated these streets are *not* considered "on campus." Ambiguities like this can lead to ridiculous debates over whether a student robbed while crossing a publicly-owned street bisecting a campus was definitely "on the campus." What if he or she was on the sidewalk? What if he or she was in the street when the robbery began but on the sidewalk when it was completed? What if the street parallels the campus? Is the sidewalk on the campus side "on" campus and the other side "off" campus? What if the victim had one foot on the sidewalk and the other on the campus lawn? For institutions with campuses located in business districts (e.g., many law and business schools), "campus crime" is effectively limited only to offenses occurring inside campus buildings.

IACLEA identified additional areas of ambiguity which highlight the Act's deficiencies. For example, while classroom space rented by an institution is "on campus" because the institution is controlling the space, what about "a class taught in a room in a building neither owned nor leased by the school? Does the institution control this space for the duration of the class . . . because a member of the faculty is present?" (IACLEA, 1992). Does the term "property" (used in the definition of campus) "imply only 'real' property or could it include vehicles [like] mobile medical clinics [parked] in various locations in the community?" (IACLEA, 1992). What part of a teaching hospital is a part of the campus? It could be argued that the definition be limited only to those parts of a medical complex devoted to medical school administration, classrooms, and student residences. An equally plausible argument could be made for including the entire medical complex because students receive instruction throughout the complex.

While other ambiguities abound in the Act, a final issue of concern is that the Act's definition of "campus" requires that branch campuses, schools within an institution, or administrative divisions not in a "reasonably contiguous geographic area" must be regarded as separate campuses for reporting purposes. One only need quote the phrase "reasonable contiguous geographic area" to open a bona fide Pandora's box of interpretive possibilities.

Because the Act currently excludes reporting of the most frequently occurring campus crimes and because it is ambiguous in important areas, it is my conclusion the Act fails to contribute either to uniformity or consistency in the reporting of crimes on campus. It will only create confusion.

SOME RECOMMENDATIONS

The above review of the Crime Awareness and Campus Security Act identifies some positive sides of the legislation. These include: (1) the required security report has the potential for increasing awareness about crime on campus, (2) the report focuses on crime prevention, and (3) it may lead to an improvement in, and recognition of, campus security. However, I also described serious flaws with the statistics-reporting section of the Act, especially its failure to include important data and its definitional ambiguities. These observations lead to two primary recommendations:

> (1) The sections of the Act describing and requiring an annual report of campus security policies and procedures be retained; and
> (2) The Act be amended to remove section (a)(6) as to the collection of statistics on campus crime for submission to the Department of Education and to congressional committees.

The first recommendation is offered for the reasons described in the first part of this chapter. I would add one additional comment, however. The requirement that this be an annual report (even if repetitive from year to year) is useful because it forces an annual review of policy and thus avoids complacency.

The second recommendation deserves more extended comment. Some might be tempted to offer suggestions for improving the statistical section of the Act, like requiring the inclusion of more representative offenses, requiring that data be presented as crime rates, and that "off-campus" crimes actually occurring in a clearly defined campus area be included. If these changes were added to the Act, there is no certainty the data would be accurate, complete, and consistent. The collection and reporting of crime data has always been fraught with methodological and interpretive problems (Kempf, 1990; Hindelang, 1974; Black, 1970). Thus, it is unrealistic to expect campus crime statistics would be any better. Additionally, because schools may fear students and their parents will use the reports in selecting colleges or universities, there may be an irresistible temptation for some institutions to be less than complete, accurate, and consistent in reporting their campus crime figures.

The collection and reporting of campus crime data for a nationally disseminated periodic report or for congressional review serves no constructive purpose. The extent and nature of campus crime is related to a host of variables whose relationships, though difficult to describe in a national report, are vital to understanding the issue. These variables include (but are not limited to) the physical design and size of the campus, its location (e.g., urban, rural, suburban, small town), the number of buildings constructed with crime prevention in mind (compared to nineteenth century esthetics), the nature and extent of interaction with the surrounding community, the nature of law enforcement on and around the campus, the demographic makeup of the students, the aptitude of security personnel, and the nature of security policies and procedures.[6] These variables might best be assessed through on-site visits, where crime statistics for a single campus and the surrounding area could be presented and reviewed.

Let me emphasize that I am *not* recommending that campus crime data should not be collected and analyzed. In fact, I strongly encourage its collection. I see no value, however, in either national or statewide dissemination because the inevitable comparisons made across campuses do more harm than good and undermine the process. It could even be argued that removal of the statistics requirement allows excluding crime data from the annual report. While possible, it is likely that more and not less data will be included. A case in point is a comparison of security reports distributed to the campus community at Loyola University of Chicago in 1990 (the year before the Act took effect) and the 1992 report (the first distributed under the Act). The 1990 report contained data on index crimes *including* theft and it reported a comprehensive list of nonindex crimes. The 1992 report was limited to the index crimes required by the Act.

The Crime Awareness and Campus Security Act is a well-intentioned attempt to address a variety of issues related to campus crime. The Act's requirement for the preparation and dissemination of an annual report on security policies and procedures and the requirement that crime prevention programs be identified are especially useful because they are

·likely to increase awareness of the fact and the threat of crime on any campus and perhaps improve security personnel and procedures. The Act's requirements about dissemination of crime statistics are not useful because the statistics are incomplete, misleading, and serve no useful purpose. This requirement should be dropped from the Act.

NOTES

(1) The *Federal Register* (July 10, 1992) notes "The Secretary wishes to emphasize that . . . institutions are free to develop and adopt whatever policies and procedures relating to campus crime and safety they choose."

(2) I requested copies of the most recent report from a small, convenience sample of colleges and universities, selected to illustrate a variety of institutional characteristics (e.g., urban and rural, large and small, public and private, high crime location and low crime location, and four-year and two-year institutions). I refer to these reports throughout the chapter.

(3) Before August 1, 1992, the term, "rape" was to be used. After August 1, 1992, "sexual offenses" were to be classified as forcible or nonforcible to conform with the National Incident-Based Reporting System.

(4) Schmalleger (1993), in his most recent text on criminal justice, makes the same observation, suggesting that my colleagues and I were not alone in this expectation.

(5) I informally talked with security directors and other security personnel when requesting the reports. While such anecdotal data are not generalizable, they are often useful in identifying operational flaws in policy and procedures.

(6) For an inclusive list of campus and security force variables that affect campus crime rates, see Sloan (1994), Bromley (1992), and Bromley and Territo (1990).

REFERENCES

Black, D.J. (1970) "Production of Crime Rates." *American Sociological Review 35*(4): 733–757.

Bromley, M.L. (1992) "Campus and Community Crime Rate Comparisons." *Journal of Security Administration 15*(2):49–64.

Bromley, M.L. and Territo, L. (1990) *College Crime Prevention and Personal Safety Awareness.* Springfield, IL: Charles C Thomas.

Burd, S. (1992) "Colleges Issue Federally Required Reports on Campus Crime Rates." *The Chronicle of Higher Education,* September 2, p.A25.

Chicago Police Department (1993) *Annual Report.* Chicago, IL: Chicago Police Department.

Federal Register (1992), July 10, p.30828.

Fernandez, A. and Lizotte, A.J. (1995) "An Analysis of the Relationship Between

Campus Crime and Community Crime: Reciprocal Effects?" In B.S. Fisher and J.J. Sloan, III (eds.) *Campus Crime: Legal, Social and Policy Perspectives.* Springfield, IL: Charles C Thomas.

Fox, J.A. and Hellman, D.A. (1985) "Location and Other Correlates of Campus Crime." *Journal of Criminal Justice 13*(2):429–444.

Gottis, M. (1993) "Security Reports Low University Crime Rates." *The Loyola Phoenix,* November 3, p. 4.

Hindelang, M.J. (1974) "The Uniform Crime Reports Revisited." *Journal of Criminal Justice 2*(1):1–17.

International Association of Campus Law Enforcement Administrators (1992) *News Letter,* July 23, pp.1–4.

Kempf, K.L. (1990) *Measurement Issues in Criminology.* New York: Springer-Verlag.

Lederman, D.J. (1993) "Colleges Report 7,500 Violent Crimes on Their Campuses in First Annual Statements Required Under Federal Law." *The Chronicle of Higher Education,* January 20, pp. A32–A43.

Rodenhouse, M.P. (ed.) (1992) *Higher Education Directory.* Falls Church, VA: Higher Education Publications.

Schmalleger, F. (1993) *Criminal Justice Today.* Englewood Cliffs, NJ: Prentice-Hall.

Seng, M.J. (1994) "The University's Response to Campus Crime: A Study of Compliance with the Crime Awareness and Campus Security Act." Paper presented at the 1994 Annual Meetings of the Academy of Criminal Justice Sciences.

Seng, M.J. and Koehler, N.S. (1993) "The Crime Awareness and Campus Security Act: A Critical Analysis." *Journal of Crime and Justice 16*(1):97–110.

Sigler, R. and Koehler, N.S. (1993) "Victimization and Crime on Campus." *International Review of Victimology 2*(1):331–343.

Sloan, J.J. (1994) "The Correlates of Campus Crime: An Analysis of Reported Crimes on College and University Campuses." *Journal of Criminal Justice 22*(1):51–61.

—— (1992) "Campus Crime and Campus Communities." *Journal of Security Administration 15*(2):31–48.

Smith, M.C. (1988) *Coping With Crime on Campus.* New York, Macmillan.

U.S. Department of Justice, Federal Bureau of Investigation (1990) *Crime in the United States 1990: The Uniform Crime Reports.* Washington, DC: U.S. Government Printing Office.

—— (1992) *Crime in the United States 1992: The Uniform Crime Reports.* Washington, DC: U.S. Government Printing Office.

Wooldredge, J.D., F.T. Cullen, and E.J. Latassa (1992) "Victimization in the Workplace: A Test of Routine Activities Theory." *Justice Quarterly 9*(4):326–337.

APPENDIX
CRIME AWARENESS AND CAMPUS SECURITY ACT BASIC PROVISIONS[1]

(a) An institution shall by, September 1, 1992, and each year thereafter, prepare, publish, and distribute, through appropriate publications or mailings, an annual security report that contains, at a minimum, the following information:

(1) A statement of current campus policies regarding procedures and facilities for students and others to report criminal actions or other emergencies occurring on campus and policies concerning the institution's response to such reports

(2) A statement of current policies concerning security and access to campus facilities including campus residences

(3) A statement of current policies concerning law enforcement, including:

(i) the enforcement authority of security personnel, including their working relationship with state and local police agencies; and

(ii) policies which encourage the accurate and prompt reporting of all crimes to campus police and the appropriate police agency.

(4) A description of the type and frequency of programs designed to inform students and employees about campus security procedures and to encourage students to be responsible for their own and other's security.

(5) A description of programs designed to inform students and employees about the prevention of crimes,

(6)(i) Statistics concerning the occurrence on campus of the following criminal offenses reported to local police agencies and to any official of the institution who has significant responsibility for student and campus activities:

(A) murder

(B) rape (prior to August 1, 1992) or sex offenses, forcible or nonforcible (on or after August 1, 1992)

(C) robbery

(D) aggravated assault

(E) burglary

(F) motor vehicle theft[2]

---

[1]Provisions of the Act presented here have been edited in the interests of brevity and focus. A complete version of the Act is published in the *Federal Register* (1994) v. 59 (April 29), pp. 2318–22321.

[2]The Act requires that definitions of these offenses conform to those used in the *Uniform Crime Reports.* More recent definitions conform to the National Incident-Based Reporting System.

(7) A statement of policy concerning the monitoring and recording through local police agencies of criminal activity in which students engaged at off-campus locations of student organizations recognized by the institution, including those student organizations with off-campus housing facilities.

(8)(i) Statistics concerning the number of arrests for the following crimes occurring on campus—

(A) liquor-law violations

(B) drug-abuse violations

(C) weapons possessions.

(Sections 9–12 and Appendix not included.)

Chapter 4

STATE-LEVEL INITIATIVES AND CAMPUS CRIME

Michael C. Griffaton

Sunlight's said to be the best of disinfectants.

—Louis Brandeis, 1933

For I must talk of murders, rapes, and massacres, Acts of black night, abominable deeds.
—William Shakespeare, 1594

INTRODUCTION

The 1986 rape and murder of Jeanne Ann Clery in her dormitory room by a fellow student at Lehigh University in Pennsylvania helped unite divergent interests who were insisting more information be released about campus crime and security. Jeanne Ann's parents successfully lobbied their state for the nation's first campus security reporting law—the Pennsylvania College and University Security Information Act of 1988. The succeeding years have witnessed an increasing awareness among students, colleges, and state legislatures of the need for information on the extent of campus crime. As a result, fourteen states have enacted campus security reporting legislation.

This chapter describes and analyzes the three-pronged division campus security reporting laws commonly use: information gathering, information access, and enforcement provisions. Additionally, because the statutes vary in scope and content, the chapter explores common problems among these statutes, including interpreting and reporting statistics and reporting of crimes to the police, and suggests possibilities for improvement. Finally, the chapter explains the importance of campus security reporting laws, describes their implications for campus administrators, and discusses what can be learned from them.

CAMPUS SECURITY LEGISLATION

Pennsylvania's College and University Security Information Act was the nation's first campus security reporting law (Pa. Cons. Stat. Ann., 1992). It requires colleges to compile the type and number of crimes occurring on their campuses and provide information about security procedures to campus community members. With some variation, California, Connecticut, Delaware, Florida, Kansas, Louisiana, Nevada, New York, Tennessee, Virginia, Washington, West Virginia, and Wisconsin have modeled their campus security reporting legislation on the Pennsylvania law. While Massachusetts had also enacted a law identical to Pennsylvania's, it was repealed after passage of the federal Crime Awareness and Campus Security Act of 1990 (Mass. Gen. L., 1992). These statutes, in general, contain three operative sections that specify what information must be compiled, how to distribute the information, and what happens to a college failing to comply with the requirements of the first two sections.

Compiling Campus Crime Information

Most campus security reporting laws require colleges to gather information about their security procedures and crimes occurring on their campuses. Some states mandate that limited information be compiled, while others have more comprehensive requirements.

Campus Crime Statistics

Connecticut's and Pennsylvania's reporting laws require colleges to annually report their campus crime statistics to the state police for publication in the Federal Bureau of Investigation's *Uniform Crime Reports* (Conn. Gen. Stat. Ann., 1993; Pa. Cons. Stat., 1992; U.S. Department of Justice, 1993). The crime statistics must be submitted on forms and in the format prescribed by the state police. In addition, each institution reports crime statistics for the three years immediately preceding the current reporting year.

Like Pennsylvania and Connecticut, Delaware's college security reporting law requires its colleges to annually report to the state police crimes occurring on their campuses (Del. Code Ann., 1993). The Delaware statute also prescribes each college to prepare a monthly report detailing the number and type of reported crimes occurring on school property. When combined with a yearly crime statistics report, the monthly reports furnish additional notice to a college community about the presence of criminal activity.

The reporting provisions of the California and Wisconsin campus security laws require the compilation of state *and* national campus crime statistics; however, both states emphasize additional facets of campus crime. California, for example, also requires its colleges to compile information about all criminal and noncriminal acts and arrests involving "hate" crimes (Cal. Educ. Code Ann., 1994). Wisconsin, on the other hand, addresses rape and acquaintance rape by requiring its colleges to separately assemble statistics on those crimes (Wis. Stat., 1992).

Several states limit the statistics their colleges may report. In Florida and West Virginia, colleges have to report crime statistics only for the most recent three-year period (Fla. Stat., 1993; W. Va. Code, 1993). This requirement is less stringent than the monthly, annual, and three-year reports imposed by Delaware, but is more stringent than New York which does not require its colleges to report *any* crime statistics (N.Y. Educ. Law, 1994). West Virginia also requires its schools to collect and distribute campus crime statistics as a component of its "statewide report card," used for intrastate, regional, and national school comparisons (W. Va. Code, 1993). The "report card" combines campus crime statistics, test scores, information about athletic programs, and graduation rates. All this information, however, may detract from the material on campus crime. Further, the law applies *only* to West Virginia's sixteen public colleges. Consequently, the state's twelve private schools (which annually enroll nearly 8,000 students) are exempt from the law (Chronicle of Higher Education, 1993).

Other states' legislation is different. For example, in Virginia, colleges are obliged to report only those crime statistics already compiled for inclusion in the *Uniform Crime Reports* (Va. Code Ann., 1991). In Nevada, campus crime statistics are gathered only for the schools in the University of Nevada system (Nev. Rev. Stat., 1993). This narrow reporting domain of the Virginia and Nevada laws may adversely affect thousands of students; only two of the nine colleges in Nevada and nineteen of the eighty-three colleges in Virginia disclosed campus crime statistics to the FBI in 1993 (U.S. Department of Justice, 1993; Chronicle of Higher Education, 1993). Consequently, if the school to which a student applies or currently attends does not report its statistics, the student will be unaware of the incidence of crime at that campus.

Off-Campus Statistics for Crimes Against Students

Tennessee is the only state that currently requires its colleges to collect statistics for reported crimes against students that occurred *off campus.* The statistics are compiled from police reports and student accounts and reporting is limited to off-campus crimes committed in the county where the school is located (Tenn. Code Ann., 1994). In addition, the reports also name the victim's school.

Tennessee's off-campus reporting requirement could be improved by requiring schools to compare their crime rates with those of the surrounding community found in the *Uniform Crime Reports.* Combining the statistics for on-campus and off-campus crimes gives students a better picture of the number of crimes occurring at and near their colleges.

Other states should amend their campus security reporting laws to mandate compiling statistics for off-campus crimes committed against students and crimes of the surrounding community because these statistics are important in helping students, faculty members, and staff gauge the safety of their college and its environment. Most colleges cannot board all students in campus housing; moreover, the boundaries between a college's property and that of the local community often are blurred. Therefore, data for off-campus incidents involving students may alert students to crime problems that must be confronted when living and traveling off campus.

Security Policies and Procedures

The Pennsylvania law requires colleges to report detailed information on security policies and procedures (Pa. Cons. Stat., 1992). Colleges must collect data on crime-reporting procedures (both to police and to school authorities), institutional responses to those reports, as well as policies on the use of alcohol, weapons, and illegal drugs on campus. In addition, Pennsylvania colleges compile information about safety considerations and how security information is communicated to the campus community. Colleges maintaining student housing facilities must also describe both the security personnel assigned to patrol housing, their training, and the type and frequency of programs used to inform residents about housing security and enforcement policies. Several states (California, Delaware,

Louisiana, Tennessee, and Washington) have laws almost identical to Pennsylvania's (Cal. Educ. Code, 1994; Tenn. Code. Ann., 1994; Del. Code Ann., 1993; La. Rev. Stat. Ann., 1993; Pa. Cons. Stat., 1992; Wash. Rev. Code, 1993).

Police Department Information

Nevada's campus security reporting law requires colleges in the University of Nevada system to disclose comprehensive facts about each campus police department or security force in the system (Nev. Rev. Stat., 1993). Included are details on officer training, the equipment officers are permitted to use, and each department's policy on the use of force. The schools are also required to compile the number of complaints alleging the use of excessive force by the police and whether those reports were substantiated. Finally, each department must report activities undertaken to improve or maintain public relations between the campus and the community.

Statistical Reliability and Effective Use of Information

Campus security reporting laws vary considerably in the security policies and procedures that must be reported. Florida and Virginia, for example, require little more than a recitation of their campus crime statistics reported to the FBI (Fla. Stat., 1993: Va. Code Ann., 1991), while Pennsylvania mandates the disclosure to students of comprehensive policies (Pa. Cons. Stat., 1992). New York requires the reporting only of policies on sexual assaults that occur on campus (N.Y. Educ. Law, 1994), and Virginia's campus law does not mention security policies (Va. Code Ann., 1991).

Thirty-six states currently lack even rudimentary campus security reporting legislation. States debating whether to enact or improve campus security reporting laws can find models in the campus security and sexual assault policies described in the Pennsylvania, California, and New York laws (Cal. Educ. Code Ann., 1994; N.Y. Educ. Law, 1994; Pa. Cons. Stat., 1992). It is possible that students could interpret stricter campus security reporting laws to mean that a campus crime epidemic is occurring which could damage schools' recruitment and retention efforts. However, as students and their parents become more concerned with crime on campus and consider campus safety when selecting colleges, the presence of the laws may become an incentive to enroll at the school.

One problem with interpreting campus crime statistics involves understanding what the numbers mean. Thus, the statistics should be reported in a comprehensible manner. West Virginia, for example, requires that all information contained in its statewide report cards, including campus crime statistics, be written in brief, concise, and nontechnical language (W. Va. Code, 1993). Technical or explanatory material is placed in a separate appendix available to the public on request. States also could ensure the reliability and accuracy of crime statistics by providing colleges with an annual crime reporting update that describes typical errors in school crime reporting procedures and effective methods of monitoring and recording school crime data.

Accessing Campus Crime Information

Campus crime statistics and security information, if not distributed, would not inform students, faculty members and staff about crime on their campus. States differ in what information they require colleges to report as well as how the information is distributed. Moreover, campus security reporting laws often distinguish between enrolled students and applicants for admission in the procedures by which they can acquire campus crime information.

Notice Requirements and Information Availability

Pennsylvania's college security reporting law (Pa. Cons. Stat., 1992) and the laws of California (Cal. Educ. Code Ann., 1994), Connecticut (Conn. Gen. Stat. Ann., 1993), Tennessee (Tenn. Code Ann., 1994), and Washington (Wash. Rev. Code, 1993), illustrate one way of informing the college community and prospective applicants of campus crime:

> Upon request, the institution shall provide the report to every person who submits an application for admission to either a main or branch campus and to each new employee at the time of employment. In its acknowledgment of receipt of the formal application of admission, the institution shall notify the applicant of the availability of such information. The information shall also be provided on an annual basis to all students and employees.

The dissemination requirement, however, is triggered by the "request" of the applicant after her "formal application." This weakens the efficacy of several campus security reporting laws because the burden of inquiry is placed on the applicant (who may neglect to request the information) and not the college. The laws would be more effective in apprising applicants of crime on campus if colleges were required to supply that information in its recruitment literature.

Further, the nonrefundable fee that accompanies many college applications effectively means that applicants must pay for the campus crime information when deciding to apply to a college. If colleges supplied this information in recruitment literature, applicants could narrow their choices and save application fees. If campus administrators are concerned that students will use campus crime as the sole criterion for evaluating a college, they could publicize (with the crime data) facts about security procedures and crime-awareness programs. This policy could prove an enrollment *incentive*, especially if the other schools the student is considering do not have similar programs.

Delaware's campus security reporting law ensures that its colleges will inform students about campus crime, though college applicants do not receive any notice that campus crime information is available. The law specifies that campus crime statistics are public records, available to any person on request; presumably, applicants, students, and even members of the public can access college crime information (Del. Code Ann., 1993). Crime statistics and crime rates must be published annually in a campus newspaper or other suitable method to inform the campus community. A monthly publication requirement could improve these notice guidelines further.

Louisiana law does not provide for the dissemination of campus crime information to currently enrolled students or applicants; its campus security reporting law says that reports detailing campus crime statistics are a "public record" (La. Rev. Stat. Ann., 1993). A similar notice provision appears in the Florida law, which says that colleges must "announce" the campus crime report is available on request (Fla. Stat., 1993). Unfortunately, the statute fails to specify to whom notice must be given or the manner in which notice is to be given. Virginia directs an institution of higher education to furnish a copy of *UCR* statistics relating to Virginia's colleges to any interested person on request (Va. Code Ann., 1991). Without informing current and prospective students of the availability of campus crime information, it is unlikely they will request it.

New York's campus security reporting law is silent on the issue of campus crime statistics (N.Y.S.B. 2295 1993). At least one New York state senator has criticized the inadequacy of New York's law, and legislation has been introduced in the New York General Assembly to require compliance with the Federal Crime Awareness and Campus Security Act of 1990 (Editorial, 1990). On the positive side, New York's is the only law explicitly prohibiting hazing. The law requires colleges and universities to develop rules prohibiting, during initiation into any organization, "reckless" or "intentional" endangerment to health or forced consumption of alcohol or drugs (N.Y. Educ. Law, 1994). These rules are automatically included in every campus organizations' bylaws, a distinctive approach that helps ensure notice of the regulations and the sanctions imposed for their violation.

The fundamental purpose of campus security reporting laws is to reduce the incidence of campus crime by increasing students' awareness. That purpose, however, is circumvented if colleges fail to provide students with either campus crime statistics or rules for acquiring them. Thus, states must enact legislation ensuring access to that information. Each college should be required to publicly notify members of its community (in its brochures, newspapers, and by other suitable means) that crime reports are available on request to any applicant, current student, or employee.

Delaware, Louisiana, and Washington require their colleges to report their monthly and annual crime facts (Del. Code Ann., 1993; La. Rev. Stat. Ann., 1993; Wash. Rev. Code, 1993). However, no state law currently requires that campus community members be told about criminal incidents *as they occur*. To remedy this, colleges could post announcements detailing the crime and where it occurred soon after the incident. Students would then be reminded of the danger, especially if the suspect had not yet been apprehended.

Campus Security Task Forces

In New York, each of its colleges and universities must create an advisory committee on campus security, which reviews current policies and procedures for reporting sexual assault (N.Y. Educ. Law, 1994). Washington requires a similar task force for its colleges, but it focuses on general campus security (Wash. Rev. Code, 1993). In both New York and Washington, schools appoint representatives to the advisory committee from the school's administration, as well as from its faculty and staff, student organizations, and campus police; in New York, at least one-half of the representatives are required to be women. To increase the effectiveness of campus security task forces, states should require colleges to solicit comments from the campus and surrounding community and to publish its findings.

Because students are often the victims of campus crime, their input is particularly important for assessing the effectiveness of anti-crime programs, security measures, and in determining where improvements are needed. For similar reasons, women should serve on the task force and their input be sought in evaluating whether a college's sexual assault and rape awareness programs and its response to those crimes are effective. Finally, campus administrators should involve local civic, business, and church leaders and law enforcement authorities in a campus security task force; such a community-college partnership can create many benefits, including funding and speakers for crime awareness programs, new perspectives on how to confront campus crime, offenders, and victims, and good public relations.

Special Information Programs

California, New York, and Wisconsin mandate the disclosure of comprehensive procedures on sexual assault, including its definition, preventive measures, and policies to address the victim and the offender. Similarly, the Kansas legislature passed a resolution encouraging, though not mandating, its colleges to introduce and implement rape and sexual assault awareness programs.

California's law institutes a victim-centered model of responding to sexual assault. Each college in California is obligated to adopt a written policy containing, at a minimum, the following information:

(1) Policy regarding sexual assault on campus;

(2) Campus personnel who should be notified and procedures for doing so with the victim's consent;

(3) Legal reporting requirements, and procedures for fulfilling them;

(4) Services available to victims, and personnel responsible for providing these services, such as the person assigned to transport the victim to the hospital, to refer the victim to a counseling center, and to notify the police, with the victim's concurrence;

(5) A description of campus resources available to victims, as well as appropriate off-campus services;

(6) Procedures for ongoing case management, including procedures for keeping victims informed of the status of any disciplinary proceedings in connec-

tion with the sexual assault, and the results of any disciplinary action or appeal, and helping the victim deal with academic difficulties that may arise because of the victimization and its impact;

(7) Procedures for guaranteeing confidentiality and appropriately handling requests for information from the press, concerned students, and parents; and

(8) Each victim of sexual assault should receive information about the existence of at least the following options: criminal prosecutions, civil prosecutions, the disciplinary process through the college, the availability of mediation, alternative housing assignments, and academic assistance alternatives (Cal. Educ. Code, 1993).

Beyond these procedures, California included several recommendations in its campus security reporting law that focus on rape, acquaintance rape, and sexual assault occurring on campus. For example, colleges are requested to provide seminars on rape and sexual assault to athletes, student organizations, and residence hall advisors.

First-year student orientation programs in New York and Wisconsin include sexual assault information. These programs are an effective way of ensuring that students receive the information. For example, the New York law specifies the following information *must* be given to new students:

(1) the applicable laws, ordinances and regulations on sex offenses;

(2) the penalties for commission of sex offenses;

(3) the procedures in effect at the college for dealing with sex offenses;

(4) the availability of counseling and other support services for the victims of sex offenses;

(5) the nature of and common circumstances relating to sex offenses on college campuses and

(6) the methods the college employees to advise and to update students about security procedures (N.Y. Educ. Law, 1993).

Colleges in New York must inform new students about sexual assault prevention measures using programs (e.g., workshops, seminars, and discussion groups) to disseminate information about sexual assault and encourage the prevention and the reporting of sexual assault incidents. Providing new students with information about sexual assault helps colleges dispel myths surrounding sexual assault, including gender differences in communication and general naivete about the offense (see Belknap and Erez, 1995).

The Kansas legislature, while not enacting a campus security reporting law, passed a concurrent resolution to encourage its colleges to create rape and sexual assault awareness information and seminars (Kan. H.C.R., 1993).

Orientation programs are invaluable sources of information for new students, and they provide campus administrators the opportunity to present their policies on campus crime. The seminars should stimulate student interest and emphasize the importance of crime awareness and prevention. However, since new students may be overwhelmed by the abundance of information during orientation, the seminars should be regularly repeated. Likewise, information about campus security procedures should also be distributed to students several times during the year.

Campus Security Logs

Only Tennessee's campus security reporting law refers to campus crime "logs" kept by campus law enforcement; the logs contain the type and number of crimes and the identities of offenders. The security department of each college must maintain a daily log of all crimes reported to the department including: time and location of the crime, whether an arrest was made, and the identity of arrestees. Not included in the logs are the names of victims and witnesses, as well as suspects not yet arrested (Tenn. Code Ann., 1994). Unless state or federal law prohibits disclosure of this information, the campus crime logs are public records.

Thus far, courts have differed on whether campus crime logs and the records of campus disciplinary proceedings are public records or whether they are sealed educational records. The Department of Education had designated campus crime logs as "educational records." This designation brought the logs under the purview of the Family Educational Rights and Privacy Act of 1974 (FERPA) (USC, 1993). Information protected by FERPA cannot be disclosed publicly without the possibility that the Department of Education would penalize the college by withholding federal funds. Therefore, students were unable to obtain crime logs maintained by campus police.

In *Student Press Law Center v. Alexander* (1991), student journalists challenged the Department of Education's designation of campus crime logs as "educational records." The court held that FERPA, as applied to the campus crime logs, violated the students' First Amendment right to receive the information in the logs and enjoined the Department of

Education from withholding or threatening to withhold federal funds from colleges that release campus crime logs.

State and federal courts in Florida and Missouri have reached similar conclusions, ruling campus police reports are *not* educational records protected by FERPA. The courts ruled that when it comes to reporting criminal activity, a student enrolling at a college does not have any greater privacy right than members of the public (see *Bauer v. Kincaid,* 1991; *Campus Communications v. Criser,* 1986). The courts explained the public's interest in greater access to information is highest in personal safety and crime prevention matters. This interest outweighs the interest of college students in protecting their record of campus criminal activity. Accordingly, the courts in both cases ruled that a college's failure to release campus crime logs violated state open meeting laws and the First and Fifth Amendments of the Constitution. For similar reasons, the Georgia Supreme Court held that records of campus disciplinary proceedings are not protected by FERPA; therefore, they must be disclosed under the state's Sunshine Law (see *Red & Black Publishing Company, Inc. v. Board of Regents,* 1993).

The United States District Court for the Western District of Arkansas dismissed a case for want of federal jurisdiction in a case in which a prospective student sought access to campus police records (*Norwood v. Slammons,* 1991). In that case, the federal court expressly disagreed with the conclusions set forth by the *Bauer* court that the First Amendment guarantees a right of access to campus crime logs. However, the court left open the possibility that information contained in campus crime logs could be disclosed under the Arkansas Freedom of Information Law.

College Noncompliance

Seven of the fourteen campus security reporting laws discussed above contain sanctions in the event a college fails to adhere to the law's provisions. Among these states, there is variation in the methods used to promote compliance; sanctions range from criminal and civil penalties to the removal of state funding.

In California, any person requesting campus security information from a college, but has been denied the information, may bring a civil action against the college (Cal. Educ. Code, 1994) and the plaintiff can recover damages of up to $1,000 from the school. Although not explicitly authorized by the campus security reporting law, the California Code of

Civil Procedure provides for the awarding of attorney fees if the following criteria are met: (1) the action has resulted in the enforcement of an important right affecting the public interest; (2) a significant benefit has been conferred on the public or a large class of people; (3) the necessity and financial burden of private enforcement make the award appropriate; and (4) the fees should not, in the interest of justice, be paid out of the recovery (Cal. Code Civ. Proc., 1994). A student suing to enforce a state campus security reporting law vindicates the public interest in college safety and confers a significant benefit (crime information about the college community). Other benefits arising from student lawsuits to acquire crime information may impel the lobbying efforts in states currently without campus security reporting laws to enact them.

No other state authorizes private actions similar to those available in California. However, two states permit their attorney general to bring action against a college to compel compliance with a campus security reporting law. In Pennsylvania and Delaware, if an institution has willfully violated the law or has failed to promptly conform with a compliance order, a civil penalty of up to $10,000 may be imposed (Pa. Cons. Stat., 1992; Del. Code. Ann., 1993).

States could amend their campus security reporting laws to permit students to sue for the release of campus crime information and to authorize the award of attorney's fees for students who prevail in the suit. Private enforcement actions serve several functions, including: (1) encouraging student vigilance in policing the public interest in a safe, secure college environment; (2) educating others about a current issue of public importance; and (3) inducing college compliance with campus security reporting laws (Smith, 1990). The threat of potential lawsuits may also promote college administrators to develop effective anti-crime measures and programs.

Beyond enforcement actions by students and attorneys general, states may impose criminal sanctions on college administrators who fail to comply with a law's provisions. In Tennessee, any official responsible for overseeing a college's obligations under the campus security reporting law, and fails to do so, is guilty of a Class C misdemeanor punishable by up to 30 days imprisonment, a fine not to exceed fifty dollars, or both (Tenn. Code Ann., 1994). Wisconsin imposes similar requirements on campus administrators for violating any part of its campus security reporting law, although the fine and length of possible incarceration are greater: violators may be imprisoned for up to 90 days, fined up to $500, or both (Wis. Stat., 1992).

States can also encourage compliance by overseeing college security departments. Louisiana forbids any private or public college from commissioning a college police officer until the state determines the college has complied with the campus security reporting law. As campus safety becomes a recruiting point for colleges and a selection (and retention) consideration for applicants, as well as attracting and retaining faculty members and staff, it is unlikely an institution would ignore statutory reporting requirements if its lack of security was publicized.

The threat of withholding financial aid possibly creates the greatest incentive for compliance with a campus security reporting law since it is unlikely that colleges could continue operations without state financial assistance. New York law states that a college whose administrators fail to follow the dictates of the campus security reporting law will be ineligible for *any* state financial aid until it comes into compliance (N.Y. Educ. Law, 1994); in New York, state aid amounts to approximately $4 billion of the $14 billion in college expenditures.

In 1992, the states with campus security reporting laws supplied almost $19 billion to the $59 billion for operating costs, student financial aid, and research and development grants expended by the colleges in those states (Chronicle of Higher Education, 1993). The state of Louisiana, for example, provided 65% of the money on which its colleges needed to operate (Barbett, 1992). A state withdrawing this money could financially force an institution into compliance. Moreover, the Department of Education's success in compelling compliance with FERPA by threatening to remove federal funding conclusively demonstrates this fact. Although there have been at least 150 formal violations of FERPA, through the leverage of withdrawing all federal money, the department has obtained voluntary compliance in every case before having to take official action (*Alexander v. Student Press Law Center,* 1991).

Finally, though no state has yet done so, it is possible to connect compliance with a college's accreditation. If the college fails to report crime statistics or does not report or institute minimal security procedures, the state could threaten to withhold accreditation. Without state imprimatur, an institution's enrollment and recruitment efforts could be seriously jeopardized.

FURTHER CONSIDERATIONS

With the spiraling cost of college tuition, according to Davenport (1985), students "are more likely to view their college education as a financial investment requiring a more careful and business-like analysis." Consequently, students deserve as much information as possible, including fundamental facts about the incidence of crime on campus, to aid in their analysis. Under current campus security reporting laws, however, considerable difference occurs in the statistics colleges report and how this information is disseminated to the campus community. Generally, states have not addressed the issues of compiling statistics for off-campus student victimizations (excluding Tennessee), the need for additional criteria for evaluating campus crime statistics, and the potential for misinterpretation of crime statistics.

Colleges are not furnishing students with the information necessary to make intelligent, informed choices about their safety if campus crime statistics are easily misunderstood or inaccurately portray campus crime. Thus, information is needed to place crime statistics in perspective; otherwise, students may wrongly believe crime is prevalent, or may believe it is not prevalent and fail to take precautions.

The Scope of Campus Security Reporting Laws

Almost 90% of the nation's colleges and universities have no state-level statutory duty to divulge campus crime information to their students, and several campus security reporting laws only apply to public colleges (U.S. Department of Justice, 1993; Chronicle of Higher Education, 1993). While the passage of the federal Crime Awareness and Campus Security Act ensures minimum disclosure and security standards for most institutions of higher education, states remain in the best position to require their public and private colleges to adopt specific policies or procedures. For example, several state-level security reporting laws only focus on public colleges. To ensure that all students and applicants have access to facts about campus crime, private colleges must be brought under the purview of state-level campus security reporting laws. This could be done by making adherence to the law a prerequisite of the college receiving state financial assistance or state accreditation.

Off-Campus Crime Statistics

No state currently requires the reporting of crime statistics for the community in which the school is located, and only Tennessee requires the reporting of off-campus crimes involving students (Tenn. Code Ann., 1994). States should amend their campus security reporting laws to require their colleges to compare *UCR* statistics for the area surrounding the college with on-campus statistics to provide students with a better gauge of safety on and around the campus.

Reporting *UCR* statistics for the surrounding vicinity also may offset disadvantages urban schools encounter by disclosing campus crime statistics. Urban schools, compared to nonurban institutions, may have higher crime rates *on their campuses* but lower crime rates than the surrounding area. Thus, a student could compare the relative safety of a college with the relative safety of its surrounding environment (based on *UCR* figures), as well as comparing the relative safety of an urban college (which might have a lower crime rate than the surrounding area) with that of a rural or suburban college (Griffaton, 1993). Finally, most colleges cannot board all students in campus housing; thus, students may fail to assess the safety of their chosen college if they do not consider whether they will live on campus or off campus. Community crime statistics may alert students to crime problems they must contend with when living and traveling about off campus (see Fernandez & Lizotte, 1995).

The money colleges would expend to disseminate *UCR* statistics for on-campus and off-campus crimes is probably minimal. The *UCR* is compiled by the FBI and a college would incur little cost in reprinting that information. Moreover, the experience of Pennsylvania's colleges operating under the college security reporting law underscores the fact that any additional expense incurred by reporting crime information is outweighed by heightened student awareness. Bruce Jordan, President of Pennsylvania State University, explained: "The process has been workable and reasonable. The major goal of the legislation—to inform the university community—has been achieved. It is one step that will help students and staff make informed choices about their own security" (Cong. Rec., 1990).

Reporting Campus Crimes to Law Enforcement Authorities

A major deficiency with current state-level campus security reporting laws is their failure to require campus security or college administrators to report crimes occurring on campus to local law enforcement authorities. Although campus disciplinary proceedings have neither the ability nor the jurisdiction to adjudicate felonies, nevertheless, colleges routinely process crimes that would subject students to criminal sanctions if they were committed off campus. If a victim of date rape, for example, selects a disciplinary hearing before a college judicial board and does not report the incident to the police, the rape allegations may never be made public and the offender may never be brought to justice. Obviously, if the rape was committed off campus, the local police would not submit the student-offender to the college disciplinary process. Further, if the offense was committed on campus by a non-student, the college would not submit the case to its judicial board.

Tennessee is the only state to have questioned whether college officials must report campus crimes to the local police (Op. Atty. Gen., 1991). The Tennessee Attorney General concluded that statutory grants of power to municipalities and state colleges gives both the responsibility to maintain and enforce state laws on college grounds. Therefore, campus security personnel are not required to notify municipal authorities of the commission of on-campus felonies or misdemeanors. However, college officials are bound by obstruction of justice laws (Model Penal Code, 1962; USC, 1969).

States can and should amend their campus security reporting laws to mandate that administrators report campus crimes to the local police. Otherwise, student-offenders who commit crimes on campus could be dismissed (at worst) while student-offenders and non-students who commit crimes off campus could face imprisonment. This distinction raises equal protection issues similar to those over whether to release information contained in campus police logs. Students should not possess a greater degree of protection from sanctions for criminal violations than others by virtue of their status as students who committed a crime on campus. An argument possibly could be made that while a college could discipline students who commit misdemeanors like alcohol violations, there appears no justification for leaving felony rape, theft, drug abuse, and aggravated assault cases in the hands of a campus judicial proceeding. Since felonies are the most serious breaches against both the victim and society, society should judge any offender (students included) in the legal system.

Making Sense of the Numbers

The use of campus crime statistics, like the use of statistical evidence in general, is replete with opportunities for misinterpretation. While deliberate misrepresentation by a college sounds improbable, an unintended distortion of campus safety may result when students and applicants misinterpret a college's campus crime statistics. These statistics, for example, fail to describe the severity of reported crimes, as the same figures reporting the incidence of theft on campus include the theft of both automobiles and stamps (Reford, 1989). Consequently, crime statistics need to be disseminated so everyone can understand them.

Campus crime statistics also do not reveal the forces contributing to campus crime. A college whose *UCR* statistics report an increase in the number of rapes or thefts, for example, may not be implying an escalation in the incidence of campus crime. Instead, the increase may be the result of more vigilant enforcement and prosecution by campus security and administrators, increased disclosure by students, or a combination of these elements. As more states require their colleges to adopt security policies that encourage student reporting of crimes, the number of reported campus crimes probably will increase (Griffaton, 1993). However, high crime rates may instead reveal a college with ineffective enforcement, lax security procedures, or apathetic students; a college reporting low crime rate faces similar problems.

State campus security reporting laws should require colleges to disclose, besides their crime statistics, details on variables that may contribute to crime on campus. Colleges can include material on student and community demographics, the percentage of full-time students, the number of students residing on campus, and the number of male students. Each of these variables significantly correlates with a high campus crime rate and should be disclosed (see Sloan, 1994; Fox & Hellman, 1985).

Without some way to differentiate which components influence campus crime, college students will be unable to make informed choices about their safety. Since it is likely that students will use and rely on these statistics in choosing a school, states should compel their colleges to provide students with a means for calculating their significance. States considering whether to enact campus security reporting laws, as well as those states seeking to improve current laws, could follow West Virginia's lead in requiring the use of brief, concise, and nontechnical language in reporting campus crime information (W. Va. Code, 1993). By ensuring that this information is nontechnical, the definition of theft used by the reporting agency probably would reflect the general public's perception of that crime; at the least, it recognizes the difference between legal definitions and public perceptions. States also could inform colleges of problems in compiling and reporting statistics; crime reporting should be standardized and the procedures for data collection validated. Standardized reporting of crime statistics encourages and simplifies comparison of crime trends across campuses. Administrators could use the knowledge garnered from these comparisons to develop effective crime awareness programs and security procedures.

CONCLUSION

State campus security reporting laws provide several alternatives by which to address the problem of campus crime. College administrators in the fourteen states that have enacted campus security reporting laws have a legal duty to abide by and conform to those laws; enforcement provisions are found in seven of the states' laws to ensure compliance (Cal Educ. Code Ann., 1994; Del. Code Ann., 1993; La. Rev. Stat. Ann., 1993; N.Y. Educ. Law, 1994; Pa. Cons. Stat., 1992; Tenn. Code Ann., 1994; Wis. Stat., 1992). Notwithstanding the presence of an enforcement provision, it is necessary that campus administrators not only comply with the dictates of a campus security reporting law, but also develop effective security procedures.

Colleges governed by campus security reporting laws have the opportunity to garner public recognition of their crime prevention efforts. Under the Crime Awareness and Campus Security Act, the Secretary of Education is authorized to recognize security procedures that have been effective in reducing crime or helping crime victims (USC 1992); the Secretary also may disseminate that information to other colleges regulated by the Act. This provides campus administrators with an incentive to develop and implement security procedures and shares with other colleges successful anti-crime programs.

Security procedures may also help reduce the possibility of campus crime. Several courts have held that colleges have a duty to protect their students from reasonably foreseeable criminal assaults. By providing students with campus crime information and by establishing safety features like security doors, improved lighting, and campus escort and bus services, a college may reduce the likelihood that crime will occur. A court may be less likely to find a college liable for a failure to warn about or protect students from campus crime if it has taken such precautions.

Finally, the experience of college administrators operating under the fourteen state campus security reporting laws affords administrators in the other thirty-six states, as well as administrators already operating under those laws, with opportunities to learn from their colleagues' successes and failures. The laws of New York and California, for example, provide administrators with excellent models of campus anti-rape programs; Pennsylvania's law illustrates campus security measures and procedures. While these campus security reporting laws are not panaceas for the campus crime problem, they symbolize a significant step toward reducing possible student victimization by apprising them of campus crimes and basic security precautions.

REFERENCES

Barbett, S.F., R. Korb, M. Black, and M. Hollins (1992) *State Higher Education Profiles.* Washington, DC: National Center for Education Statistics.

Brandeis, L. (1933) [1986] *Other People's Money, And How the Bankers' Use It* (2 ed). New York: Kelley.

Davenport, D. (1985) "The Catalog in the Courtroom: From Shield to Sword?" *Journal of College & University Law 12*(2):201–203.

Editorial (1990) "Students Need Better Campus Security." *The New York Times,* September 20, p. 20.

Fernandez, A. and A.J. Lizotte (1995) "An Analysis of the Relationship Between Campus Crime and Community Crime: Reciprocal Effects?" In B.S. Fisher and J.J. Sloan, III (eds.) *Campus Crime: Legal, Social and Policy Perspectives.* Springfield, IL: Charles C Thomas.

Fox, J. and D. Hellman (1985) "Location and Other Correlates of Campus Crime." *Journal of Criminal Justice 13*(4):429–438.

Griffaton, M. (1993) "Forewarned is Forearmed: The Crime Awareness and Campus Security Act." *Case Western Reserve Law Review 43:*525–590.

Note (1986) *"Campus Communications v. Criser." Medical Law Reporter 13:*1398.

Reford, M. (1989) "Pennsylvania's College and University Security Information Act: The Effect of Campus Security Legislation on University Liability for Campus Crime." *Dickenson Law Review 94:*179–196.

Shakespeare, W. (1594) [1966] *Titus Andronicus.* New York: Penguin Books.

Smith, M.C. (1990) "College Liability Resulting from Campus Crime: Resurrection for *In Loco Parentis?" Western Education Law Reporter 59:*1–25.

—— (1988) *Coping with Crime on Campus.* New York: Ace Books.
The Chronicle of Higher Education (1993) *Almanac.* Washington, DC: Chronicle of Higher Education.
U.S. Department of Justice, Federal Bureau of Investigation (1993) *Crime in the United States 1992: The Uniform Crime Reports.* Washington, DC: U.S. Government Printing Office.

Cases and Statutes Cited

Bauer v. Kincaid, 759 F. Supp. 575 (1991).
Cal. Code Civ. Pro., § 1021.5 (1994).
Cal. Educ. Code Ann., §§ 67380, 67390 to 67393, 94380 (1994).
Cal. Penal Code, §§ 628. to 628.6 (1994).
136 Cong. Rec. H3122 (daily ed. June 5, 1990) (remarks of Rep. Goodling) 91-74.
Op. Atty Gen., Aug. 20, 1991 (Tenn.).
Conn. Gen. Stat. Ann. §§ 10a-55a to 10a-55c (1993).
Crime Awareness and Campus Security Act, 20 U.S.C. § 1092 (1992).
Del. Code Ann. Title 14, §§ 9001 to 9005 (1993).
Family Educational Rights and Privacy Act 20 U.S.C. § 1232g (1990).
Fla. Stat. ch.240.2683 (1993).
Kan. H.C.R. No. 5019 Kan. Sess. Laws 300 (1993).
La. Rev. Stat. Ann. § 17:3351(3) (1993).
Mass. Gen. L. ch.22, § 16 (1992).
Model Penal Code § 242.1 (1962).
N.Y. Educ. § 6450 (McKinney 1985 and Supp. 1994).
N.Y. S.B. No. 2295 (Feb. 22, 1993).
Nev. Rev. Stat. § 396.340 (1993).
Norwood v. Slammons, 788 F. Supp. 365 (1991).
24 Pa. Cons. Stat. § 2501-1 (Purdon 1992).
Red & Black Publishing Co., Inc. v. Board of Regents, 262 Ga. 848 (1993).
Student Press Law Center v. Alexander, 778 F. Supp. 1227 (D.C.Cir. 1991).
Tenn. Code Ann. § 49-7-2203 (1994).
Va. Code Ann. § 23-9-1.1 (Michie Supp. 1991).
Wash. Rev. Code § 28B.10.569 (Supp. 1993).
W. Va. Code § 18B-1-8a (Supp. 1993).
Wis. Stat. § 36.11(22) (West Supp. 1992).
18 USC § 4 (Supp. 1990).

PART II
THE SOCIAL CONTEXT OF CAMPUS CRIME

INTRODUCTION TO PART II
THE SOCIAL CONTEXT OF CAMPUS CRIME

Only recently have social scientists begun to systematically examine campus crime. Some of these studies are exploratory, seeking to answer basic questions about campus crime. Other studies, theoretically driven and using sophisticated methodology, seek to model the causal dynamics of campus crime. Still others examine perceived risk and fear of victimization among students, faculty members, and staff.

These studies, however, all share a common orientation. They seek to understand the scope, extent, and nature of crime (or fear of crime) on college and university campuses. Their results, in turn, can be used as input for administrative decision making by policymakers.

This part of the book presents five chapters examining the social context of campus crime. In Chapter 5, "An Analysis of the Relationship Between Campus Crime and Community Crime: Reciprocal Effects?" by Adriana Fernandez and Alan Lizotte, the authors examine whether there is a relationship between crime rates in communities surrounding college campuses and campus crime rates and vice versa. Using official data, Fernandez and Lizotte describe and explain how the characteristics and crime rates of communities surrounding campuses, and the characteristics and crime rates of college and universities, affect one another.

John Wooldredge, Francis Cullen and Edward Latessa, in Chapter 6, using data from a faculty victimization survey, explore whether the demographic characteristics of faculty members or their "routine activities," or some interaction of the two, best accounts for victimization patterns among faculty.

In Chapter 7, Patricia Brantingham, Paul Brantingham and Jayne Seagrave examine the problem of campus crime at a Canadian university. They first present a theoretical framework (pattern theory) for studying crime and fear of crime on campus, and then describe victimization and fear of crime patterns among a sample of Canadian university students.

Chapter 8, "The Victimization of Women on College Campuses: Courtship Violence, Date Rape, and Sexual Harassment," by Joanne Belknap and Edna Erez, synthesizes more than twenty years worth of published research on the rape, battering, and sexual harassment of women on college campuses in this country. After reviewing this research, they present suggestions on stopping violence against women at colleges and universities.

We conclude this part of the book with a chapter by Bonnie Fisher, John Sloan and Deborah Wilkins. Their study examines perceived risk and fear of victimization at an urban university campus in the South. In their study, they review five models developed to explain perceived risk and fear of victimization in other contexts. Following this, they test the utility of these models to explain fear and perceived risk of victimization on campus.

These five chapters address different issues and use different theoretical perspectives and methodologies. However, each of them is an example of current research and each incorporates discussion of the policy implications of their findings.

Chapter 5

AN ANALYSIS OF THE RELATIONSHIP BETWEEN CAMPUS CRIME AND COMMUNITY CRIME: RECIPROCAL EFFECTS?

ADRIANA FERNANDEZ AND ALAN J. LIZOTTE[1]

INTRODUCTION

Recently there has been much concern, in both the popular press and the social sciences, about crime on campus. Today, post-secondary institutions no longer resemble serene ivory towers isolated from the harmful influences of crime and violence apparent in the rest of society. The problem of crime on campus has eroded this image. In response to concerns by parents, students, and university administrators, Congress has passed the *Crime Awareness and Campus Security Act of 1990* (20 USC 1092), which mandates that all colleges and universities receiving federal funds publish their crime statistics yearly. Now, institutions face the challenges of both crime prevention and publicly reporting crime statistics, while trying to project the image of a safe haven to parents, students, and faculty. In addition, these newly published data provide a vehicle for analyzing the correlates and causes of campus crime.

Although the rate of crime on the campus is generally much lower than that of its surrounding community (Lizotte & Fernandez, 1993; Bromley, 1992), the occurrence and reporting of crime still pose formidable problems to college administrators for several reasons. First, a safe environment is vital for learning and doing research. Second, colleges have been successfully sued by campus crime victims; these suits are not only costly but set precedent for future cases (Smith, 1988).[2] Third, an institution's ability to recruit students, faculty, and staff can be affected by lawsuits, reporting its crime statistics, and the resulting unflattering publicity. Finally, given the diverse population of the campus community, administrators have the difficult task of addressing the varying risks and security needs of its members.

One reason campus crime is a major concern is because students are

79

young and naive; as a result, they make easy victims. For many first-year students, college is their first extended excursion away from home and parental control. This heightens parents' concerns about many issues including crime. Undoubtedly, parents want their children to be safely insulated from the harmful influences of the outside world. However, crime has become a part of the campus life and parents know it. A survey of college students conducted by the Towson State University's Campus Violence Prevention Center showed that approximately 40% of the respondents were victims of campus crime at least once during their college experience. Furthermore, 88% of the respondents knew a victim of violence on campus (Siegel & Raymond, 1992).

Of course, parents and students are concerned not only with crime on campus but with the level of crime in the community in which the campus is located and the extent that community crime spills on campus. These concerns raise questions about how characteristics of campuses and their surrounding communities affect various types of crime for both the campus and the community.

Although studies of campus crime have identified the characteristics of victims, few have considered how the characteristics of institutions and their surrounding communities may determine the extent and nature of crime occurring on campus. Studies have also neglected to study crime spillover from the community onto the campus and from the campus into the community. The present study is designed to fill this gap by analyzing the reciprocal association between crime levels on campus and crime levels in the community where the campuses are located. Characteristics of both the campus and the community are used to predict these reciprocal effects.

THEORETICAL FRAMEWORK

Campuses may be the ideal target for offenders from both the campus and the community. Students may be easy prey for offenders because they often make poor guardians of themselves and their property. Potential offenders may consider campuses and students low-risk targets compared to other high-risk targets where the certainty of discovery and punishment is more likely. Hakim and Rengert (1981), for example, found that crime "spills over" from one neighborhood to another because potential offenders devote less time to crime opportunities in high-risk areas and move instead to lower-risk areas; this spillover may also be limited to particular crimes. If students' naivete and campus life-style make them crime targets, it would be reasonable to assume that crime may spill over from the community onto the campus. Further, crime may spill from the campus into the community because the opportunities surrounding student life function like a crime magnet.

Of course, those of college age (18–24) have life-styles associated with higher risk of victimization (Bureau of Justice Statistics, 1992:260). However, the physical and demographic characteristics of the institution also need to be considered. According to ecological research, the environment may be influential in determining whether a crime occurs by providing opportunities to potential offenders (Brantingham & Brantingham, 1981, 1993; Siegel & Raymond, 1992; Sherrill & Siegel, 1989; Davidson, 1981; Harries, 1980). Variables, including the percentage of students living on campus, the setting of the campus (urban, suburban, or rural), and the size of the campus population compared to the community population, may contribute to criminal events.

Both the structural characteristics of the campus and the demographic characteristics of its inhabitants may create the opportunities for crime to occur. We consider these effects, among others, in this chapter.

PAST RESEARCH ON CAMPUS CRIME

Past campus crime research has relied on victimization studies conducted using either small samples of campuses or a single campus. The studies have usually concentrated on topical areas like rape, sexual aggression, or courtship violence (Bachmam et al., 1992; Mills & Granoff, 1992; Ward et al., 1991; Koss et al., 1987; Roark, 1987; Kanin, 1984), sexual harassment (Adams, 1983; Wilson & Kraus, 1983; Metha & Nigg, 1982), and hazing (Smith & Smith, 1990; Roark, 1987). Recently, researchers have also paid attention to linkages of drugs and alcohol with the occurrence of violence on campus (Siegel & Raymond, 1992; Nichols, 1987; Powell, 1981). Linkages between alcohol and drug abuse and campus crime has been acknowledged in congressional testimony on campus crime, where experts said, "ninety-five percent of the offenses involved alcohol or drugs" (Sloan 1992:32).

These victimization studies typically survey students and have identified important characteristics of victims and have influenced campus crime policy. Colleges and universities, aware of the extent of student victimization occurring on campus, have instituted safety and crime prevention programs including escort services, installation of call boxes or emergency telephones throughout the campus, card-key access systems, and educational programs on date rape and sexual harassment (Spitzberg & Thorndike, 1992; Nichols, 1987; Powell, 1981). Additionally, the last two decades have seen the professionalization of campus law enforcement which has enabled campus law enforcement personnel to design programs that effectively meet the needs of their distinctive environments (Peak, 1995; Spitzberg & Thorndike, 1992).

However, victimization studies do little to identify the institutional characteristics producing crime on campus. Crime occurs as a product of the physical characteristics of places and the demographic characteristics of people living there. Knowing which campus or community characteristics are correlated with campus crime can develop explanations of why crime rates are high or low on diverse campuses.

Generally, campus crime researchers have neglected to take into account the characteristics of the community in which the college is located. Because the college is part of the larger community, it would be logical when studying campus crime to take into account the larger community environment which provides both the opportunities for and deterrents against crime.

There have been only two published studies of campus crime that considered how the characteristics of post-secondary institutions *and* their surrounding communities affected the level and type of crime on campus. McPheters (1978) analyzed data from 38 four-year schools using a model that approximated the simultaneous effects of campus and community crime. While the small unrepresentative sample of institutions and limited explanatory variables make generalizations from this work difficult, McPheters found that higher percentages of students living on campus, higher unemployment rates in surrounding communities, and higher levels of expenditures on security per student were all associated with higher rates of crime on campus.

Fox and Hellman (1985) conducted a more extensive study of the relationship between campus and community crime at 222 colleges and universities in this country. They used data from the early 1980s describing the demographic, socioeconomic, scholastic, and environmental features of the campuses. They found campus size and scholastic quality were associated with campus crime and concluded (as did McPheters, 1978) that few community characteristics had a direct effect on campus crime rates, but one of the characteristics had a small influence on the crime mixture (violent crime as the proportion of all crime). They found that as communities became more urban, the crime mixture on campus became more violent.

Fox and Hellman (1985) and McPheters (1978), however, failed to analyze explicit *types* of property and violent crimes. To their credit, they did conduct separate analyses for violent and property crimes; however, analyses need to be done for particular crime types (e.g., robbery, burglary, or theft).

Grouping campus crimes together disregards the subtleties of particular types of crime and gives undue emphasis to frequently occurring crimes regardless of their seriousness. For example, Lizotte and Fernandez (1993) compared larceny and motor vehicle theft rates at a large sample of campuses. They found that larceny among students occurred frequently and constituted about 85% of all property crime occurring on the campuses (Lizotte & Fernandez, 1993). The rate of larceny (usually students stealing from one another) appeared driven by the college's enrollment, the percentage of students residing on campus, and tuition costs. Students living in dormitories have many lightweight durable goods easily brought to campus and easily stolen. Additionally, students who can afford to pay high tuition costs typically bring more valuable possessions with them on campus.

On the other hand, motor vehicle theft, which occurred less frequently, may be associated with the number of students who drive their cars to school, the wealth of the students, and the existence of an automobile theft ring in the nearby community. As more students drive their cars to school, especially if they are expensive, the more cars community thieves can target. While larceny and motor vehicle theft are both property crimes, they differ in frequency of occurrence and are affected by diverse causal forces.

A MODEL OF CAMPUS CRIME

This study examines the structural causes and correlates of particular crime types at a sample of colleges and universities. Figure 1 shows the structure of models we developed for each crime type.[3] Solid lines indicate relationships between community characteristics and rates of community crime and between campus characteristics and rates of campus crime that can be deduced from previous research. For example, community characteristics like income, percent minority, and population size are associated with community crime rates (Sampson, 1986; Davidson, 1981; Harries, 1980). Similarly, campus characteristics like enrollment and percentage of students living in dormitories are related to campus crime rates, especially larceny (Sloan, 1994, 1993; Bromley, 1993; Lizotte & Fernandez, 1993; Fisher, 1992; Fox & Hellman, 1985; McPheters, 1978).

Dotted lines in Figure 1 indicate associations that have not been thoroughly tested. For example, despite past research efforts, we still do not know how community characteristics and the crime rate in a community correlate with campus crime rates, nor do we know if campus characteristics and the campus crime rate affect community crime rates.

FIGURE 1

HYPOTHESIZED RELATIONSHIP BETWEEN CAMPUS AND COMMUNITY CHARACTERISTICS AND CAMPUS AND COMMUNITY CRIME

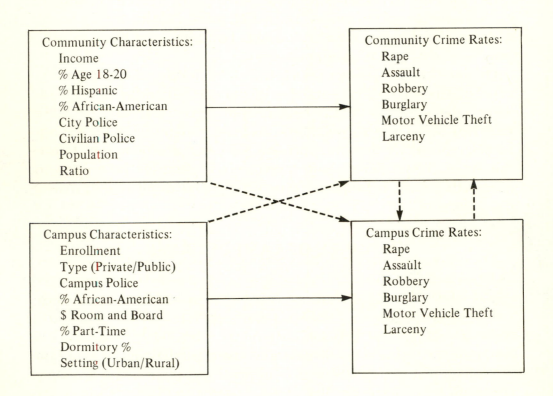

DATA AND METHODS

This study used data from 530 two-year and four-year college campuses for the 1991–1992 academic year and the communities in which they were located. Using these data, we analyzed the reciprocal effects for rape, aggravated assault, robbery, burglary, motor vehicle theft, and larceny on campus and in the community. The sample contains approximately 16% of the colleges and universities in this country and approximately 34% of all college students (U.S. Department of Education, 1993).

The data set was compiled by the Consortium for Higher Education Campus Crime Research (CHECCR), a nonprofit research organization at the School of Criminal Justice at the University of Albany. Campus and community crime data were obtained from the *Uniform Crime Reports* (U.S. Department of Justice, 1992) and from CHECCR members. We supplemented the crime information with descriptive data for the schools obtained from *Peterson's Guide* (Lahmen, 1991) and other authoritative sources. We obtained data on the characteristics of the communities in which the schools were located from the 1990 U.S. Census (Bureau of the Census, 1990).

Characteristics of the Sample

Eighty-four percent of the campuses are four-year schools and eighty-five percent are public institutions. Approximately 51% of the campuses are located in an urban area. The mean enrollment at the schools was 11,586; the range was from 240 students to 56,350 students. On average, 22% of the students lived in dormitories; the range was from 0% to 80%. The mean percentage of part-time students at the schools was 29% and the mean percentage of in-state residents was 85%. The mean annual costs at the schools were $2,543 for tuition and $2,578 for room and board.

The average population of the communities in which the schools were located was 264,896 people. On average, the schools had a property crime rate of 6,089 reported offenses per 100,000 population and an average violent crime rate of 923 per 100,000 population. The average property crime rate on the campuses was 2,766 offenses per 100,000 students, and the average violent crime rate was 76 offenses per 100,000 students. For the communities, Hispanic and African-Americans, on average, comprised 9% and 17% of the population. On average, five percent of the households in the community were headed by females. The average percent of people between the ages of 18 and 24 living in the community was twenty percent. Although the data set contains several hundred variables, only those theoretically appropriate were included in the equations.[4]

Table I shows the coding of variables used in the analysis. The coding of most variables is straightforward and need not be discussed; however, some of the variables need a brief introduction. Rates of rape, assault, robbery, burglary, motor vehicle theft, and larceny for both the campus and the community are the endogenous variables.[5] Most schools report comparatively low levels of crime. However, the distributions are skewed to the high end. That is, while a small number of schools reported high crime rates, the differences between a campus with a high crime rate and one with an even higher rate were not as important as the difference between a campus with a low crime rate and a campus having a slightly higher rate. To correct this problem, all crime rates were logged. Using the natural logarithm of these variables assumes that differences between cases at dramatically high values are not as important as differences between cases at less extreme values. In the analyses that follow, logging the crime rate variables significantly improved the estimation of equations, as we expected.

Additionally, the equations included dummy variables indicating for each crime type whether the campus or community was in the top 25 percent of the crime rate distribution. For example, "high campus rape" indicates that the campus was in the top twenty-fifth percentile of campus rape rates. These variables measure whether high rates in one arena (e.g., the community) produced more crime in the other (e.g., the campus).[6]

Table I also presents the campus and community characteristics that, theoretically, could influence crime. Campus characteristics include variables like size of enrollment, percent African-American students, percent part-time students, and dollar cost of room and board.[7] Community characteristics include, among other variables, average household income, percent African American, population size, and city police and civilian police.[8]

The variable *ratio* is the ratio of student enrollment to community population. High values of this variable indicated the population of the campus was large compared to the population size of the community.

We expected two possible effects of this variable on community crime rates. First, if crime spilled from the campus to the community because

TABLE I
CODING OF VARIABLES USED IN THE ANALYSIS

Variable	Coding of Variable	Mean	SD
Campus Crime Rates			
HC Rape	Campus Rape 0 = no 1 = yes (top 25%)	1.23	.42
Campus Rape	Logged Campus Rape (per 100,000)	1.01	1.43
HC Assault	Campus Assault, 0 = no 1 = yes (top 25%)	.22	.42
Campus Assault	Logged Campus Assault (per 100,000)	2.64	1.90
HC Robbery	Campus Robbery, 0 = no 1 = yes (top 25%)	.22	.42
Campus Robbery	Logged Campus Robbery (per 100,000)	1.55	1.67
HC Burglary	Campus Burglary, 0 = no 1 = yes (top 25%)	.22	.42
Campus Burglary	Logged Campus Burglary (per 100,000)	4.69	1.92
HC MV Theft	Campus MV Theft, 0 = no 1 = yes (top 25%)	.22	.42
Campus MVT	Logged Campus MV Theft (per 100,000)	3.03	2.06
HC Larceny	Campus Larceny, 0 = no 1 = yes (top 25%)	.21	.41
Campus Larceny	Logged Campus Larceny (per 100,000)	7.33	1.11
Community Crime Rates:			
HI Rape	City Rape, 0 = no 1 = yes (top 25%)	.21	.40
City Rape	Logged City Rape (per 100,000)	3.49	1.34
HI Assault	City Assault, 0 = no 1 = yes (top 25%)	.22	.42
City Assault	Logged City Assault (per 100,000)	5.71	1.35
HI Robbery	City Robbery, 0 = no 1 = yes (top 25%)	.21	.40
City Robbery	Logged City Robbery (per 100,000)	4.85	1.79
HI Burglary	City Burglary, 0 = no 1 = yes (top 25%)	.21	.41
City Burglary	Logged City Burglary (per 100,000)	6.91	1.08

TABLE I (Continued)

Variable	Coding of Variable	Mean	SD
HI MV Theft	City MV Theft, 0 = no 1 = yes (top 25%)	.21	.41
City MV Theft	Logged City MV Theft (per 100,000)	5.94	1.39
HI Larceny	City Larceny, 0 = no 1 = yes (top 25%)	.20	.40
City Larceny	Logged City Larceny (per 100,000)	7.90	1.15
Community Characteristics:			
Income	Average household income ($\times$ 1000)	26.32	12.65
% Age 18–20	Percent age 18–20	10.30	9.97
% Hispanic	Percent Hispanic	9.3	15.3
% African-Amer.	Percent African-American	16.9	17.8
City Police	City police (per 100,000) ($\times$ 1000)	.94	15.97
Civilian Police	Civilian Police (per 100,000) ($\times$ 1000)	.24	3.89
Population	City population ($\times$ 1000)	264.90	732.12
Ratio	Student population/ community population	.35	.55
Campus Characteristics:			
Enrollment	Student enrollment total ($\times$ 1000)	11.60	9.875
Type	School type, 1 = public 2 = private	1.12	.32
Campus Police	Campus police (per 100,000)	270.0	458.0
% African-Amer.	Percent African-American students	9.11	17.6
$ Room and Board	Cost of room and board ($\times$ $1000)	2.58	1.44
% Part-time	Percent part-time students	28.90	25.00
Dormitory %	Percent living in dormitories	.22	.19
Setting	Setting of campus 1 = urban 2 = rural	1.46	.50

of students, the ratio variable should be positively correlated with community crime rates. On the other hand, if students make good neighbors, the ratio variable should be inversely related to community crime rates. Of course, this variable could also predict crime rates on campus to the extent that crime in the communities overwhelmed the campuses.

For each type of crime, three-stage least squares simultaneous equations were used to estimate the reciprocal relationships between campus and community crime, controlling for the characteristics of *both* the campus and the community.[9] In general, the model hypothesized the demographic and economic characteristics of both campus and community would affect community crime rates *and* campus crime rates. Further, community and campus crime rates could affect one another in a causal loop.[10]

ANALYSES AND RESULTS

Table II shows the standardized regression coefficients for three-stage least squares equations predicting the rates of various types of crime on campus. Similarly, Table III (discussed below) shows equations predicting rates of the same crimes for communities. The equations in these tables allowed us to assess the reciprocal effects of campus and community crime. In addition, both community and campus characteristics were used to predict crime rates for *both* communities and campuses. For example, the campus rape rate was predicted from campus characteristics, community characteristics, and from the community rape rate. Similarly, community characteristics, campus characteristics, and the campus rape rate were used to predict the community rape rate.

Table II, with two exceptions, shows only coefficients which achieved statistical significance; that is, we "trimmed" from the models all non-significant predictor variables. Initial equations were estimated using predictor variables (except the instruments). We reestimated the equations after trimming non-significant variables. Table II also reports the reciprocal effects of campus crime and community crime and variables indicating high campus or community crime regardless of the coefficients' statistical significance. Finally, the "ratio" variable (which measures campus size compared to community size) was also included in the models.

Table II shows that, in general, community crime rates and community characteristics had little effect on campus crime rates. Campus characteristics, on the other hand, had strong and consistent effects on campus crime rates.

Community crime rates have no statistically significant influence on campus rape, assault, burglary, and larceny rates; however, robbery and motor vehicle theft rates in the community do affect campus robbery and motor vehicle theft rates. Additionally, when robbery rates were extraordinarily high in the community, robbery rates on campus also increased; further, as robbery rates increased in the community, they also increased on campus. Similarly, when motor vehicle theft rates were extraordinarily high in the community, they also increased on campus. These relationships may have occurred because robbery and motor vehicle theft were more likely than other crimes to have been committed by criminals from off campus who targeted *both* students and community residents.

Few community characteristics affected campus crime rates. For example, a high concentration of minorities in the community was related to higher rates of motor vehicle theft on campus. In addition, the ratio variable shows that as campuses become large (compared to community size), campus robbery and burglary rates also increased.[11] Perhaps when campuses become a sizable part of the larger community, perpetrators from the community become more familiar with the campus, which produces suitable targets for them. This familiarity could also make it easier for community perpetrators to come and go from the campus.

In contrast to the small influence of community characteristics, campus characteristics had a much greater effect on campus crime rates. We are not saying, however, that perpetrators of campus crime are *necessarily* members of the campus community. The characteristics of the campuses *themselves* could encourage or discourage perpetrators coming on campus from the community. For example, excluding motor vehicle theft rates, where students spent most of their time affected the rates of *all* forms of campus crime. Campuses with high concentrations of part-time students had lower rates of assault, robbery, burglary, and larceny; because part-time students spend less time on campus, their exposure to victimization decreases.

On the other hand, high dormitory populations were associated with high rates of campus rape and larceny. When students live on campus, every phase of their lives becomes associated with the campus. Their education, social activities, and housing all have campus foci; this could increase the likelihood of rape and theft occurring. Given this, one might expect high dormitory populations on campus to be associated with low crime rates in communities, a relationship we discuss below. Additionally, larger enrollment was associated with higher levels of all crimes except burglary. Large institutions could provide more targets for attack and more anonymity for prospective offenders.

TABLE II
PREDICTORS OF CAMPUS CRIME[a]

| | Campus Crime Rates: | | | | | |
	Rape	*Assault*	*Robbery*	*Burglary*	*MV Theft*	*Larceny*
Community Crime Rates						
High Rape	−.05					
	(−.17)					
Rape	−.27					
	(−.29)					
High Assault		.08				
		(.33)				
Assault		−.11				
		(−.16)				
High Robbery			.14*			
			(.29)			
Robbery			.31**			
			(.56)			
High Burglary				−.07		
				(−.27)		
Burglary				.25		
				(.45)		
High MV Theft					.33**	
					(1.55)	
MV Theft					−.09	
					(−.12)	
High Larceny						.04
						(.07)
Larceny						−.01
						(−.00)
Community Characteristics:						
Income						
% Age 18–20						
% Hispanic					.21**	
					(.03)	
% African-Amer.					.17**	
					(.02)	
City Police						
Civilian Police						
Population						
Ratio	−.05	−.01	.15*	.14*	.04	−.01
	(−.13)	(−.04)	(.43)	(.44)	(.12)	(−.00)

TABLE II (Continued)

Campus Characteristics:

Enrollment	.22**	.16**	.21**		.22**	.20**
	(.0)	(.0)	(.0)		(.0)	(.0)
Type	−.15**					
	(−.63)					
Campus Police				.19**		.39**
				(.0)		(.0)
% African-Amer.		.30**	.12**	.10*		
		(.03)	(.01)	(.01)		
$ Room and Board	.25**		.22**	.44**	.13**	.31**
	(.0)		(.0)	(.0)	(.0)	(.0)
% Part-time		−.28**	−.15**	−.20**		−.19**
		(−.02)	(−.01)	(−.02)		(−.0)
Dormitory %	.20**					.22**
	(1.63)					(.96)
Setting						

* p < .05 ** p < .01

[a]Unstandardized coefficients are reported in parentheses; standardized are not.

Perhaps the strongest and most consistent effect on campus crime rates was the measure of wealth of the students—dollar costs of room and board. Campuses with higher room and board costs had higher rates of all forms of crime having an economic motivation. Robbery, burglary, motor vehicle theft, and larceny rates all increased as the cost of room and board increased. Students who paid higher room-and-board costs could have high-quality goods to steal at comparatively little risk for the offender. In addition, rape rates were directly related to costs of room and board. Rape could be an afterthought to some forms of economic crimes (e.g., burglary of a dorm room) or the economic crimes could be an afterthought to rape.

To summarize, Table II shows that community characteristics and crime rates had little effect on campus crime. Instead, campus crime rates were strongly affected by campus characteristics like the time students spent on campus, where they lived, the size of the campus, and the wealth of the students.

Table III shows equations predicting crime rates in the communities where the campuses were located. Campus crime rates, community characteristics, and campus characteristics were used as predictors in these equations. Recall that campus characteristics were, by and large, the biggest influence on campus crime. Similarly, community crimes were extensively influenced by community characteristics. Rates of campus crime, generally, had no influence on community crime rates for the offenses of rape, assault, robbery, and larceny. However, rates of campus burglary and motor vehicle theft did influence burglary and automobile theft rates in the community. For example, when campus burglary rates were extraordinarily high, they were also high in the community. Similarly, higher levels of motor vehicle theft on campus were associated with higher rates of motor vehicle theft in the community. Also recall that high rates of automobile theft in the community had a significant influence on campus rates of motor vehicle theft.

Taken together, these results show a reciprocal relationship between campus and community motor vehicle theft rates. That is, when community motor vehicle theft rates were extremely high, campus motor vehicle theft rates were higher. In turn, as campus motor vehicle theft rates increased, so did community motor vehicle theft rates.

There are at least two interpretations for this reciprocal relationship. One explanation could be that students are the unwitting targets of automobile theft because they are careless. They may park in undesirable areas, leave their cars unlocked, or their keys unguarded. Alternatively, when motor vehicle theft rings operate in communities, they may not differentiate between the larger community and the campus, which would increase rates of motor vehicle theft both in the community and on campus.

We found that community crimes were largely the result of community characteristics. As shown in previous research, income levels, population size, age structure, size of minority population, and level of police strength (city police and civilian police) all affected levels of community crime (Sampson, 1986; Davidson, 1981; Harries, 1980). In addition, the ratio variable had a consistent and inverse relationship to community crime rates. That is, crime rates in the community were low when the campus population was large (compared to community population size). This could mean students were less likely than community members to engage in serious forms of crime. Thus, high concentrations of students depressed rates of serious crimes in the community. In this sense, campuses make good neighbors. However, for less serious public-order crimes (like disorderly conduct and public drunkenness), this finding may not hold.

We also found campus characteristics had few significant effects on community crime rates. First, rural campuses had lower rates of all forms of crime than did urban campuses. Second, recall that campus crime

TABLE III
PREDICTORS OF COMMUNITY CRIME[a]

| | Community Crime Rates: | | | | | |
	Rape	Assault	Robbery	Burglary	MV Theft	Larceny
Campus Crime Rates:						
High Rape	−.32					
	(−.96)					
Rape	.05					
	(.04)					
High Assault		−.13				
		(−.38)				
Assault		.15				
		(.10)				
High Robbery			.14			
			(.55)			
Robbery			.18			
			(.19)			
High Burglary				.17*		
				(.39)		
Burglary				.02		
				(.01)		
High MV Theft					.10	
					(.30)	
MV Theft					.54**	
					(.36)	
High Larceny						−.03
						(−.08)
Larceny						−.01
						(−.01)
Community Characteristics:						
Income		−.18*		−.20**		
		(−.0)		(−.0)		
% Age 18–20		−.17*	−.16*	−.15**	−.19**	
		(−.02)	(−.03)	(−.02)	(−.03)	
% Hispanic						
% African-Amer.	.19**	.34**	.31**	.18**	.13**	
	(.02)	(.03)	(.03)	(.01)	(.01)	
City Police				.09**	.10**	.09**
				(.0)	(.01)	(.0)
Population	−.14**			−.16**	−.12**	−.21**
	(−.0)			(−.0)	(−.0)	(−.0)
Ratio	−.26**	−.13	−.21**	−.16**	−.17**	−.34**
	(−.61)	(−.30)	(−.66)	(−.28)	(−.42)	(−.60)

TABLE III (Continued)

	Community Crime Rates:					
	Rape	Assault	Robbery	Burglary	MV Theft	Larceny
Campus Characteristics:						
Enrollment Type					.13* (.50)	
Campus Police						
% African-Amer.						
$ Room and Board						
% Part-time	−.17** (−.01)					
Dormitory %	−.18** (−1.34)	−.10* (−.72)	−.19** (−1.84)	−.17** (−.98)	−.19** (−1.44)	
Setting	−.16** (−.43)	−.21* (−.55)	−.23** (−.80)	−.29** (−.58)	−.21** (−.55)	−.36** (−.74)

* p < .05 ** p < .01
[a]Unstandardized coefficients are reported in parentheses; standardized are not.

rates were high when students spent more time on campus. This suggests community crime rates would be lower when dormitory populations were high. High populations of dormitory residents imply that students spend less time in the community and were, therefore, less likely to be victims of crime in the community. Table III confirms this: high dormitory populations were related to lower rates of rape, robbery, burglary, and motor vehicle theft in the community.

Thus, Table III illustrates that community characteristics had the largest influence on community crime rates and (excluding burglary and motor vehicle theft rates) campus crime rates had no effect on community crime rates. There were two campus characteristics that had significant influences on community crime rates. First, we found the higher the dormitory population on campus, the lower the rates of community crime. Second, rural campuses were associated with lower rates for all forms of community crime.

RECOMMENDATIONS

Our results suggest that when universities and colleges develop and implement campus safety and crime prevention programs, they need to consider student demographic characteristics, the structural characteristics of the campus, and the structural characteristics of the community.

How these elements interact and influence one another may vary across campuses; without additional research exploring these differences, it becomes difficult to discuss campus crime policy recommendations except in general terms. Because campuses are distinctive environments, effective security and crime preventive programs have to address the special needs of an individual campus, yet keep in mind how structural characteristics affect campus crime rates.

Security strategies and programs that educate the students about campus safety should account for the structural characteristics of the campus (e.g., where students spend their time and their level of wealth). For example, campuses with large dormitory populations should focus their security and crime preventive strategies toward campus rape and larceny. This emphasis, of course, would vary depending on whether the campus was residential or a commuter school. Because of varying structural characteristics, the two types of campuses (residential compared to commuter) had varying campus crime rates. We found residential campuses had higher rape and larceny rates while commuter campuses had lower rates of rape and larceny but higher rates of motor vehicle theft and robbery.

Campus administrators should also know the demographic composition of the students, and the percentage of part-time students also have implications for security policy. Our results indicated that campuses with a higher percentage of part-time students had lower rates of assault, robbery, burglary, and motor vehicle theft. Consequently, post-secondary schools with large populations of part-time students could shift their focus to more crucial security concerns that they may have while still maintaining control over the more serious campus crime. However, campuses that by and large have a higher percentage of full-time students need to focus their security programs on all forms of campus crime.

Of course, there are structural characteristics difficult for campuses to change. However, if administrators are aware of their potentially harmful influences, campus officials can modify their security and crime prevention programs. Two structural characteristics that may dictate type of security and crime preventive programs are cost of room and board and size of enrollment. Both were positively correlated with most types of campus crime. For example, we found campuses with large enrollments had higher rates of crime; a campus with many students provides more targets for prospective offenders and allows them to walk around unobserved. Therefore, security policies at campuses with large enrollments will have to incorporate these facts into their strategies.

Campuses with higher room and board costs generally need to focus their policies on all crimes *except* assault. While room and board costs are a structural characteristic that is difficult to change, administrators can make wealthy students aware of the risks of property crime that they face, just as campus security can focus on preventing property crime.

Knowing which structural characteristics are significantly related to campus crime, either low or high, has important policy implications for campus administrators. Having this information allows campuses to determine whether their crime rate is typical (compared to similar campuses) or if it is driven by other forces. For example, some campuses may naturally have higher crime rates because they have structural characteristics associated with higher crime rates (e.g., sizable enrollment). However, a problem arises when a campus has high crime rates yet has structural characteristics associated with low crime rates. The issue becomes determining what it is about that campus that is driving the crime rate and what can be done about it.

CONCLUSION

Many previous studies of campus crime focused on the characteristics of *victims* and not the characteristics of the *campus.* This focus ignores how structural characteristics of the campus and the community in which it is located could influence one another. These structural characteristics are important because they create opportunities for criminal events.

In this chapter, we have described and explained the relationship between college campuses and their communities by studying the effect of community characteristics and crime rates on campus crime rates and vice versa. The study examined whether crime in the community "spills over" to the campus and whether crime from campus "spills over" into the community.

We did not find much evidence of a reciprocal relationship between campus crime rates and community crime rates; we did, however, find a reciprocal relationship between campus motor vehicle theft rates and community motor vehicle theft rates. We also found community characteristics and community crime rates had little effect on campus crime rates. Only two community crimes, robbery and motor vehicle theft rates, had any significant influence on campus crime rates. This result could be expected because these crimes occur outside, where perpetrators are free to come and go.

By and large, *campus* crime rates are influenced by *campus* characteristics like enrollment size, percent African-American students, cost of room and board, percent part-time students, and percent of students residing in dormitories. More generally, our findings suggest that where students spent their time and their wealth determined their exposure to diverse types and levels of campus crime. For example, institutions with more full-time students had higher rates of assault, robbery, burglary, and larceny; campuses with high percentages of students residing in dormitories had higher rates of rape and larceny. A strong and direct effect on campus crime came from the costs of room and board (our proxy measure of students' wealth). Our analyses found that as room and board costs increased, so did rates of economically motivated campus crimes. This result may show that wealthier students provide more lucrative targets for economically motivated crimes.

Excluding campus rates of robbery and burglary, the size of the campus population (compared with the population of the community) was not a statistically significant predictor of campus crime rates. Perhaps when campus populations are large (compared to community populations), campuses are better able to insulate themselves from many types of crimes.

Similar to past research, we found community crime rates were primarily affected by community characteristics. Few campus characteristics had any effect on community crime rates. For example, burglary and motor vehicle theft appeared to "spill over" from the campus into the community. The percentage of students living in dormitories and urban settings also had significant effects on community crime rates. The results support the hypothesis that an increase in the time students spend on campus (especially living in dormitories) is associated with decreases in community rape, robbery, burglary, and motor vehicle theft rates. Further, recalling the analyses of the ratio variable, we found if the student population is large (compared to the community population), *all* community crime rates decreased. This may be because students are "good neighbors" and do not commit serious crimes in the community. However, future research should consider the impact of public-order crimes on campus and in the community. We found campus crime does not significantly contribute to a community's serious crime rate; however, the campus may pose other problems for the community by increasing their rates of public-order crime. While public-order crimes are not as serious as the crimes studied at present, they could still create problems for some communities.

Our findings, while contributing to understanding the causes and correlates of campus crime, open many future research paths. With a larger sample size, additional analyses and relationships can be explored. For example, the size of the student population compared to the size of the community population needs further analysis. One might expect that the causes and correlates of campus crime differ for small campuses located in large communities compared to large campuses located in small communities. The location of the campus (rural or urban) may have a large effect on the size of the reciprocal effects between campus and community crime rates. Although we found no two-way effects (excluding motor vehicle theft), we are not suggesting these effects may not occur in other situations. If we focus our analysis on particular forms of crime in distinct situations, it is possible two-way effects may be operating. More detailed analyses could lead to more specific policy recommendations.

NOTES

(1) We thank the Consortium for Higher Education Campus Crime Research (CHECCR) for providing the data used in the analyses and Pam Porter for helpful advice on earlier drafts of this chapter.

(2) Discussion of the status of the law in this area can be found in Smith (1995). Discussion of state-level initiatives to address campus crime are found in Griffaton (1995).

(3) Independent variables shown in Figure 1 were meant to be illustrative. Additional variables were used in the analyses.

(4) Many variables were initially tested in the equations. Variables reported were those of prime theoretical importance or statistically significant in at least one equation.

(5) We were concerned that reciprocal relationships between specific types of campus and community crime could be a methodological artifact because campuses could have reported their crimes to both the FBI and to local police. In turn, the local police could report them to the FBI a second time as part of their local crime figures. To correct for this and to evaluate the seriousness of the problem, we subtracted campus crime community crimes before calculating rates. If this resulted in the number of crimes in the community being less than or equal to zero, we

maintained the original community crime for that case. Since these new crime rates produce results comparable with results obtained without this manipulation, we use the original coding scheme in the analyses reported in the chapter.

(6) We included both the continuous crime rate and the dummy variable indicating very high crime rate in the equations at the same time. We did this for two reasons. First, we expected lower levels of crime in one location (campus) to have continuously affected crime in the other location (community). Second, we expected extraordinarily high crime in the other place (campus) to have qualitatively increased crime in the other place (community). While the continuous crime rate and dummy high crime variables were correlated, they did not produce a collinearity problem.

(7) Dollar cost of room and board is our proxy measure for the wealth of students. These costs vary considerably and can significantly exceed tuition costs. The costs of room and board are generally higher at private schools than public schools. We assumed this cost differential is because the accommodations are nicer; for a wealthy student, nicer accommodations could be an additional reason to choose a private school. To eliminate the effect of "public" compared to "private" school differences in the analysis, we controlled for type of institution (private or public). To avoid missing data, we coded commuter schools as having "zero" room and board costs. In the analyses, we eliminated the bias this coding scheme created by controlling for whether the institution was a commuter school.

(8) The latter variables, respectively, measure the number of city police per 100,000 population and number of civilian police employees per 100,000 population.

(9) Three stage least squares allowed us to estimate the effect of a particular type of campus crime on the same type of community crime and the simultaneous effect of community crime on campus crime. These two equations are solved simultaneously. If ordinary least squares analyses were used to estimate the two equations individually, the errors in estimation would be confounded leading to improper results.

(10) In three stage least squares, instruments are required for equation estimations. An instrument is a theoretically important variable that predicts the dependent variables in one simultaneous equation (i.e., community crime) and does not predict the dependent variable in the other equation (i.e., campus crime). Both equations need an instrument. If the instruments were not included, there would be too many unknowns to solve the set of simultaneous equations. The instruments used to initially solve the equations were campus police (in the campus crime equation) and city police (in the city crime equation).

(11) To ensure that the ratio variable was not a proxy measure of community size, the initial estimation of equations included campus enrollment and community population size. With these two variables in the equations, the ratio variable had identical relationships with the crime rates as reported in the chapter. This result shows that the ratio variable is not a proxy for community size.

REFERENCES

Adams, J.W., J.L. Kottke and J.S. Padgitt (1983) "Sexual Harassment of University Students." *Journal of College Student Personnel 24:*484–490.

Bachman, R., R.J. Paternoster and S. Ward (1992) "The Rationality of Sexual Offending: Testing a Deterrence/Rational Choice Conception of Sexual Assault." *Law & Society Review 26:*343–372.

Brantingham, P.J., and P.L. Brantingham (1993) "Environment, Routine, and Situation: Toward a Pattern Theory of Crime." In R.V. Clarke and M. Felson (eds.) *Routine Activity and Rational Choice: Advances in Criminological Theory.* New Brunswick, NJ: Transaction Publishers.

—— (eds.) (1981) *Environmental Criminology.* Beverley Hills, CA: Sage.

Bromley, M.L. (1992) "Campus and Community Crime Rate Comparisons: A State-wide Study." *Journal of Security Administration 15*(2):49–64.

Bureau of Justice Statistics (1992) *Sourcebook of Criminal Justice Statistics.* Washington, DC: US Government Printing Office.

Davidson, R.N. (1981) *Crime and Environment.* London: Croom Helm.

Fisher, B. (1992) "On Crime and Fear of Crime on University and College Campuses and the Surrounding Legal Issues." *Journal of Security Administration 15*(2):1–4.

Fox, J.A., and D.A. Hellman. (1985) "Location and Other Correlates of Campus Crime." *Journal of Criminal Justice 13*(2):429–444.

Griffaton, M.C. (1995) "State-Level Initiative on Campus Crime." In B.S. Fisher and J.J. Sloan, III (eds.) *Campus Crime: Legal, Social, and Policy Perspectives.* Springfield, IL: Charles C Thomas.

Hakim, S. and G.F. Rengert (eds.) (1981) *Crime Spillover.* Beverly Hills, CA: Sage.

Harries, K.D. (1980) *Crime and the Environment.* Springfield, IL: Charles C Thomas.

Kanin, E.J. (1984) "Date Rape: Unofficial Criminals and Victims." *Victimology 9*(1):95–108.

Koss, M., C. Gidycz and N. Wisniewski (1987) "The Scope of Rape: Incidence and Prevalence of Sexual Aggression and Victimization in a National Sample of Higher Education Students." *Journal of Consulting and Clinical Psychology 55:*162–170.

Lehman, A.E. (ed.) (1992) *Peterson's Guide to Four-Year Colleges 1992.* Princeton, NJ: Peterson's Guides.

Lizotte, A.J. and A. Fernandez (1993) *Trends and Correlates of Campus Crime: A General Report.* Albany, NY: Consortium of Higher Education Campus Crime Research.

McPheters, L.R. (1978) "Econometric Analysis of Factors Influencing Crime on the Campus." *Journal of Criminal Justice 6*(1):47–51.

Metha, A. and J. Nigg (1982) "Sexual Harassment: Implications of a Study at Arizona State University." *Women's Studies Quarterly 10*(1):24–26.

Mills, C.S. and B. Granoff (1992) "Date and Acquaintance Rape Among a Sample of College Students." *Social Work 37:*504–509.

Nichols, D. (1987) *The Administration of Public Safety in Higher Education.* Springfield, IL: Charles C Thomas.

Peak, K.J. (1995) "The Professionalization of Campus Law Enforcement." In B.S.

Fisher and J.J. Sloan, III (eds.) *Campus Crime: Legal, Social, and Policy Perspectives.* Springfield, IL: Charles C Thomas.

Powell, J.W. (1981) *Campus Security and Law Enforcement.* London: Butterworth Publishers.

Roark, M.L. (1987) "Preventing Violence on College Campuses." *Journal of Counseling and Development 65:*367–370.

Sampson, R.J. (1986) "Crime in Cities: The Effects of Formal and Informal Social Control." In A.J. Reis, Jr. and M. Tonry (eds.) *Communities and Crime.* Chicago: University of Chicago Press, pp. 271–311.

Sherrill, J.M. and D.G. Siegel (eds.) (1989) *Responding to Violence on Campus.* San Francisco, CA: Jossey-Bass.

Siegel, D.G. and C.H. Raymond (1992) "An Ecological Approach to Violent Crime on Campus." *Journal of Security Administration 15*(2):19–29.

Sloan, J.J. (1994) "The Correlates of Campus Crime: An Analysis of Crimes Reported to University Police." *Journal of Criminal Justice 22*(1):51–61.

—— (1992) "Campus Crime and Campus Communities: An analysis of crimes known to campus police and security." *Journal of Security Administration 15*(2):31–45.

Smith, M.C. (1995) "The Status of the Law and Liability for Colleges and Universities." In B.S. Fisher and J.J. Sloan, III (eds.) *Campus Crime: Legal, Social and Policy Perspectives.* Springfield, IL: Charles C Thomas.

——(1989) "Institutional Liability Resulting from Campus Crime: An Analysis of Theories of Recovery." *Education Law Reporter 55:*361–368.

—— (1988) *Coping with Crime on Campus.* New York: Macmillan.

Smith, M.C. and M.D. Smith (1990) *Wide Awake: A Guide to Safe Campus Living in the 90s.* Princeton, NJ: Peterson's Guide.

Sptizberg, I.J. and V.V. Thorndike (1992) *Creating Community on College Campuses.* Albany, NY: State University of New York Press.

Student Right-to-Know and Campus Security Act (1990). Public Law No. 101–542, amended by Public Law No. 102–26, Sec. 10(e) (1991); 20 USC 1092(f).

United States Department of Education (1993) *Digest of Education Statistics for 1993.* Washington, DC: U.S. Government Printing Office.

Ward, S.K., K. Chapman, E. Cohn, S. White and K. Williams (1991) "Acquaintance Rape and the College Social Scene." *Family Relations 40*(1):65–71.

Wilson, K.R. and L. Kraus (1983) "Sexual Harassment in the University." *Journal of College Student Personnel 24:*219–224.

Chapter 6

PREDICTING THE LIKELIHOOD OF FACULTY VICTIMIZATION: INDIVIDUAL DEMOGRAPHICS AND ROUTINE ACTIVITIES

John D. Wooldredge, Francis T. Cullen and Edward J. Latessa

INTRODUCTION

Recent media attention (e.g., Lederman, 1993) to the problem of crime on college and university campuses neglects the fact campus crime affects not only college students but faculty members as well. However, it is probably unwise to assume the likelihood of victimization for faculty members is the same as for students. Although both groups may share the physical space of a college campus, students and faculty members differ in the privacy of their work environments, with whom they interact, the time spent in these work environments, and their routine activities in these environments. In turn, these differences may differentially influence the likelihood of victimization for the two groups. It is important to examine victimization among faculty members to provide a more comprehensive picture of the magnitude and possible causes of their on-campus victimization.

College faculty may be more vulnerable than students to campus victimization, given their work routines and the time they spend on campus. In contrast to students, faculty (1) spend more hours each day working alone in classroom buildings, (2) are exposed to larger numbers of students and staff (given the nature of their work), and (3) compared to students, their routines are much more structured and easier to monitor. Although the likelihood of victimization for students may be influenced by the same variables affecting faculty victimization, these forces differ dramatically between the two groups. In turn, these differences could lead to varying likelihoods of victimization for faculty members compared with students.

This chapter describes and explains possible causes of faculty victimization at an urban university and the relative importance of individual demographic characteristics compared to life-style characteristics for shaping the likelihood of faculty victimization.

ROUTINES COMPARED WITH DEMOGRAPHICS IN PREDICTING VICTIMIZATION

Several studies' results have supported routine activities theory as an explanation for individual-level differences in the likelihood of victimization (Collins, Cox, & Langan, 1987; Felson, 1986, 1987; Lynch, 1987; Sampson & Wooldredge, 1987; Cohen & Felson, 1979, 1981; Hindelang, Gottfredson, & Garofalo, 1978). However, some researchers have found that individual demographics like gender, race, and age are stronger predictors of the likelihood of victimization when compared to an individual's daily routine activities which affect his or her opportunities for victimization (Clarke, Ekblom, & Mayhew, 1985; Gottfredson, 1984). Yet, one theme in these studies is finding greater support for routine activities theory when researchers examine victimization in distinct social domains (e.g., work, school, home, or leisure) with precise measures of routine activities occurring in those domains. For example, Lynch (1987) has argued that individual demographics merely proxy the significant effects of various unmeasured routine activities on likelihood of victimization. For example, if men are more likely to work in occupations with greater victimization risks (like unskilled blue-collar positions), then general studies of victimization may reveal significant correlations between gender and victimization *if* type of occupation is not controlled. More properly specified models with domain-specific measures of routine activities may yield less support for the importance of demographics and greater support for routine activities in predicting likelihood of victimization.

A recent study of victimization among faculty members at an urban university revealed that, controlling for routine activities particular to faculty, the demographics of gender, age, and race were not significant predictors of personal and property victimization (Wooldredge, Cullen, & Latessa, 1992). Furthermore, substantial support was found for the significance of daily activities in predicting the likelihood of property and personal victimization of faculty while on campus. However, the possible utility of individual demographics for predicting the likelihood of victimization should not be disregarded entirely. Criminologists must recognize the possibility that demographic characteristics may *interact* with select routines to produce significant differences in likelihood of victimization. In other words, it is possible that limited *types* of routine activities may increase the likelihood of victimization for members of some demographic groups but not others.

This chapter explores the possible use of interactions of individual demographic characteristics (gender and race) and domain-specific routines for predicting a faculty member's likelihood of criminal victimization. Data for the present study are from a larger analysis of faculty victimization described above (Wooldredge, Cullen, & Latessa, 1992).

ROUTINE ACTIVITIES THEORY

Routine activities theory posits the likelihood of victimization is heavily influenced by one's daily (routine) activities which affect his or her opportunities for victimization (Felson, 1986, 1987; Cohen & Felson, 1979, 1981). Four concepts, central to the theory, are related to routine activities: *exposure* of one or one's property to potential offenders, *guardianship* over one and one's property, *target attractiveness,* and *proximity to offenders* (Cohen & Felson, 1979; Hindelang, Gottfredson & Garofalo, 1978). Greater exposure, less guardianship, more attractive targets, and closer proximity to offenders should correspond with significant increases in likelihood of victimization. The concept "offender proximity" is difficult to operationalize; many researchers use "perceived dangerousness" as a proxy (Lynch, 1987). Generally, researchers assume people who perceive greater victimization risks for themselves or their property are close to potential offenders.

As discussed above, previous victimization studies have not included properly specified models of domain-specific routine activities. In addition, many previous studies have included analyses of survey data involving how many times respondents were victimized during select periods (Garofalo, 1987). The difficulty with this technique is that the specific domains of victimization are unknown, so it becomes difficult to estimate actual relationships among domain-specific routines and the likelihood of victimization (Lynch, 1987). Studies which explore activities and victimizations converging in time and space may be more likely to yield support for routine activities theory (Sherman, Gartin, & Buerger, 1989; Collins, Cox, & Langan, 1987; Garofalo, Siegel, & Laub, 1987; Maxfield, 1987; Block, Felson, & Block, 1984; Gottfredson, 1981, 1984).

Correcting for these problems in a study of campus victimization among faculty at the University of Cincinnati, Wooldredge, Cullen, and Latessa's (1992) results supported *exposure, guardianship,* and *perceived dangerousness* as predictors of the likelihood of property victimization (e.g., office burglary, theft of office property, and damage to office property). However, in predicting the likelihood of victimization for personal crimes (e.g., robbery, aggravated assault, sexual assault, and assault with a deadly weapon), their results supported only *exposure* and *perceived dangerousness* as predictors of victimization.

The differences between the two models (i.e., comparing property to personal victimization) could be because of operational concepts related to *guardianship* (which focused only on the guardianship of property). Further, the lack of significance of *target attractiveness* in predicting personal victimization could have resulted from the model including only one operational concept related to the theoretical construct.

Despite these differences, results from both models revealed no relationships among a faculty member's gender, race, and age and likelihood of either property or personal victimization. Wooldredge et al. (1992) suggested the results support the idea that "improvements in measurement and model specification corresponding with domain-specific analyses of victimization may reduce the importance of demographic variables in those models" (p. 332).

To fully test the usefulness of demographics for predicting the likelihood of victimization, the next logical step would be to examine whether demographic characteristics *interact* with differences in routines to produce differences in the likelihood of victimization. The original argument supporting the primary effects of demographic characteristics on likelihood of victimization said that explicit demographic groups may be more vulnerable to victimization because these groups are more *vulnerable* to victimization. For example, potential offenders may perceive women as easier targets than men and minorities may be more likely to reside and interact in geographic areas with higher crime rates (because of income differences between non-whites and whites).

The logic behind race as a predictor of victimization ties into the argument that individual demographics are correlated with distinctive routines which may, in turn, increase both an individual's exposure of self and his or her proximity to offenders. Therefore, controlling for vulnerability (as influenced by routine activities) should significantly reduce variation in likelihood of victimization between whites and non-whites.

This logic does not apply to gender differences in the likelihood of victimization because the argument related to gender centers on the idea that women are *perceived* by potential offenders as "more vulnerable" than men. The argument related to gender differences in victimization may therefore be valid for distinct *types* of routine activities which could enhance perceptions of vulnerability. In short, an individual's gender may influence the likelihood of victimization only in limited contexts involving select social routines while gender may be irrelevant in other contexts.

STUDY SITE AND SAMPLE

The University of Cincinnati is an urban campus with approximately 36,000 students spread over two campuses. The East and West campuses are located two miles from the central business district of the city. Faculty from the East campus were not included in the study because this campus constitutes the medical college—the environments of the two campuses could themselves contribute to differences in likelihood of victimization. Therefore, the study's target population included all full-time faculty on the West campus during the 1990–91 academic year.

The West campus contains all colleges except the medical college. All classrooms, office buildings, and dormitories are in the same geographic area and within 30 minutes walking distance of one another. Campus businesses and student apartments constitute the perimeter of the West campus.

Because the University of Cincinnati is an urban campus, the results of the present study cannot be generalized to suburban, small town, or rural campuses because the prevalence of crime and victimization varies significantly across different geographic areas based on the population densities of those areas (see Sloan, 1994). In short, larger concentrations of people on a campus correspond with higher likelihood of victimization.

The sample for the current study consisted of 427 full-time faculty working on the University of Cincinnati's West campus between September 1, 1989 and December 31, 1990 (the original sample consisted of 422 faculty members).[1] The sample comprised 51% of the target population. Crime victimizations suffered by faculty members during the study period included *personal crimes* (robbery, aggravated assault, sexual assault, and assault with a deadly weapon) and *property crimes* (office burglary, theft of personal property, and damage to office personal property). Five percent of the faculty in the sample were victimized by personal crimes during the study period while 27 percent of sample members were the victims of property crimes.

The logic behind individual demographics as important for predicting likelihood of victimization implies demographic variables are more appropriate to studies of personal victimization and not property victimization. Therefore, the present study only included an analysis of personal victimizations.

Of the 427 respondents in the study, 21 were the victims of personal crime. This figure reflects enough variation to generate internally valid results; the external validity of the results is questionable. As a result, the purpose of this study is to examine whether interactions of individual demographics and routine activities should be used in future research examining faculty (or student) victimization on college or university campuses.

RESEARCH HYPOTHESES

Main Effects

Measures of *exposure* in the university domain included: the average number of weekday nights (Monday through Friday), each week during the study period, a faculty member spent on campus; the average number of Saturdays spent on campus each month; the average number of Saturday nights spent on campus each month; the extent a faculty member walked alone on campus during the study period (aside from walking to and from classes); and whether a faculty member socialized with students outside classes during the study period.

We hypothesized a faculty member's likelihood of victimization would increase with an increase in the frequency of number of weekday nights, Saturdays, and Saturday nights on campus; an increase in the frequency of walking alone on campus; and if the faculty member socialized with students outside classes.

Several measures of *guardianship* were also created (although these operational concepts may be more applicable to studies of property victimization). Nonetheless, their inclusion in the model is important because property victimizations can lead to personal victimizations (e.g., a burglary can lead to the assault of the property owner). These measures included: the extent other faculty are in shouting distance of a faculty member's office; whether a faculty member teaches all his or her classes in the same building where his or her office is located; and whether a faculty member's office is in the most secured and best-lit building on campus. We hypothesized that victimization would be more likely: (1) among faculty whose offices are removed from others' offices (i.e., removed from "shouting distance"), (2) among faculty who do not teach in buildings housing their offices, and (3) among faculty whose office buildings are less secure.

The concept *target attractiveness* is likewise more appropriate to studies of property victimization, but its inclusion in current study is important for the same reason as guardianship. Target attractiveness was measured as whether a faculty member's office is in a "high status" building (i.e., buildings housing the departments with the largest amounts of capital resources, including biology, chemistry, computer science, engineering, law, and music). Because of the presence of easily convertible goods (e.g., musical instruments, computers, or laboratory equipment), faculty in these "high status" buildings could be more susceptible to victimization. It should be noted, however, that none of these buildings includes the "most secured" building mentioned above.

The concept *proximity to offenders* was measured by the degree a faculty member generally "felt safe while on campus." We hypothesized that the likelihood of victimization is higher among faculty who feel less safe on campus.

Demographic variables included gender and race (white-Anglos compared to all others). We hypothesized the direct effects of these demographic variables would not be statistically significant predictors of likelihood of victimization.

We did not include age because of difficulty in interpreting interaction effects between age and routine activities (given the operational concepts examined). In pooled models, interaction terms are the products of the original variables. Thus, age multiplied by the number of weekday nights on campus would not yield a very useful scale. For example, a forty-year-old faculty member who spent an average of three weekday nights on campus receives the same value (120) as a faculty member aged 60 who spent two nights on campus each week. The direct effect of age was weak and was not statistically significant in the original study—its exclusion from the complete model did not alter the coefficient estimates of the remaining variables.

For the present analyses, we also excluded two operational concepts from the original study: *aggregate students in classes* and *months on leave* from the university during the study period. We omitted these variables from the new model because they did not maintain significant relationships in the original model, either with property or personal victimization, and their exclusion did not significantly alter coefficient estimates of the remaining variables.

Interaction Effects

In this study, we examined four interactions of demographics and routine activities. We should note, however, given their theoretical rationale, the interactions are relevant only for the theoretical concept *exposure.* The specific *measures* of exposure we used concern exposure of faculty members to potential offenders, whereas measures of *guardianship* and *target attractiveness* apply to faculty members' offices and property.

We also note the variables related to nights and Saturdays spent on campus were combined to prevent multicollinearity (see discussion in the next section). Further, interactions involving "frequency of walking alone on campus" could not be examined for the same reason (also discussed in the next section). Thus, the interactions we examined included the following: gender by "nights and weekends spent on campus," gender by "socialize with students," race by "nights and weekends spent on campus," and race by "socialize with students outside classes."

We hypothesized the likelihood of victimization would be highest among women spending time on campus "after hours," among women who "socialize with students" outside classes, among non-whites spending time on campus "after hours," and among non-whites who "socialize with students" outside classes.

Women may be more vulnerable in situations where they are exposed to potential offenders, thereby increasing their likelihood of victimization *only* in these situations. On the other hand, non-whites may more likely be victims in these situations because of the greater opportunities offered potential offenders to victimize minorities.

RESEARCH METHODOLOGY

Every faculty member on the West campus of the University of Cincinnati was sent a self-report survey which contained questions about personal and property victimizations occurring on campus between September 1, 1989 and August 31, 1990. The questionnaire also asked faculty members about their demographic characteristics as well as their "routine activities" and feelings of safety on campus (a complete discussion of the sample and data set is found in Wooldredge, Cullen & Latessa, 1992).

The dependent variable for the current study is whether a faculty member was a victim (yes/no) of a personal crime (e.g., robbery, aggravated assault, sexual assault, or assault with a deadly weapon) during the 12-month period described above. Few faculty were victimized more than once during the period; therefore, the number of times a faculty member was victimized could not be examined as a dependent variable.

Table I presents the definitions, categories, and univariate descriptives for the variables used in the analyses. Table I shows that women comprised 23% of the sample and minorities comprised 10% of the sample. These figures are comparable to the population of faculty on the West campus (roughly 20% percent female and 10% minority). The descriptives also reveal that, generally, faculty spent some (but not much) time on campus after hours and on weekends and while on campus, they walk alone. Additionally, 55% of the faculty members claimed they socialized with students outside classes; most were in offices in shouting distance of other faculty; and 69% teach all of their classes in the building housing their office. Finally, 8% of the faculty teach in the most secure building on campus, 39% teach in a "high status" office building, and most faculty (generally) felt safe on campus.

These figures reveal significant variation in the "routine activities" variables. If the likelihood of victimization is influenced by these variables, the descriptives in Table I suggest the sample includes a wide range of faculty at "high," "medium," and "low" risk of suffering victimization.

The variables representing "weekdays nights" (Monday through Friday), "Saturdays on campus," and "Saturday nights on campus" were not separately included in the complete model to prevent multicollinearity (faculty who spent more weekday nights on campus were also likely to have spent more weekends on campus). Therefore, we created a "composite variable" from the three separate variables by summing the standardized scores for all three variables. This new variable is standardized with a mean of zero with a standard deviation of approximately 3.00. The procedure adjusted for the differences in scales among the three separate variables; larger values on this composite variable reflect additional time spent "after hours" on campus by a faculty member.

TABLE I
DEFINITIONS AND UNIVARIATE DESCRIPTIVES FOR ALL VARIABLES

Variable	Categories	Mean	Median	SD
Dependent:				
Victim of personal crime	0 = no 1 = yes	0.049	0.000	0.216
Demographics:				
Gender	0 = male 1 = female	0.230	0.000	0.423
Race	0 = white 1 = other	0.102	0.000	0.303
Exposure:				
Average number of weekday nights on campus each week; Average number of Saturdays and Saturday nights on campus each month	Range: −2.06 to 10.68 (composite)	0.000	−0.471	2.838
Frequency of walking alone on campus, aside from trips to class	1 = never 2 = sometimes 3 = often	2.591	3.000	0.562
Socialize with students outside of classes	0 = no 1 = yes	0.554	1.000	0.498
Guardianship:				
Colleagues within shouting distance from office	1 = never 2 = sometimes 3 = often	2.515	3.000	0.704
Teach all classes in office building	0 = no 1 = yes	0.693	1.000	0.462
Office in most secured building on campus	0 = no 1 = yes	0.076	0.000	0.265
Target Attractiveness:				
Office in "high status" building	0 = no 1 = yes	0.390	0.000	0.488

TABLE I (Continued)

Variable	Categories	Mean	Median	SD
Perceived Dangerousness:				
Agreement with statement: "I generally feel safe on campus"	1 = strongly disagree 2 = disagree 3 = agree 4 = strongly agree	3.191	3.000	0.599
Interactions:				
Gender (x) On campus after hours	Range: −2.06 to 10.29	−0.014	0.000	1.052
Gender (x) Socialize with students	0 = all others 1 = female and socializes	0.092	0.000	0.290
Race (x) On campus after hours	Range: −2.06 to 10.68	0.132	0.000	1.105
Race (x) Socialize with students	0 = all others 1 = non-white, socializes	0.049	0.000	0.215

N = 427

Before including the six interaction terms in the model, we explored them for evidence of multicollinearity. Four of the six interactions included in the model without producing multicollinearity problems were: gender by nights and weekends on campus, gender by "socialize with students," race by "nights and weekends on campus," and race by "socialize with students." The remaining interactions were too highly correlated ($r > .70$) with their components and were dropped from the model.

We created two models for this study: one with and one without interactions. We did this to alleviate any other concerns about multicollinearity in the model with interactions.

We used logit analysis (Aldrich & Nelson, 1984) to estimate the models. This method of analysis is appropriate for dichotomous dependent variables with marginally skewed distributions (see Aldrich & Nelson, 1984). Logit models have been used in related studies of victimization because most of these studies have included similarly skewed dependent variables (see Sampson & Wooldredge, 1987).

RESULTS AND DISCUSSION

Table II presents the results of the complete models predicting personal victimization. Despite differences in this and the original studies' sample size and number of variables examined, the results for statistical significance and strength of fit are consistent between the two studies. In the model without interaction terms, neither gender nor race were statistically significant while the variables tapping exposure and perceived dangerousness were statistically significant. The results reveal that a faculty member's likelihood of personal crime victimization significantly *increases* with (1) more evenings and weekends spent on campus, (2) increased frequency of walking alone on campus, (3) increased social interactions with students, and (4) a decline in feelings of safety on campus.

The results for the model with the interaction terms reveal that two of the four interactions were statistically significant, but the effect of one of the interactions was in a direction opposite to that hypothesized. Women who spent more evenings and weekends on campus were significantly *less* likely to be victimized by personal crimes compared to any other subgroup examined. This result contradicts the relationship we hypothesized for this interaction. A separate crosstabs analysis (not presented) revealed the substantive significance of the gender interaction term is with the difference between men spending more evenings and weekends on campus compared with women doing the same. Interestingly, compared to members in the former group, members in the latter group were *less likely* to be victimized.

In contrast, the interaction of race and number of evenings and weekends spent on campus was statistically significant *and* in the hypothesized direction: compared to the other subgroups, minorities who spent more evenings and weekends on campus were more likely to be victimized by personal crimes.

This interpretation is, however, not intuitively obvious from Table II because the interaction coefficient's sign is *negative* suggesting just the opposite conclusion. Additionally, the independent effect of race on personal victimization is now statistically significant and much stronger (compared to the model without the interaction term). This effect is a consequence of adding the interaction terms involving race to the complete model (see following discussion). The main effect of race is in the expected direction, indicating higher likelihood of victimization for

TABLE II
LOGIT ANALYSIS OF FACULTY MEMBERS' PERSONAL VICTIMIZATIONS

Variable	Model without interactions	Model with interactions
	Logit Coefficient (SE)	Logit Coefficient (SE)
Constant	−1.462 (2.126)	−1.420 (2.201)
Gender	−1.056 (0.820)	−2.249 (2.003)
Race	0.946 (0.696)	1.907** (0.912)
On campus after hours	0.217** (0.106)	0.359** (0.119)
Walk alone on campus	1.091* (0.650)	1.228* (0.698)
Socialize with students	1.506** (0.678)	1.405* (0.818)
Colleagues within shouting distance	−0.189 (0.449)	−0.273 (0.463)
Teach in office building	−0.095 (0.564)	−0.182 (0.576)
Office in most secured building	−0.009 (1.143)	−0.651 (1.298)
Office in "high status" building	0.220 (0.558)	0.240 (0.568)
Generally feel safe	−1.220** (0.446)	−1.368** (0.476)
Gender (x) Nights on campus	—	−1.723* (1.145)
Gender (x) Socialize with students	—	5.365 (20.989)
Race (×) Night on campus	—	−0.388* (0.223)
Race (×) Socialize with students	—	0.397 (1.524)
Model chi-square	38.29 (10 df)	45.83 (14 df)
−2 (×) log likelihood	117.74	109.95
Gamma	0.659	0.750

* 1.5 times standard error
** 2.0 times standard error

non-whites (compared to whites). In any logit model, however, the interpretation of the dependent variable (in this case, likelihood of victimization) must involve an evaluation of the *entire model* and not separate evaluation of the individual variables in the model (also discussed below). However, the results for both interaction terms were statistically significant only when a critical region of .10 was used, suggesting the interactions were marginally significant. Neither interaction term comprising whether faculty socialize with students outside classes was statistically significant.

These findings provide only partial support for the idea that interactions of individual demographics and domain-specific routine activities may be important for predicting the likelihood of personal victimization. However, the results do suggest that demographic characteristics may be important predictors of victimization in the context of *distinctive* routine activities and not *all* routine activities.

As noted above, race becomes statistically significant in the complete model *only* when the interaction terms are included. This should not be surprising, however, given the nature of the analysis—inclusion of interaction terms sometimes inflates the magnitude of the coefficients for the individual variables because of non-zero correlations among them (Hanushek & Jackson, 1977). This happens to the individual variables which comprise the statistically significant interactions. Thus, in the present model, the direct effect of race on victimization was a consequence of the method of analysis. This situation illustrates why it is important to estimate models with *and* without interaction terms. Finally, the consistency between the two models (statistical significance and coefficient estimates for the remaining variables in the models) indicate that multicollinearity is not a problem.

The dependent variable in the logit analysis was the natural log of the ratio of the probability of personal crime victimization p, to the probability of nonvictimization $(1-p)$, or $\ln[p/(1-p)]$. Taking the natural antilog and solving for p therefore provides the exact probability of victimization for individual faculty profiles.

This procedure provides a useful interpretation of the results. We can, for example, calculate the exact probabilities of victimization for people sharing all the same characteristics (except gender). Comparing males to females who spent the *most* time on campus after hours and using the median values of the remaining independent variables for the calculations, the likelihood of victimization for males in the sample was equal to:

$\ln[p/(1+ -p)] = -1.420 - 2.249(0) + 1.907(0) + 0.359(10.68) + 1.228(3) + 1.405(0) - 0.273(3) - 0.182(1) - 0.651(0) + 0.240(0) - 1.368(3) - 1.723(0) + 5.365(0) - 0.388(0) + 0.397(0)$

$\ln[p]/1-p] = 0.993$

$p/(1-p) = 2.6993203$
$p = 0.730.$

The likelihood of victimization for females in the sample was equal to:

$\ln[p/(1-p)] = -1.420 - 2.249(1) + 1.907(0) + 0.359(10.68) + 1.228(3) + 1.405(0) - 0.273(3) - 0.182(1) - 0.651(0) + 0.240(0) - 1.368(3) - 1.723(10.29) + 5.365(0) - 0.388(0) + 0.397(0)$
$\ln[p/(1-p)] = -13.62069$

$p/(1-p) = 0.0000012$
$p = 0.0000011.$

This dramatic difference in likelihood of personal crime victimization suggested a male faculty member's likelihood of victimization increased dramatically *if* he spent many nights and weekends on campus (the largest value for the composite variable relating to nights and weekends on campus was used in the equations—this accounted for the dramatic difference in the likelihood of victimization).

Given the stronger effect of race in the model with interaction terms, the probability of personal victimization for non-white male faculty members who spent the most evenings and weekends on campus was 0.945 compared to 0.730 for white males who spent the most evenings and weekends on campus. While not as dramatic a difference as we found for gender-based groups, the difference in likelihood of victimization was still significant between race groups who spent the most time on campus after hours.

Using the equation *without* interactions (see Table II), we calculated the probabilities of victimization for white males, white females, non-white males, and non-white females at high, average, or low risk of victimization. This alternative analysis allowed us to determine whether the *interactions* of gender and race corresponded with significant differences in the likelihood of victimization when all variables related to routine activities were *simultaneously* manipulated in the equation. We also did this to provide a more useful comparison of victimization likelihood for all four demographic groups. The probabilities are presented in Table III; definitions of high, average, and low risk are also found in Table III.

TABLE III
PROBABILITIES OF VICTIMIZATION FOR FACULTY MEMBERS
BY DEMOGRAPHIC AND RISK GROUPS

	Demographic Group			
	White Males	White Females	Black Males	Black Females
Risk Group:				
Average[a] Risk	0.104	0.231	0.039	0.095
Lowest[b] Risk	0.0017	0.0044	0.0006	0.0015
Highest[c] Risk	0.987	0.988	0.995	0.968

[a]*Average Risk:* Mean values of variables related to exposure, guardianship, target attractiveness, and perceived dangerousness were used in the calculation of the logit equation predicting the likelihood of personal victimization.
[b]*Lowest Risk:* Values representing the lowest amount of exposure, the highest levels of guardianship, the least attractive targets, and the least amount of perceived dangerousness were used in the calculation of the logit equation predicting the likelihood of personal victimization.
[c]*Highest Risk:* Values representing the greatest amount of exposure, the lowest levels of guardianship, the most attractive targets, and the greatest amount of perceived dangerousness were used in the calculation of the logit equation predicting the likelihood of personal victimization.

The results presented in Table III provide important qualifications to the above discussion. The findings revealed that the greatest differences among demographic groups in likelihood of victimization occurred for faculty with an "average risk" of victimization. This result was important because faculty at an "average risk" of victimization were "typical cases" in the sample. This means there were significant differences in likelihood of victimization between demographic groups among faculty with the "most typical" daily routines. White *females* were the most likely targets of personal victimization (23%), followed by white males (10%), black females (10%), and black males (4%). In contrast to the above discussion, *female* members of the sample (regardless of their race) were the most likely victims of personal crime when *all* variables in the model were assigned their mean values. Further, in contrast to the above discussion, black males had the *lowest* risk of victimization when all variables were assigned their mean scores.

The results in Table III show (1) the importance of gender and race for predicting victimization and (2) *how* these characteristics pertain to victimization depend on a faculty member's daily routine. They also highlight gender and race as important predictors of victimization in specific social contexts.

The finding for black males contrasts with the victimization literature which suggests black males are *generally* at higher risk of victimization (compared to any other gender or racial group). The above results are not necessarily contradictory findings, however, because this study examined a subgroup (black male university faculty) of the general population. The results emphasize the importance of examining victimization in different environmental settings.

We also note that the finding of gender differences in victimization *only* applies to faculty at average risk of victimization. Gender is *not* a significant predictor of personal victimization in Table II because the results in Table II are not specified by victimization risk.

POLICY IMPLICATIONS

These findings suggest that several steps could be taken to reduce a faculty member's risk of personal victimization while he or she is on campus:

(1) Increase building security for faculty who work after hours (e.g., lock outside doors after a definite time, create better lighting).

(2) Upgrade external campus lighting for people walking on campus alone after dark.

(3) Reduce faculty members' interactions with students in social settings.

(4) Enhance faculty members' feelings of safety on campus by improving external lighting after dark, expanding building security, and by installing emergency call boxes.

These implications may only be applicable to reducing faculty victimizations on urban campuses. Campuses located outside of urban areas (i.e., not located in the center of a large city) may be safer places for faculty because they are removed from high-crime areas more generally.

CONCLUSIONS

There are three important recommendations emerging from this research. First, the possible importance of interactions of individual demographic characteristics with routine activities should not be ignored in studies of personal victimization. Second, it is possible individual demographics play important parts in predicting personal victimization in the context of particular routine activities. Finally, researchers need to be wary of multicollinearity problems that could result from studies of interaction effects.

The current study's results provide two important qualifications to the original analysis of personal victimization of faculty in a university setting (Wooldredge et al., 1992). First, individual demographics may be important for predicting the likelihood of personal victimization among university faculty, *but only in the context of some (not all) routines.* For example, males and non-whites may be subjected more to victimization (compared to females and whites) in situations where faculty members are isolated from the presence of other faculty *and* from students. Second, individual demographics may be important only to predicting the likelihood of personal victimization among faculty *who maintain typical daily routines.* However, because we examined a small sample of victimizations, the results are actually meant to provide researchers with incentive to examine such interactions in future research. The results presented here provide partial support for the idea that analyses of interactions may be necessary to properly specify models of personal victimization in limited domains.

Besides the results for the interactions we examined, our results suggest faculty have considerable control over their likelihood of personal victimization (offenses like aggravated assault and sexual assault). This observation underscores the importance of establishing the significance of interactions of individual demographics with routine activities in predicting personal victimization in work domains like a university campus. The significance of these interactions will reveal if personal victimization is in the control of the individual, or if the likelihood of victimization is partly influenced by various unalterable characteristics *in combination with* domain-specific routines.

NOTES

(1) The five additional cases for the study presented here resulted from not including a faculty member's age in the complete model. The five additional cases had missing data related to age.

(2) Given the nature of logit analysis and how the results are interpreted, the statistical significance of race is not merely a statistical artifact. Its significance has meaning concerning the interpretation of the interaction term. When calculating the effect of any single variable on the dependent variable of a logit model, it is necessary to include *all* remaining variables in the calculations. Including the variables must be done because the results for any particular variable must be interpreted contingent on the results for all other variables in the equation (see Hanushek & Jackson, 1977).

REFERENCES

Aldrich, John and F. Nelson (1984) *Linear Probability, Logit, and Probit Models.* Beverly Hills, CA: Sage.

Block, R., M. Felson, and C.R. Block (1984) "Crime Victimization Rates for Incumbents of 246 Occupations." *Sociology and Social Research 69*(4):442–51.

Clarke, R.P., M.H. Ekblom, and P. Mayhew (1985) "Elderly Victims of Crime and Exposure to Risk." *Howard Journal of Criminal Justice 24*(1):81–89.

Cohen, L.E. and M. Felson (1979) "Social Change and Crime Rate Trends: A Routine Activities Approach." *American Sociological Review 44*(4):588–608.

—— (1981) "Modeling Crime Trends: A Criminal Opportunity Perspective." *Journal of Research in Crime and Delinquency 18*(1):138–64.

Collins, J., B. Cox, and P. Langan (1987) "Job Activities and Personal Crime Victimization: Implications for Theory." *Social Science Research 16*(2):345–60.

Felson, M. (1986) "Linking Criminal Choices, Routine Activities, Informal Social Control, and Criminal Outcomes." In D. Cornish and R. Clarke (eds.), *The Reasoning Criminal,* pp. 119–28. New York, NY: Springer-Verlag.

—— (1987) "Routine Activities and Crime Prevention in the Developing Metropolis." *Criminology 25*(4):911–32.

Garofalo, J. (1987) "Reassessing the Lifestyle Model of Criminal Victimization." In M. Gottfredson and T. Hirschi (eds.), *Positive Criminology: Essays in Honor of Michael J. Hindelang.* Beverly Hills, CA: Sage, pp. 23–42.

Garofalo, J., L. Siegel, and J. Laub (1987) "School-Related Victimizations Among Adolescents: An Analysis of National Crime Survey (NCS) Narratives." *Journal of Quantitative Criminology 3*(2):321–38.

Gottfredson, M. (1981) "On the Etiology of Criminal Victimization." *Journal of Criminal Law and Criminology 72*(3):714–26.

—— (1984) *Victims of Crime: The Dimensions of Risk.* London: Her Majesty's Stationary Office.

Hanushek, E.A. and J.E. Jackson (1977) *Statistical Methods for Social Scientists.* San Diego, CA: Academic Press.

Hindelang, M.J., M.R. Gottfredson, and J. Garofalo (1978) *Victims of Personal Crime: An Empirical Foundation for a Theory of Personal Victimization.* Cambridge, MA: Ballinger.

Lederman, D. (1993) "Colleges Report 7,500 Violent Crimes on Their Campuses in First Annual Statements Required Under Federal Law." *The Chronicle of Higher Education,* January 20, pp. A32–A43.

Lynch, J.P. (1987) "Routine Activity and Victimization at Work." *Journal of Quantitative Criminology 3*(2):283–300.

Maxfield, M.G. (1987) "Household Composition, Routine Activity, and Victimization: A Comparative Analysis." *Journal of Quantitative Criminology 3*(2):301–20.

Sampson, R. and J.D. Wooldredge (1987) "Linking the Micro- and Macro-Level Dimension of Lifestyle-Routine Activity and Opportunity Models of Predatory Victimization." *Journal of Quantitative Criminology 3*(2):371–93.

Sherman, L.W., P.R. Gartin, and M.E. Buerger (1989) "Hot Spots of Predatory Crime: Routine Activities and the Criminology of Place." *Criminology 27*(1):27–55.

Sloan, J.J. (1994) "The Correlates of Campus Crime: An Analysis of Reported Crimes on College and University Campuses." *Journal of Criminal Justice 22*(1):51–61.

Wooldredge, J.D., F.T. Cullen, and E.J. Latessa (1992) "Victimization in the Workplace: A Test of Routine Activities Theory." *Justice Quarterly 9*(2):325–35.

Chapter 7

CRIME AND FEAR OF CRIME AT A CANADIAN UNIVERSITY

Patricia Brantingham, Paul Brantingham and Jayne Seagrave

INTRODUCTION

As in the United States, the characteristics of Canadian university campuses—open access (compared to business, industrial, and government establishments of similar size and working populations), continuous day and nighttime activities, freely moving groups of people, and situations that force people into isolated activities at unconventional times—create strong potentials for criminal victimizations and fear of victimization. In Canada, the fear potential has been reinforced by several highly publicized murders that have occurred on different campuses across the country. Growing research interest in date rape and dating violence among university students has also heightened concerns about crime on campus. This chapter explores the little that is presently known about crime and fear of crime on Canadian campuses. It presents a framework for future studies of campus crime and campus fear. Finally, it presents the results of an application of this framework in a victimization survey conducted at Simon Fraser University in British Columbia.

BACKGROUND

Campus crime is a matter of growing fear and public concern in Canada. This growth is almost certainly tied to media coverage of several murders that have occurred on college and university campuses in recent years and to increased academic attention to the issues of date rape and gender violence that has focused on violence on university and college campuses.

Three sensational killings, and the mass media coverage of them, have helped create a popular feeling in Canada that campus crime levels are high. The most terrifying was a mass killing at LeEcole Polytechnique at the University of Montreal in 1989. A lone gunman entered the school and used assault weapons to kill 14 female engineering students before committing suicide. The killings at LeEcole Polytechnique, by themselves, accounted for more than two percent of all the homicides that occurred in Canada that year (Ouimet, 1992). In a murder at Concordia University in 1992, a disaffected faculty member concluded a long series of arguments with colleagues in an office shooting spree that killed and wounded administrators, faculty and support staff. In January, 1993, a female student at the British Columbia Institute of Technology (BCIT) in metropolitan Vancouver was stalked by an assailant as she walked to her car in a campus parking lot after attending evening classes; she was shot and killed by a crossbow bolt.

The focus of Canadian date rape research on the campus situation may, in part, be tied to the working location of most researchers, but it is also linked to concerns about women's access to education, to changes in the Canadian Criminal Code that eliminated *rape* as a crime and replaced it with the far broader offense of *sexual assault*, and to general social concerns about abuse of and violence (using very broadly based definitions of "abuse" and "violence") against women (Currie & Maclean, 1993). Such studies have received extensive media coverage in recent years and support a public perception that campuses are dangerous places for women.

CRIME ON CANADIAN CAMPUSES: THE LITTLE THAT IS KNOWN

The Picture in Official Data

Despite the development of public concern about crime and violence on college and university campuses, there is presently no systematic collection of information about campus crime in Canada. There is nothing similar to the campus crime data now collected and published by colleges and universities in the United States (Sloan, 1994; Siegal & Raymond, 1992). Officially recorded campus crimes known to the police are typically subsumed within and reported as part of municipal crime totals. Only occasionally does a Canadian university or college constitute a separate police jurisdiction for which official crime statistics are publicly available.

Even when officially known crime figures can be found, they can be situationally misleading. The University of British Columbia's officially reported crime rates, for instance, are calculated using the number of students residing in dormitories on campus (about 4,000 people). This calculation gave UBC the second highest reported crime rate—at 404 crimes per 1,000 population—among the 185 separately reporting police jurisdictions in the province in 1992, and suggests that UBC is a particularly dangerous place (Police Services, 1993).

This picture is badly misleading, of course, because UBC has more than 30,000 students and, with faculty, staff and visitors, probably has a daily average population at risk (DAPAR) in excess of 50,000 people. If crime rates were calculated using UBC's 30,000 students (and not just the 4,000 students living in dormitories), then UBC's crime rate would have been only 65 crimes per 1,000 population in 1992, making it the eighth lowest rather than second highest among British Columbia's 185 separately reporting police jurisdictions. If crime rates were calculated using UBC's DAPAR, then its crime rate would have been 38 per 1,000 in 1992, second lowest of all BC jurisdictions. Either of these alternative calculations makes the UBC campus appear especially safe rather than especially dangerous.

There is no requirement that Canadian university security departments use a standardized system for recording the crime incidents reported to them; these records, as a result, are frequently incompatible from campus to campus.[1] Thus, it is currently not possible to use official statistics to determine if there are any crime trends across or crime differences among Canadian campuses (Seagrave, 1993).

Address level official data as presently collected in Canada make it impossible either to explore the spatial patterns of campus crime or to analyze the behavior settings in which campus crimes take place. Through media reports, mass murders and other rare but serious crimes that occur on campuses usually have discrete locations attached to them. More generally, common crimes and fear of crime are only amorphously attached to distinct locations on university and college campuses in Canada (Brantingham & Brantingham, 1994c). Even when detailed address level crime data such as calls for police services are made available for research (Brantingham & Brantingham, 1991), reported campus crimes are generally recorded as having occurred at only a few addresses of convenience. For example, Burnaby Royal Canadian Mounted Police (RCMP) assigns a single address and single geographic coordinate to all crimes reported at Simon Fraser University, regardless of where on campus the offense actually occurs.[2]

The Picture in Survey Data

Surveys have not, so far, solved the problems posed by official data for comparison of campus crime rates across Canada. Surveys have helped, conceptually, to raise researchers' interest in crime and fear on campus. Despite much concern about female victimization, particularly in male-female interactions, the national and multi-site campus crime surveys done in Canada to date are so full of conceptual problems that little can actually be said except that there have been several surveys and that there appears to have been general agreement among those doing them that female respondents report a high *prevalence* of "abuse."

Unfortunately, the surveys conducted to date have used widely varied definitions of "abuse" and "violence" in reaching this conclusion. Incidents counted as "abuse" have ranged from incidents of "insults or swearing" to incidents in which a male "threatened you with a knife or gun" (DeKeseredy & Kelley, 1993). Even with broad-ranging definitions, to date, most analyses of Canadian survey results have involved the construction of aggregate categories of "abuse" combining all the different types of behavior identified. To arrive at some total count of "abuse" for analytic and policy prescription purposes, instances in which a woman has been "insulted" by someone are treated identically with instances in which a woman has been threatened with a gun or hospitalized as the result of a beating.

Most campus crime surveys conducted in Canada to date have been flawed in several additional ways. For instance, many have been flawed in focusing mostly on violence against students as if faculty, support staff, and others who spend time on campus are either not at risk or do not matter. The focus on violence characteristic of many studies suggests that property crime is not a problem, although American studies suggest that property crimes constitute the largest component of campus crime (Sloan, 1994; Siegal & Raymond, 1993; Fox & Hellman, 1985). The focus on female victimization suggests that males are either at less risk or that their victimization matters less. Most Canadian surveys conducted to date have also failed to distinguish between events that occur on campus, events that occur off campus as a culmination of some situation or activity that began on campus, and events that occur wholly off campus and are connected to campus solely because they involve some member of the campus community such as a student or a professor.[3]

It is worth noting that the most recently published national victimization survey conducted in Canada, which interviewed more than 10,000 respondents in 1988, identified such a small number of sexual assaults that Statistics Canada declined to publish reported incident counts and was unable to make either incident or rate estimates using acceptable statistical techniques (Sacco & Johnson, 1990). Since no estimates could be made for the prevalence or incidence of sexual assaults among the entire respondent population, it follows that Statistics Canada was unable to make estimates for subgroups by sex, age or other demographic characteristics. While the low reporting rates may relate to the difficulties people have in responding to victimization questions on sensitive topics over the telephone, they may also indicate that the sexual assault problem is, numerically, a small one. While more campus-specific surveys need to be done, in most situations the focus for campus crime surveys in Canada should probably be on fear and not actual crime.

The Picture in the Media

As already indicated, Canadian media give prominent attention to serious and bizarre crimes when they occur on college and university campuses. Serious campus crimes have news value because of their relative rarity. The media also report campus incidents involving examples of racism, sexism and intolerance in general. For example, in 1992 Canadian media gave prominent attention to anti-female graffiti scrawled on structures at the University of Alberta. Such crimes attract media attention because they contrast with a popular image of rational behavior, tranquil contemplation and focused study that is the good side of life viewed from an "ivory tower."

The pattern of crime on Canadian campuses cannot be extracted from media coverage any more than American campus crime patterns could be extracted from American media coverage. The media do not cover routine campus crimes any more than they cover routine crime in society at large: thefts and vandalism may be important to their victims, but make uninteresting fare for most readers and viewers.

The Canadian Picture: A Summary

The problems with current official data and survey research findings point out the need for a much better framework for studying the patterns of campus crime in Canada. This is particularly important when it comes to developing some understanding of fear of crime on Canadian campuses. Based on what is known about fear of crime at present, many Canadian university and college campuses are designed and structure their activities in ways likely to expose many campus users to situations in which they *fear* they are at risk of criminal attack regardless of their *actual* risk (Fisher, 1993; Nasar & Fisher, 1992; Skogan & Maxfield, 1981). In addition, on some urban campuses the cues that elicit fear may also be tied to sites and situations where the individual is at substantial *real* risk of criminal attack (Brantingham & Brantingham, 1978, 1981).

A better framework is needed to shape research that can help colleges and universities respond effectively when crime and fear problems are identified. The study of crime and fear of crime on campus is important not only because many criminological researchers work on campuses but also because the university offers a setting in which crime and fear prevention experiments may be more feasible and less costly to society than they would be in the less controlled environments beyond the campus perimeter. Analysis of the sites, situations and behavior settings where fear and actual crimes occur on campuses, if done at multi-dimensional levels, may pay off in development of better techniques for crime and fear prevention in areas beyond campus (Brantingham & Brantingham, 1993a, 1993b; Nasar & Fisher, 1993).

A FRAMEWORK FOR CRIME AND FEAR STUDIES ON COLLEGE CAMPUSES

A framework for studying crime on Canadian campuses must consider university and college campuses at the macro-level, meso-level, and micro-level simultaneously and at least be aware that campuses are both similar in general and dissimilar in particular. Crime may be a problem on a campus located in a high crime part of a city; crime may be low on a nonurban campus. Fear may be high on both urban and nonurban campuses regardless of the actual underlying risks of crime. Campus crimes will be committed by both **insiders** (students, faculty and staff, alumni, and others who spend a lot of time on campus) and **outsiders** (neighborhood residents and workers who have little or nor other contact with campus; people who occasionally visit campus; and people who come to the campus specifically to find crime targets).

Pattern Theory

Crime does not occur randomly across neighborhoods or social groups, nor during daily activities or during an individual's lifetime. Crime clusters and bunches. It is high in some places and low in others. It is high on some nights and low on others. It is high during the teenage years and low during the retirement years (Gottfredson & Hirschi, 1990; Wilson & Herrnstein, 1986; Brantingham & Brantingham, 1984). Neither is fear of crime randomly or uniformly distributed in time and space. It varies by time, place, situation, demographic characteristics, experience and personality. Even with this variability, clear patterns in crime and fear of crime frequently emerge.

An understanding of what shapes the patterns in crime and fear must be developed by looking at detailed and general pictures of variation simultaneously. There is an interconnectedness of the general and the specific; of the physical and the conceptual; of the past and the present. Recognizing this interconnectedness involves the cognitive process of "seeing" similarities, "seeing" prototypes or templates, and understanding how local conditions can distort or modify more general patterns in events (Brantingham & Brantingham, 1993a).

Patterns are sometimes obvious. For example, bars on windows may make passersby think that the buildings so equipped are frequently targeted by burglars. Bars on windows engender the highly reasonable assumption that property crimes are common in the area. While such an awareness might trigger discomfort or fear in the passerby at night, it might not do so during the day when a lot of people are present unless also accompanied by signs of daytime problems such as litter and graffiti. Litter, graffiti and bars on windows viewed together in a joint, holistic sense could easily trigger daytime fears about a neighborhood. Crime and fear cues work conjointly (Brantingham & Brantingham, 1993b; Macdonald & Gifford, 1989).

The "bars on windows" example can be seen against many layers of the environmental backcloth. When a person walks through a commercial area where most ground floor windows have bars, that person may develop a general feeling about the risk of the area. If only a single building has installed bars, the passerby might think there is something about that particular building that attracts burglars. There ought to be no general fear for the safety of the neighborhood, day or night.

Crime and fear patterns are sometimes discernible only through researcher insight that is embedded within the environment as a whole. The environment (social, cultural, legal, spatial, and temporal) is also understood as patterns. Crime and fear patterns can, therefore, sometimes only be understood as patterns within patterns within patterns.

Understanding patterns can sometimes be a difficult task. The environmental backcloth upon which particular situations and events are arrayed and against which patterns must be discerned is never static. As shown by Nasar and Fisher (1993), for example, student choice of walking paths on campus varies by time of day. The choice of campus path also probably varies by day of week, by time of year, with the weather in general.

A criminological framework for analysis of campus crime and fear must be flexible and should make it easier to recognize and understand individual and aggregate patterns of behavior at many levels of aggregation and resolution (Brantingham & Brantingham, 1993a, 1993b; Nasar & Fisher, 1993; Brantingham et al., 1976). An explanation of how crime or fear of crime changes as the backcloth varies should produce clear patterns, but such an explanation requires a focus on change itself. Fear varies by site, situation, and history. Criminal behavior is influenced by site, situation, and the experiences of both the offender and the victim.

Influences on the Pattern

In general, the pattern is influenced by the *event process,* the *activity backcloth and mental template,* and the *readiness of offenders* and *susceptibility of potential targets.*

The Event Process

The event process is a sequence of behaviors, set on the environmental backcloth, that produces a crime-related result. A behavioral sequence leads to a critical event occurs that *triggers* an extant desire or willingness to commit a crime or *triggers* the potential fear of being a victim. For instance, a crime trigger might be the discovery by a potential thief of an unguarded purse in a library study carrel. Fear might be triggered in a female student who, leaving a campus pub in the evening, notices a group of males leaving the pub a few moments after her and walk behind her in the same general direction.

The Activity Backcloth and the Mental Template

While forming patterns in the foreground, the event process rests on a general environmental backcloth that is the ever-changing context that surrounds the daily lives of individuals. The activity backcloth on campus might include the paths routinely followed to and from classes, the normal rhythms of campus schedules, and campus insiders' general expectations of social interactions in the campus setting.

The template[4] is a set of cognitive images: normal expectations about particular sites and situations created by experience or learned from various sources, then shaped by routine. The campus safety template, for instance, could be keyed to a series of environmental cues that trigger feelings of safety or risk (Nasar & Fisher, 1992; Macdonald & Gifford, 1989) or a set of environmental cues that indicate to potential offenders the presence of suitable targets in unguarded conditions (Hackler, 1994; Brantingham & Brantingham, 1978, 1993b; Cohen & Felson, 1979).

Readiness/Willingness/Susceptibility

Whether a crime-related result is triggered by a particular event arrayed on a particular configuration of the environmental backcloth depends, in part, on the *readiness* or *willingness* (Cornish & Clarke, 1986) of potential offenders to offend and on the *susceptibility* to fear and *vulnerability* to crime of the potential victim. Criminal behavior is more likely to be triggered from a given opportunity if the potential offender is highly motivated. Fear is more likely to be triggered in a given situation as the anticipated impact of crime on the potential victim increases.

The state of susceptibility of the potential victim is related to a mental template of risky situations. The vulnerability of a potential victim is related as assessment of the personal impact of the anticipated crime (Fattah, 1991).

The activity backcloth, the template, the event process and both readiness and susceptibility should be considered at varying spatial levels of analysis. Generally, there is a geometry of crime (Brantingham & Brantingham, 1981) that is clearly visible at many levels in the geographic cone of resolution (Brantingham et al., 1976). Behavior is tied to actions and movements. The actions and movements can be analyzed at low levels of resolution, at intermediate levels of resolution and at very high levels of resolution. Research can operate at the *macro* level, looking at behavior aggregated across a large set of college and university campuses (Sloan, 1994; Siegel & Raymond, 1992; Fox & Hellman, 1985). Research can operate at the *meso* level, comparing common features across campuses without aggregating the data. Research can operate at the *micro* level, analyzing crime and fear patterns across areas within a particular campus (Nasar & Fisher, 1992, 1993). A framework for analyzing campus crime should include multiple levels of analysis.

LEVELS OF ANALYSIS

The Macro-Level

Crime and fear patterns can generally be understood through application of a conceptually straightforward aggregate movement model. People routinely live in one location and take regular routes to school or work, shopping centers and friends' residences, to entertainment sites and other activity nodes (Felson, 1994; Brantingham & Brantingham, 1981; Chapin, 1972). There are always exceptions to these routine activity patterns. Changes is people's lives over time create new attractors and new pathways. Still, the activity backcloth, the template, the event process and both readiness and susceptibility should be interpreted within a routine spatial movement context.

Most persons who commit crimes do so within personal awareness spaces formed by routine activity. Target choices are generally made within these awareness spaces. The places that generate fear of victimization are those in normal activity spaces that fit a fear template or that fit some different fear template about a less well defined place outside the normal activity space.

In studying campus crime it is important to examine the macro-movement patterns of known offenders, victims, and fearful people. A university campus may serve a particular person as home, school, or work, and major extracurricular activity center all rolled into one, or it may just serve the school or work location for students, faculty members and staff who live off campus (Table I). It may be nothing more than a pathway to someplace else for those who live or work near the campus but have no other university connection. For example, a high proportion of students (and possibly faculty and staff) at a rural, dormitory-based university will be major users of campus. They will live on campus, work there, and organize most of their nonacademic activities on campus as well. At the other extreme, most students, faculty members, and staff at an urban commuter college will be minimal users of the campus. Surveys of students and staff should include spatially and temporally compatible questions about both the use of campus and the location of victimizations and fear-producing sites.

TABLE I
CAMPUS USE AND CRIME

Campus User Category	Use as Home	Use for School or Work	Major Extra-curricular Activity Center	On Campus Crime Level[1]
Major User	X	X	X	High
Moderate User				
Type 1	X	X		Moderate
Type 2		X	X	Moderate
Minimal User		X		Low

1. Relative to other campus use categories.

Activity patterns will vary within any user group and will be associated with a range of personal and sociodemographic characteristics. Much more background information ought to be collected than is now collected in most campus crime surveys.

Meso-Level

Campus users are not identical. Some have been victims or have felt fear; others have not. Prior experience helps shape an individual's activity pattern and cognitive template of "trouble spots" or "trouble situations."

Campuses are not identical. Some are located in urban areas; some are located in rural areas; some are located in high-crime areas and some are located in low crime areas. Some campuses have highly permeable edges; some have nonpermeable edges. What happens on any campus depends both on what happens *around* the campus and on *where* commuting students, faculty and staff live.

The permeability of the campus border is particularly important (Beavon et al., 1994; White, 1990). An *edge effect* almost certainly shapes crime and fear at the campus boundary. When a campus has a sharp border with its surroundings (from walls or from sharp socioeconomic differences for instance), people who neither work nor go to classes on the campus probably stand out as different whenever they are present. Such people become identifiable *outsiders*. They may generate fear within the confines of the campus because they are seen as "different" or as "intruders." *Outsiders* are much more likely to be present at the edge of a campus that at its center.

This "boundary effect" is a more generalized version of the ecological discomfort effect felt by burglars who venture into strange neighborhoods (Crowell et al., 1991; Rengert & Wasilchick, 1985; Brantingham & Brantingham, 1975) which has long been recognized by urban planners and environmental psychologists concerned with the design of neighborhoods (Lynch, 1960). Crimes by outsiders are most likely to occur and fear generated by the presence of outsiders is most likely to be situated on the edge of the campus and in areas adjacent to the campus edge.

Most people make the insider/outsider distinction. We want people who cause problems to look different from "us." Campus insiders seem to believe this though data indicate that most campus crimes are committed by campus insiders (Sloan, 1992; Fox & Hellman, 1985). The important point about the surroundings of a campus and the permeability of the campus border is that crime and fear may be generated by a mixture of insiders and outsiders or may be generated by situations created by insiders alone.

It is also important to note that the use of the insider/outsider distinction really comes from where the observer is located on the environmental backcloth. In areas around either a highly permeable campus border or a nonpermeable border, the residents and workers adjacent to campus see themselves as *neighborhood* insiders and may view the university students, faculty and staff as neighborhood outsiders and intruders.

The permeability of the campus boundary is greater when a campus blends with its surrounds. In such situations students, staff, and faculty members may move in and out of the major user category in the macrolevel of analysis. University insider activity levels are high both on and near campus.

At highly permeable urban campuses, residents and workers in the surrounding areas also probably use campus space. In fact, what is and is not campus space may not be well defined. There are often public roads and walkways that traverse the campus. Such public paths through a campus have been shown to constitute major crime concentrators (Brantingham, Brantingham & Molumby, 1977; Molumby, 1976). Area permeability has been shown to be a major contributor to general crime rates (Beavon et al., 1994; White, 1990; Bevis & Nutter, 1977).

A lack of boundary can produce personal confusion whether a specific fear or risk relates to the campus. Fear in the parking lot or at the transit stop may be seen as a campus fear, but it is really an off-campus fear. A student may live on campus, for instance, but go to a restaurant off campus. If that student is robbed just outside the restaurant, he or she may see it as a university problem. American courts have certainly interpreted some such situations as "campus crimes" in the sense that they have held the university liable for damages to students criminally attacked on public streets near campus (Nasar & Fisher, 1993).

At the *meso-level* it is important to examine *movement patterns* on and near campus. It is also important to consider how the university sits within its surroundings. Table II presents a minimum framework for *meso* analysis of fear and crime on campus. Three simplified categories of characteristics are considered: boundary permeability, surrounds, and dominant campus utilization patterns. The "+" and "−" symbols used in Table II present the expected range of fear and crime levels for each meso-level characteristic treated in the table.

In Table II, boundary permeability is treated as two categories: permeable and nonpermeable. Although campus locations can be much more finely categorized (Sloan, 1994; Fox & Hellman, 1985), at present, campus surrounds are divided into only two categories: small town and urban. Campus utilization by students, faculty and staff is divided into three categories: major use, mixed use, and minor use (see Table I for description).

Any particular campus should be seen as a combination of these and other characteristics. For example, fear levels would probably be lowest in a small-town campus with a clear campus boundary, but located in a middle-class area with most students living on campus. Crime rates might be highest on an urban campus that has permeated into a surrounding low socioeconomic status area. Problems might be particularly high when students live both on campus and in nearby apartments and when there are many day and nighttime activities on campus and in the surrounds that generate a lot of movement on and off campus.

Crime is higher on urban campuses since the potential offender pool, including campus outsiders, is larger. On rural and small-town campuses

TABLE II
CAMPUS PROBLEMS AND MESO-LEVEL CAMPUS CHARACTERISTICS

Campus Characteristics	Small Town		Urban	
	Fear	*Crime*	*Fear*	*Crime*
Boundary Permeable	−/+	−/+	+/++	+/++
Boundary Non-Permeable	on edge + in center −	activity nodes+	on edge ++ activity nodes −	activity nodes ++
Surrounds Similar	−	−	−/+	−/+
Surrounds Dissimilar	−	−	+/++	+/++
Students, Faculty, Staff (Major Users Only)	−	−	−/+	−/+
Students, Faculty, Staff (Mixed Use)	−/+	−/+	+/++	+/++
Students, Faculty, Staff (Minor Users Only)	−	−	+/++	+/++

the offenders are more likely to be students, faculty members and staff, with fewer outsiders intruding onto the campus: a smaller pool of potential offenders creates a smaller crime problem.

Fear is higher whenever campus insiders are faced with the unknown; whenever there are large differences between the social characteristics of faculty, staff and students on the one hand and nearby residences and workers on the other; and whenever there is a conceptual blurring of on-campus and off-campus situations. Fear probably increases as campus permeability increases. People seen by students, faculty and staff as outsiders become more common as campus permeability increases. At similar levels of permeability, urban campuses should have higher levels of fear than rural campuses because the urban surrounds increase the pool of outsiders who might come onto the campus. Urban campus boundaries may be much less certain than rural campus boundaries because they blend into the urban surrounds, creating mixed use zones of campus insiders and outsiders, where, simultaneously, everyone belongs and no one belongs.

Classifying campuses at the meso-level is important. Failure to do so may result in inept and confusing cross-campus crime and fear comparisons. Worse, failure to do so may lead to the adoption of singularly inappropriate security policies.

Micro-Level

Cross comparisons at the macro-level and meso-level require careful considerations of the activity backcloth, the process and the readiness/willingness or susceptibility of campus users. At the *micro-level* these background characteristics or backcloth structures must still be considered, but quasi-experimental design is possible. Even on a low crime or low fear campus, there will be locations that have high crime levels and places that generate a lot of fear (Nasar & Fisher, 1992, 1993). On high-crime campuses, there will also be hot spots and cool areas. Micro-level analysis looks at the event process and at crime and fear triggers against a varying backcloth. What is the difference between high-fear and low-fear spots on campuses? Is there any similarity between campuses? While one campus may have more high-fear areas than another, are the fear areas similar in physical design, in social usage, in temporal placement? Micro-level analysis of crime and fear on campus can focus on the construction of fear or crime templates and triggering events, but should place these templates on the routine travel paths and should analyze them against the results of meso-level and macro-level analysis.

The work of Nasar and Fisher (1992, 1993) presents an American micro-level study that should be replicated widely on many campuses. Nasar and Fisher found, among other things, that fear of particular sites and situations on the campus they studied was related to potentials for offender concealment, to blocked view angles (lack of prospect), and to lack of alternative escape pathways in case of confrontation (boundedness). Of course, concealment areas and boundedness increase while prospect decreases with the fall of night.

Fear probably also increases in situations that present sequences of event cues carrying unknown or unpredictable consequences: a sound from around a corner when you can see no one; a person walking behind you when you are alone; walking by a person or group whose characteristics make you uncomfortable. Conversely, comfort and feelings of safety increase with increases in the known and the predictable.

Actual crime patterns are frequently different from fear patterns (Brantingham, Brantingham & Molumby, 1987). When searching for a robbery site, for instance, an offender may want a place that offers both concealment before the attack and a good escape path following the attack, but that also provides good prospect from the hiding position so the presence of guardians can be detected (Felson, 1994). A suitable theft target is usually nothing more than accessible property. This makes libraries, cafeterias, classrooms, and parking lots the best sites for property crime, especially when they are in moderately heavy use (Angel, 1968).

SIMON FRASER UNIVERSITY
VICTIMIZATION AND FEAR STUDY

Simon Fraser University (SFU) is located on the top of a small mountain in Burnaby, British Columbia, some 35 minutes drive to the east of downtown Vancouver. It is surrounded by forested parkland. One edge of the campus is a high cliff that drops off sharply to an ocean inlet. The other edges are on sharp inclines on the side of the mountain. Although Burnaby is a well-developed suburb of Vancouver, the university is isolated from development by its terrain and the parks that cover the flanks of the mountain. Sitting almost at the exact population center of gravity for a metropolitan region approaching two million population, the university is more like a rural campus than an urban one. This is striking because it is a commuter and not a residential campus.

Simon Fraser University was built in the late 1960s in an architectural style that features connected buildings and walkways. The basic design is a linear arrangement of buildings, malls and quadrangles of different sizes along the mountain crest. Viewed from the air, the SFU campus resembles the motherboard of a personal computer. This architectural plan produces an almost endless series of paths across campus that require constant turns around blind corners, walks down long corridors of limited prospect containing many concealing niches, and constant entry into enclosed concrete stairwells. There are several open quadrangles, but these are usually empty of people during the day and very dark at night. Smaller quadrangles are filled with shrubbery. Larger quadrangles have fewer plantings, but are conceptually enclosed.

Funding for the university's development stopped before most planned residences could be built. While the SFU campus has more than 13,000 students, it has residence space for only about 400 people. Consequently, most students commute. The area around Vancouver has a growing but limited public transit system (DesChamps et al., 1991). Most students, faculty members, and staff drive to campus. Parking lots are vast and placed, primarily, at the eastern edge of the campus. The parking lots stair-step down the mountainside. They have been built as a series of linear strips of different elevations. To maintain the "green" effect, different parking strips are separated by runs of trees and dense underforest growth. It is possible to see ahead along the particular strip the viewer is on, but vision to either side is constricted by elevation and greenery.

The demand for parking space on campus far exceeds the parking space available. Many students have to park at the base of the mountain and hitchhike or ride a bus up to campus. Those with parking passes have to hunt for parking in the large lots at the distant edge of campus. When their classes run late or when they must stay into the night to work in labs or the library, they have to walk long distances through largely empty parking lots to get to their cars.

Because of the high number of commuters, there is comparatively little nighttime activity on the SFU campus. Even those who live in the few campus residences usually leave campus during the evening for shopping or entertainment. Parking difficulties keep many students from coming to campus on days when they do not have classes.

Simon Fraser University in the Framework

Macro-Level

SFU primarily has minor users. Faculty members, staff, and students spend a large portion of their time off campus. Faculty member, staff, and student victimizations (and campus offending patterns) should be low. Crimes are most likely to be daytime property crimes.

Meso-Level

SFU would best be classified as a rural campus. It is surrounded by forest. It is likely to have less crime than an urban campus since offenders are most likely to be insiders. The pool of potential offenders is not increased in numbers by outsiders who have easy access to the campus. The campus is marked by low levels of permeability. The edge of the campus, however, with its surrounding forest, is a likely area to create feelings of fear. The campus edge is truly an unknown and largely unknowable area. At the meso-level, then, SFU should experience low crime but have comparatively high-fear areas near its edge.

Micro-Level

The SFU campus is full of micro-sites characteristic of sites and situations known to generate fear (Nasar & Fisher, 1992, 1993). Students frequently commute alone and consequently walk to and from parking alone. Since classes end on a predictable schedule, it is easy to picture what happens in the evening: a wave of students begins moving toward the parking lots in small groups as particular classrooms at different locations on campus empty. These small groups split apart as people reach their cars or move to different parts of the parking lots in semi-random patterns, dictated by all the variants affecting the hunt for a parking space earlier in the day. Those at the far ends of the lots often end up walking alone, with other individuals, usually strangers, the remnants of *other* classroom groups following them just on the edge of auditory consciousness and peripheral vision. Especially after dark, this situation can make the person in front feel as if they are being followed or even stalked. There are few options: prospect and escape are restricted by the design of the lots, the car is in a fixed location across a lot that must be traversed. The person in front must just keep walking, but with autonomic fear reactions firing.

The fact is that comprise also adds to potential fear levels. The linear design of the SFU campus conspires to limit prospect both inside and outside most buildings. The buildings are sculpted out of a light-absorbing sandblasted concrete and feature strong vertical elements that create constant rows of shadowed niches along virtually all hallways and outside pathways. This design produces magnificent architectural vistas from many angles at most points on campus during the day, but creates limited prospect, high concealment potentials, and low escape potentials, especially outside, at night.

Based on the framework we propose in this chapter, the SFU campus should have many high-fear sites. Crime hot spots should, however, be limited. Activity centers are concentrated. Actual offenses are likely to occur in the library, in the student pub and cafeterias, and in classrooms—areas that produce sufficient concentrations of potential targets to trigger the actions of potential offenders (Angel, 1968).

STUDIES OF FEAR AND CRIME
AT SIMON FRASER UNIVERSITY

The patterns of crime and fear at Simon Fraser have been studied through a series of projects sponsored over the past five years by the Office of Traffic and Security and conducted as part of the course requirements in the introductory crime prevention seminar in the School of Criminology. These studies have included: historical analyses of campus crime incident report archives; several small pilot victimization surveys; surveys and security audits aimed at identifying parts of campus perceived as scary or safe; a survey of the physical security of campus buildings at different times; analyses of lighting levels (using light meters) in different campus locations; and formal analyses of the prospect, concealment potential, and boundedness (Nasar & Fisher, 1992, 1993) of various campus locations.

Consistent with the American literature (e.g., Sloan, 1994; Siegel & Raymond, 1992; Fox & Hellman, 1985), these student studies found that property crimes—theft and vandalism—dominate the pattern at SFU. Violent crimes are exceedingly rare. Fear appeared keyed to the physical characteristics of particular locations—their lighting levels, prospect, concealment potential, and boundedness—and not the incidence of criminal events. Crimes appeared to occur most frequently in areas in which student respondents said they felt safest. Crime locations also appeared unrelated to the physical security of particular places on campus.

Survey of Victimization and Fear

The background information provided by these student studies, coupled with the concern generated by the notorious murders that occurred on Canadian campuses and the publication of several studies on the "abuse" of university women, led to development of a large-scale campus victimization survey project. This victimization survey was a cooperative effort. The authors, members of the School of Criminology, provided questionnaire design and analysis assistance. Advice was provided by a wide array of campus organizations, including the Student Society, the Women's Centre, the Health Centre, the Faculty Association, the Office of the Harassment Coordinator, the Office of the Associate Vice-President Academic, and the Office of Traffic and Security. The overall sample frame was developed by the SFU Office of Analytic Studies and provided a three-part stratification of campus users into student, faculty and support staff subsamples. The Office of Traffic and Security hired staff who eventually conducted the actual survey by telephone interview.

During 1992, the research team developed, piloted and finalized a set of telephone interview questionnaires to collect information about the extent and nature of campus victimization and fear; the social correlates of campus victimization and fear; and the settings (macro-level, meso-level, and micro-level) of campus victimization and fear. The survey went into the field during the summer of 1993. Its questions referred to the 1992–93 academic year which ran from September, 1992 through April, 1993.

The SFU Office of Analytic Studies drew a large random sample of students ($n = 800$) from Fall, 1992 registration records. These persons were contacted by trained female members of the SFU Traffic and Security student patrol force during June and July, 1993. Samples of faculty members and staff were also drawn, but the contact rate was too low to include in this analysis.[5] Thus, this chapter only presents the results of the student survey. Over four hundred ($n = 432$) students responded to the survey.[6]

To define the macro-level setting, the questionnaire collected information about the respondent's home location; number of days spent on campus; time (in hours) spent on campus; mode of transit to and from campus; and daytime and nighttime activities on campus. Demographic information (including the respondent's age, sex, and major field of study) and self-identified minority group membership was collected. The respondents were asked whether they had been victimized by selected crimes on campus during the 1992–93 academic year and whether they had ever previously been victimized by the selected crimes either on campus or off campus. Crimes surveyed included assault, sexual assault, robbery, theft from a motor vehicle, and vandalism. The survey also included questions about incivilities and sexual harassment. Positive responses to a victimization question triggered an extended interview that collected detailed information about the geographic, social and behavioral facts for each reported victimization. Respondents were also asked a set of questions about fear on campus.

At the meso-level, respondents were also asked to identify specific locations on campus where they had been victimized, where they felt afraid, and where they felt safe. These were open-ended questions to allow analysis of the permeability of the campus.

To obtain micro-level information, respondents were asked to provide details of the events involved in their victimizations. Respondents were also asked to give detailed descriptions of the situations or cues that triggered fear or helped create a template of fear.

RESULTS OF THE SFU SURVEY

Macro-Level Analysis

While the response rate was around 50 percent, the students answering questions, in the aggregate, were not significantly different from students in general. Table III provides information about the general characteristics of student respondents and their aggregate daily activity patterns.

In general, student use of campus falls into the "minimal" category. As shown in Table III, the time spent on campus was not very dissimilar from the time spent by most people on normal daytime employment. Students arrived during the normal commuting rush hour and left at the end of the "workday." Students came to campus for classes and left campus when their "work" was over.

TABLE III
CHARACTERISTICS OF THE SAMPLE

Gender	Female	60%	Male	40%	
Visible Minority (Self-Identified)	Yes	21%	No	79%	
Mode of Transit	Car	70%	Bus	25%	Other 5%
Campus Use	Live on Campus	6%	Live off Campus	94%	
Age	Mean	29	SD	11.2	Median 24
Hours on Campus (per week)	Mean	28	SD	14.5	Median 30
Arrival Time	Mean	9:00	SD	2 hrs.	Median 8:30
Departure Time	Mean	18:25	SD	3 hrs.	Median 18:00

Victimization Patterns

As seen in Table IV, serious victimizations rarely occurred on the Simon Fraser University campus. These rates are much lower than those identified for the Canadian population as a whole in recent national victimization surveys (Sacco & Johnson, 1990; van Dijk, Mayhew & Killias, 1990:174). Students were much more likely to have been victimized off the SFU campus.

Minor thefts and vandalism to personal property (mainly cars) were the most common forms of victimization. The ten percent risk of minor property victimizations fits with a higher likelihood of minor crimes occurring during the day. Personal theft rates at SFU were higher than those reported in recent Canadian surveys of the general population, but rates of thefts from cars were much lower (van Dijk, Mayhew & Killias, 1990:174; Sacco & Johnson, 1990).

TABLE IV
PROPORTION OF STUDENT RESPONDENTS VICTIMIZED

Offense	Victim on Campus During 1992–1993 Academic Year %	Victim on Campus Before 1992–1993 Academic Year %	Victim Elsewhere Before 1992–1993 Academic Year %
Assault	0.5	1.4	4.9
Sexual Assault	0.0	0.5	1.6
Robbery	0.0	0.2	2.3
Theft from Vehicle	1.9	3.7	7.0
Other Theft	9.7	8.1	8.5
Vandalism	4.4	4.6	9.0
Sexual Assault off campus arising from situation that began on campus	0.0	1.4	N/A
Sex coerced for academic work benefit	0.2	0.9	0.9
Unwanted touching	1.2	3.3	6.3
Suggestive, racist, or offensive remarks	7.4	8.8	9.7

In addition, a significant proportion of students (7.4%) reported an on-campus victimization involving suggestive, racist, or offensive remarks. These victimization events were self-defined into these categories, then described by respondents in open-ended remarks. The victimization events described by student respondents under this category included: a group of drunk males making crude remarks such as "Hey baby!"; a woman who "came on" to the respondent; a group of male students standing outside the Women's Centre making sarcastic remarks about the Centre; a male approaching a female student while she was talking with a friend and telling her she was impolite and to "shut up"; a student being "put down" by the professor in front of the class; a male faculty member yelling at the respondent and intimidating her because she did not have some information he had requested; racist comments about "Chinese studying a lot"; and a professor making a clear remark that visible minorities were not fit for the fields of biology and chemistry and that they were stupid.

It is apparent from the previous listing that some of the events captured by this question were indeed examples of sexist or racist remarks that were clearly inappropriate within a university setting and may even be criminally actionable in Canada. Many of the victimization events reported in response to this question were, however, examples of rudeness or bad manners or poor teaching techniques and not criminal conduct. Whether particular acts of rudeness ought to be counted as some form of "abuse" and equated with racist remarks or even physical assaults is a matter of ideology or taste (see DeKeseredy & Kelly, 1993).

Fear Levels

Student daytime fear levels were low. Most students felt safe on campus during the day. As seen in Table IV, there is, in fact, little to fear on the SFU campus. This general feeling of safety on campus during the daytime was true in the aggregate for both full-time and part-time students. It was true of graduate and undergraduate students. It was true of married and single students. It was true of students who drove to campus, who took the bus to campus, and who got to campus in other ways like bicycling or hitchhiking.

As Table V shows, however, there was a significant difference ($p < .0001$) in male and female feelings of safety on campus during the day.

There was more concern among sample members about safety at night (about 30% of respondents expressed some level of fear). Interestingly, the level of nighttime fear expressed by SFU students did not vary significantly, when considered in the aggregate, by mode of transit to campus, by full-time or part-time student status, by graduate or under-

TABLE V
FEELINGS OF SAFETY ON SFU CAMPUS

	DAYTIME			
	Very Safe	*Generally Safe, Some Unsafe Places*	*Generally Unsafe, Some Safe Places*	*Very Unsafe*
Overall	59.7%	39.4%	0.7%	0.2%
Male	72.4%	27.6%	—	—
Female	50.9%	47.7%	1.2%	0.3%
	NIGHTTIME			
	Very Safe	*Generally Safe, Some Unsafe Places*	*Generally Unsafe, Some Safe Places*	*Very Unsafe*
Overall	19.4%	45.4%	23.4%	6.5%
Male	41.1%	47.0%	9.1%	2.7%
Female	7.0%	48.2%	35.2%	9.7%

graduate status, or by marital status. It did vary by gender of respondent: females were much more fearful on campus at night than males.

What is perhaps most important is that feelings of nighttime safety did not vary according to the time spent on campus or by the normal departure time of the respondent. Respondents reported higher fear levels at night than during the day, even when their nighttime presence on campus was rare.

There was one further interesting result. Self-identified minority group members did not, generally, report higher levels of nighttime fear than non-minority group members. There was one exception to this general observation: female students who identified themselves as members of the minority group *women.* While only 33 of 346 female respondents identified themselves as belonging to the minority group *women* (Table VI), this small group reported markedly higher fear levels than all other women and all other self-identified minority group members (all X^2 comparisons significant at $p < .01$).

Meso-Level Analysis

The Simon Fraser University campus is not a high-crime campus but does have some reported nighttime fear. The pattern of reported fear is what might be expected at a semipermeable rural campus.

TABLE VI
FEELINGS OF SAFETY AMONG MINORITY GROUPS

		FEELINGS ABOUT SAFETY		
	Very Safe	*Generally Safe, Some Unsafe Places*	*Generally Unsafe, Some Safe Places*	*Very Unsafe*
All Females	7.0%	48.2%	35.2%	9.7%
Self-Identified Minority Women	6.3%	28.1%	53.1%	12.5%
Other Self-Identified Minorities	16.7%	52.4%	26.2%	4.8%

Students were asked to identify the boundary of the campus. Students generally knew where the core of the campus was located, and most agreed on the location of the campus edge. Some 70% identified a ring road that circumnavigates the mountaintop as the campus edge; 8% identified the parking lots with the campus edge; some 15% named other locations; 7% said they didn't know. Depending on the situation, the "edges" defined by student respondents made conceptual sense, though none of them coincided with the boundary of the campus defined by law.

While the SFU campus may be *conceptually* permeable to campus outsiders, it is not *functionally* permeable to them. It is well off any routine commuting path that might be followed by campus outsiders. The conceptual permeability of the SFU campus is one that allows students to perceive the unknown lurking in the forests and wooded areas on the campus perimeter, though the chance of outsiders actually finding their way to the campus edge is small.

This permeability of the unknown appears strongly tied to what is located at the edge of the *built-up* campus area. Parking areas on the fringe of the *built-up* area were identified as the high-fear areas more often than any other areas (Table VII). Over 65% of the students surveyed identified parking as a site where they felt uneasy or afraid. While females indicated high levels of fear on campus at night, there was no significant difference between *categories of locations* for males and females who felt unsafe ($X^2 = 2.4$, $p = .49$). There was a significant difference by mode of transportation. While parking locations dominated the sites listed as unsafe, they were more frequently named unsafe by drivers than by bus riders ($X^2 = 17.4$, $p < .001$).

The other areas defined as fear generators were outside of buildings,

TABLE VII
PLACES WHERE STUDENTS FEEL UNEASY OR UNSAFE

Location	Percent
Any Parking	67.1%
Outside Buildings	20.3%
Inside Buildings	5.3%
Other	7.3%

not inside them. The architecture at SFU has many square shapes arranged around open courtyards. It is a campus full of empty, dark, nighttime areas. As shown in Table VIII, only around 20% of respondents expressed any fear of locations *within* buildings. The general mental template associated with fear was darkness and presence in an empty area while alone. Generally, the key fear cues identified by the student respondents were lack of people or personal isolation at the site and darkness. Over 57 percent gave isolation or lack of people as the major reason for feeling unsafe; about 25 percent named darkness or lack of light as the reason they felt unsafe. Restricted view angles or lack of prospect was identified as the reason for feeling unsafe at a particular site by about seven percent of those who named a site.

There was a noticeable difference between females and males depending on *where* they said they felt fear. About 40 to 45 percent of females identified isolation or being alone as the primary reason for feeling fear independent of the nature of the site. That is, isolation was identified as the *principal* reason for feeling unsafe in parking areas, outside buildings, and inside buildings ($X^2 = 6.0$, $p = .42$). While the number of males expressing any fear was low, among those expressing fear in relation to parking lots, some 70 percent identified lack of people as the reason for feeling unsafe, while about 30 percent named lack of lighting. For males who identified unsafe sites near buildings, the mix switched: 80 percent identified lack of lighting as the problem; 20 percent identified isolation or lack of people as the problem ($X^2 = 18.0$, $p < .01$).

This difference is worthy of more research. Darkness may increase female fear on campus, but improved lighting may not reduce it unless the improved lighting is tied to something that reduces the sense of isolation or being alone. More important, finding ways to protect women

TABLE VIII
DIFFERENCES IN FEELINGS OF SAFETY BY LOCATION,
MODE OF TRANSIT, AND GENDER

Location	Mode of Transit	
	Car	Bus
Any Parking	71.9%	57.7%
Outside Buildings	19.1%	21.2%
Inside Buildings	4.7%	4.8%
Other	4.3%	16.3%
Location	Gender	
	Female	Male
Any Parking	65.6%	71.3%
Outside Buildings	21.5%	16.7%
Inside Buildings	4.9%	6.5%
Other	8.0%	5.6%

from having to walk into empty parts of campus alone may reduce female fear levels even in dark areas.

While fear is the primary concern on the Simon Fraser University campus, it should be noted the few crimes reported in the survey were tied to the location of property crime targets. Some theft occurred in the parking lots (cars or goods in cars were the commonest parking lot targets) or at high activity nodes. Most property offenses occurred in classrooms, the student pub, the library and the university bookstore. These areas were *not* identified as high fear areas by the respondents, even when the respondents had been victimized in them.

Micro-Level Analysis

When viewed at the most detailed level, fear in the isolated edge environments is not tied to direct usage of the campus. The campus is primarily used by students who live away from it. All students were asked specific questions about what produced their fear (or feelings of safety) and what could be done to reduce fear on campus. Though the dominant reason given for fearing particular locations was "lack of people," the primary response on ways to improve safety at night was "better lighting." Security patrols and escort programs were rarely mentioned.

Theft generally takes only a moment to accomplish. The most common theft location was the university library. The design of the library features study carrels along the outer walls with book stacks filling the center of most floors. A wallet, purse or calculator would be stolen when someone went to look for a book or article and left the target object behind with other property to "mark" the study carrel so other students would not occupy it. Gym lockers were also frequent theft sites. These are designed with steel mesh fronts and sides to allow air to pass through. This design also makes the property left in the locker highly visible to all passersby. Parked cars are also popular crime targets at SFU. Other students are the most likely perpetrators in these cases; few outsiders venture into either the library or the gym. The parking lots are cognitively inaccessible to outsiders.

Feelings of fear were tied to "unusual" events, particularly unusual actions by other people. It is quite interesting that general fear of a given area was tied to darkness and isolation, yet frightening incidents reported by our respondents were usually tied to the behavior of other individuals present at the site. Virtually all frightening events were reported by female respondents. The following examples illustrate the kinds of events that made students feel uneasy or afraid, or think that they were being followed though they came to no harm:

(1) *Some incidents involved apparent "outsiders":* She was uneasy about a "suspicious looking" individual, no one else around. She heard rustling in bushes by [a parking] lot; dazed-looking man jumped out and wandered through lot. He was made nervous by a "suspicious looking" man in the parking lot, just wandering around, not doing anything special. She was eating lunch in the mall [open] area; "skin head" looking guy left at the same time, went in the same direction.

(2) *Some incidents involved the unknown:* She heard scary noises while walking to [parking] lot. She heard noises in bushes, then footsteps, but did not see anyone.

(3) *Some incidents involved groups of males:* Group of males walking behind her made her nervous. Rowdy males hanging around psych labs where she was planning to work all night made her nervous. Guys in [parking] lot after game were harassing her as she looked for her car; felt nervous. Group of males walked behind respondent.

(4) *Some incidents involved drunks:* On the way to [a classroom building] to see a professor, she passed a pub and guys who were loud and drunk made her feel nervous. She felt nervous because of drunk pub attendees urinating in a stairwell.

(5) *Some incidents involved confrontations in a work setting:* She had to work with ex-convict; it made her nervous. She (graduate student) felt uneasy about male student coming into her office, angry over grades.

(6) *Some incidents involve violations of personal space and appear much more sinister:* Instead of sitting in any of the empty carrels available, a man chose to occupy one right beside her. She was followed by person after class, who kept asking for her phone number. Person followed her from outside library, through mall [open space] to bus loop, got on bus with her; was staring at her the whole time. She was followed by man to bus stop; he bumped into her; sat by her at stop; then left. Man followed her and showed her pictures of himself in women's clothing.

This list is provided just to give some flavor of the events that trigger feelings of fear. They seem to reflect vulnerability; fear of the unknown; unusual-looking people or unusual behavior; noises in isolated environments and, generally, a feeling of lack of control in a situation. Such incidents may never be controllable in an open university where many students come and go alone.

Given that SFU students identified unusual persons as fear generators in an environment that is basically populated by university insiders, fear levels are likely to be much higher on urban campuses with high boundary permeability situated in ecologically different neighborhoods. Moreover, these high-fear levels are likely to be highest on the edges of the campus and in the non-campus areas adjacent to the campus edge.

CONCLUSIONS

Research on crime and fear of crime on Canadian campuses is very limited. The news media portray the campus crime problem in Canada as serious. Date rape studies blur campus with off-campus experiences. Official data on campus crime are not currently standardized in Canada. Victimization surveys have only rarely been conducted to date. The SFU victimization survey found low levels of crime. A best current estimate might suggest that crime is not a substantial problem on most Canadian college and university campuses.

However, because it is a new area of research, it may be possible to shape an analytic framework so useful comparisons can be made across studies and some standardized information collected at the macro-level, meso-level, and micro-level. Studies at all levels are particularly important in Canada if universities are going to develop security approaches that will reduce current levels of fear and risk on their campuses.

Crime and fear reduction strategies depend on how the campus is used by students, staff, and faculty members; how the campus is designed; the activities that occur on campus; events that trigger criminal incidents and feelings of fear; whether fear-triggering events are indicators of future crimes; and whether changes in the cues found in the fear templates actually alter responses to fear-triggering events.

NOTES

(1) It should be noted that the Office of Traffic and Security at Simon Fraser University has developed a standardized uniform campus crime reports system, derived from and compatible with RCMP sources, that it makes available to other universities and colleges to adopt.

(2) Even the detailed crime recording system developed for SFU by its Office of Traffic and Security consigns the spatial dimension of campus crime to a few geographic coordinates corresponding to a few large campus zones and not to discrete locations.

(3) See the *Journal of Human Justice* (1993) vol. *4*(2) special issue on campus crime for a general review of the Canadian "campus" violence studies. See also Seagrave (1993), Elliot et al. (1992), Finkleman (1992), and Barnes et al. (1991).

(4) The mental template is sometimes called a *prototype* or a *schematic* in the environmental psychology literature.

(5) An additional study is needed to find out why faculty and staff have so little interest in participating in a survey of campus victimization and fear, although it is not clear why they would respond to a survey about why they would not respond to a survey!

(6) The use of telephone answering machines to screen calls appeared to have a substantial effect on our ability to contact students and kept the response rate to 54%. While it will not be discussed in detail here, it appears that changes in telephone systems are starting to move telephone surveys in the direction of mail-out survey response rates. The triangulation of research methods is, as a result, becoming more important.

REFERENCES

Angel, S. (1968) *Discouraging Crime Through City Planning.* Berkeley, CA: Center for Planning and Development Research, Working Paper #75.

Barnes, G. E., L. Greenwood, and R. Sommer (1991) "Courtship Violence in a Canadian Sample of Male College Students." *Family Relations* 40(1):37–44.

Beavon, D.J., P. Brantingham, and P. Brantingham (1994) "Street Networks and Crime." *Crime Prevention Studies* 2(1):115–148.

Bevis, C. and J.B. Nutter (1977) "Changing Street Layouts to Reduce Residential Burglary." Paper presented at the Annual Meetings of the American Society of Criminology.

Brantingham, P. and P. Brantingham (1975) "Residential Burglary and Urban Form." *Urban Studies 12*(1):273–284.

Brantingham, P. and P. Brantingham (1978) "A Theoretical Model of Crime Site Selection." In M. Krohn and R. Akers (eds.) *Crime, Law and Sanctions.* Beverly Hills, CA: Sage.

Brantingham, P. and P. Brantingham (1981) *Environmental Criminology.* Beverly Hills, CA: Sage Publications.

Brantingham, P. and P. Brantingham (1984) *Patterns in Crime.* New York: Macmillan.

Brantingham, P. and P. Brantingham (1991a) "Crime and Calls for Service in Vancouver." Paper presented at the Annual Meetings of the American Society of Criminology.

Brantingham, P. and P. Brantingham (1991b) *Environmental Criminology* (2ed). Prospect Heights, IL: Waveland Press.

Brantingham, P. and P. Brantingham (1993a) "Environment, Routine and Situation: Toward a Pattern Theory of Crime." *Advances in Criminological Theory 5:*259–294.

Brantingham, P. and P. Brantingham (1993b) "Nodes, Paths and Edges: Considerations on Environmental Criminology." *Journal of Environmental Psychology 13*(1):3–28.

Brantingham, P. and P. Brantingham (1994a) "La Concentration Spatiale Relative De La Criminalité Et Son Analyse: Vers Un Renouvellement De La criminologie Environmentale." *Criminologie 27*(1):81–97.

Brantingham, P. and P. Brantingham (1994b) "Location Quotients and Crime Hot Spots in the City." In C.R. Block and R. Block (eds.) *Proceedings of the Seminar on Spatial Analysis of Crime.* Chicago: Illinois Criminal Justice Information Authority.

Brantingham, P. and P. Brantingham (1994c) "Surveying Campus Crime: What Can be Done to Reduce Crime and Fear?" *Security Journal* (In press).

Brantingham, P. P. Brantingham and T. Molumby (1977) "Perceptions of Crime in a Dreadful Enclosure." *Ohio Journal of Science 77:*256–261.

Brantingham, P., D.A. Dyreson, and P. Brantingham (1976) "Crime Seen Through a Cone of Resolution." *American Behavioral Scientist 20*(1):261–273.

Brantingham, P., S. Mu, and A. Verma (1994) "Patterns in Canadian Crime." In M. Jackson, and C. Griffiths (eds.) *Canadian Criminology* (2ed.). Toronto: Harcourt, Brace Jovanovich Canada.

Cohen, L.E. and M. Felson (1979) "Social Change and Crime Rate Trends: A Routine Activity Approach." *American Sociological Review 44*(5) 588–608.

Cornish, D.B. and R. Clarke (1986) *The Reasoning Criminal: Rational Choice Perspectives on Offending.* New York: Springer-Verlag.

Cromwell, P., J. Olson, and D. Avary (1991) *Breaking and Entering: An Ethnographic Analysis of Burglary.* Newbury Park, Ca.: Sage.

Currie, D. and B. MacLean (1993) "Woman Abuse in Dating Relationships: Rethinking Women's Safety on Campus." *Journal of Human Justice 4*(1):1–24.

DeKeseredy, W. and K. Kelly (1993) "The Incidence and Prevalence of Woman

Abuse in Canadian University and College Dating Relationships." *Canadian Journal of Sociology 18*(1):137–159.

DesChamps, S., P. Brantingham, and P. Brantingham (1991) "The British Columbia Transit Fare Evasion Audit: A Description of a Situational Crime Prevention Process." *Security Journal 2*(1):211–218.

Elliot, S., D. Odynak and H. Krahn (1992). *A Survey of Unwanted Sexual Experiences Among University of Alberta Students.* Edmonton, Alberta: Population Research Laboratory, University of Alberta.

Fattah, E.A. (1991) *Understanding Criminal Victimization: An Introduction to Theoretical Victimology.* Scarborough, ON: Prentice-Hall Canada.

Felson, M. (1994) *Crime and Everyday Life: Insight and Implications for Society.* Thousand Oaks, CA: Pine Forge Press.

Finkelman, L. (1992) *Report of the Survey of Unwanted Sexual Experiences Among Students of U.N.B.F. and S.T.U.* Fredericton: University of New Brunswick Counseling Services.

Fox, J. and D. Hellman (1985) "Location and Other Correlates of Campus Crime." *Journal of Criminal Justice 13*(4):429–444.

Gottfredson, M. and T. Hirschi (1990) *A General Theory of Crime.* Stanford, California: Stanford University Press.

Hackler, J.C. (1994) *Crime and Canadian Public Policy.* Scarborough, Ontario: Prentice-Hall Canada.

Lynch, K. (1960) *The Image of the City.* Cambridge, MA: MIT Press.

Macdonald, J.E. and R. Gifford (1989) "Territorial Cues and Defensible Space Theory: The Burglar's Point of View." *Journal of Environmental Psychology 9*(1):193–205.

Molumby, T. (1976) "Patterns of Crime in a University Housing Project." *American Behavioral Scientist 20*(2):247–259.

Nasar, J.L. and B. Fisher (1992) "Design for Vulnerability: Cues and Reactions to Fear of Crime." *Sociology and Social Research 76*(1):48–58.

Nasar, J.L. and B. Fisher (1993) "'Hot Spots' of Fear and Crime: A Multi-Method Investigation." *Journal of Environmental Psychology 13*(1):187–206.

Ouimet, M. (19) "The Polytechnique Incident and Imitative Violence Against Women." *Sociology and Social Research 76*(1):45–47.

Police Services (1993) *Police Management Information System: Summary Statistics 1977-1992.* Victoria, BC: Ministry of Attorney General, Province of British Columbia.

Rengert, G.F. and T. Wasilchick (1985) *Suburban Burglary.* Springfield, IL: Charles C Thomas.

Reppetto, T. A. (1974) *Residential Crime.* Cambridge, MA: Ballinger.

Sacco, V.F. and H. Johnson (1990) *Patterns of Criminal Victimization in Canada.* General Social Survey Analysis Series, Statistics Canada. Catalogue 11-612E, No. 2. Ottawa, ON: Minister of Supply and Services Canada.

Seagrave, J. (1993) "How Safe are Canadian Campuses?" *Canadian Security* 1993 (August/September):21–22.

Siegal, D. and C. Raymond (1992) "An Ecological Approach to Violent Crime on Campus." *Journal of Security Administration 15*(2):19–29.

Sloan, J.J. (1994) "The Correlates of Campus Crime: An Analysis of Reported Crimes on College and University Campuses." *Journal of Criminal Justice* 22(1):51–62.

van Dijk, J., P. Mayhew and M. Killias (1990) *Experiences of Crime across the World: Key Findings from the 1989 International Crime Survey.* Deventer, Nethelands: Kluwer Law and Taxation Publishers, p. 174.

White, G. F. (1990) "Neighborhood Permeability and Burglary Rates." *Justice Quarterly* 7(1):57–67.

Wilson, J.Q. and R. Herrnstein (1986) *Crime and Human Nature.* New York: Touchstone Books.

Chapter 8

THE VICTIMIZATION OF WOMEN ON COLLEGE CAMPUSES: COURTSHIP VIOLENCE, DATE RAPE, AND SEXUAL HARASSMENT

Joanne Belknap and Edna Erez

INTRODUCTION

Until recently, many people thought college campuses were safe environments for women. The little concern that existed for women's safety on campus was limited to stranger rapes, though these assaults are comparatively uncommon compared to women's victimizations by men they know (Currie & MacLean, 1993; Reilly et al., 1992; Lott et al., 1982). Although woman battering (domestic violence), stranger rape, and sexual harassment were recognized as social problems in the beginning of the 1970s, it was not until the late 1970s and early 1980s that courtship violence (woman battering in dating relationships), date rape, and sexual harassment of college students began to receive any attention (e.g., Barrett, 1982; Makepeace, 1981; Project on the Status and Education of Women, 1978).

Victimizations of college women commonly include coercive sexuality at student parties, battering by boyfriends, acquaintance/date rape, and unethical advances by professors and staff (Leidig, 1992). This chapter explores these phenomena. It presents the definitions and characteristics of aggression against college women, and addresses explanations for the frequency and persistence of these violations. It then reviews the dynamics of courtship violence, date rape, and sexual harassment and their consequences for offenders and victims. Finally, this chapter discusses policy recommendations to deter and better responsd to aggression against women on college campuses.

156

DEFINING THE CONCEPTS

Date rape, courtship violence, and sexual harassment are distinctively feminist issues. First, the victims of these offenses are predominantly women and the offenders are predominantly men. Furthermore, when females use physical aggression in intimate and dating relationships, it is rarely sexual, is usually to fight back against male aggression, and the violence is usually far less extreme than the violence men direct against women (see Makepeace, 1983, 1986; Lane and Gwartney-Gibbs, 1985). When women are "violent" in dating relationships, then it is usually to resist abuse. Moreover, not only do males report less fear and intimidation when abused by females than females report when males abuse them, but females usually "learn" that their attempts to fight back are unsuccessful (Gamache, 1991). Thus, this chapter is written from the perspective that represents the sizable majority of sexual harassment and dating violence: where the offenders are male and the victims are female.

The three forms of victimization of college women discussed in this chapter (date rape, courtship violence, and sexual harassment) are interrelated. In addition, they are largely perpetrated by men against women, and all of them involve power. While research has thus far failed to tie the three victimizations together, it is likely there is an overlap in the men who sexually and nonsexually physically abuse their girlfriends. Thus, rape becomes one more form of inflicting violence in an already abusive relationship. There is also some evidence that sexual harassment and date rape are related. A recent study found that the best predictor of college males' likelihood to rape was their tolerance for sexual harassment (Reilly et al., 1992). Further, conceptually and practically, rape is the extreme end of the continuum of behavior subsumed under sexual harassment.

The terms "sexual harassment" and "battered woman" did not exist until the 1970s. The term "date rape" was coined in the early 1980s. Although these behaviors were not named until the last two decades, their influence and prevalence is well documented. For example, what we currently call acquaintance and date rape occurred with alarming frequency in England during the eighteenth and nineteenth centuries (Clark, 1987). Similarly, research from the 1950s reported the same rate of unwanted sexual contact (including rapes) on dates as research from the 1980s and 1990s (Kanin, 1957). Early sexual harassment research in the 1970s focused on its occurrent in the workplace. In 1979, sexual harassment in academic settings first came under the scrutiny of researchers (Project on the Status and Education of Women, 1979).

The lack of labels for violence and violations against women has resulted in their prolonged invisibility (Belknap, forthcoming). Moreover, there are persistent beliefs (assumptions) that sexual harassment is just "good fun," and to be sexually assaulted by one's date is not "real rape" and is merely miscommunication or the woman changing her mind after the fact. Since the 1970s, feminist activities on behalf of women helped reverse the invisibility and misinformation about men's aggression toward women, to identify and label these problems, and to establish education and policies to deter and respond to these violations.

One of the problems in identifying and responding to offenders has been the ambiguity of the definitions. Even researchers have used different definitions of aggression and harassment (Fitzgerald, 1990; Rivera & Regoli, 1987), so it is certainly understandable that the public is often confused as to which behaviors constitute battering, rape, and sexual harassment. Are date rapes a form of acquaintance rape? Are rapes that occur during college parties date rape? Recent research has documented that much of the sexual aggression that college women experience occurs during fraternity, dormitory, house, and apartment parties, and not necessarily on a date (Ward et al., 1991; Gwartney-Gibbs & Stockard, 1989; Martin & Hummer, 1989; Warshaw, 1988; Abbey, 1987; Ehrhart & Sandler, 1985). One study further suggested that college women are most at risk of unwanted sexual contact (including rape) by male acquaintances or friends, followed by boyfriends, and least at risk by strangers (Ward et al., 1991).

An important distinction about violence occurring on dates is the one between *sexual* (e.g., molesting or vaginal, oral, or anal rape) and *nonsexual* physical violence (e.g., hitting, slapping, or beating). Terms like "dating violence" and "courtship violence" are sometimes used to include both sexual and nonsexual physical violence, and other times to refer strictly to nonsexual physical violence. In this chapter, we use the term *courtship violence* to describe nonsexual physical violence in a dating relationship; we use the term *date rape* to refer specifically to sexual victimization which occurs on a date or at a college function (e.g., a dance, a party, or a study group). Courtship violence is analogous to the woman battering commonly thought of as "domestic violence" in marital relationships. Date rape, on the other hand, includes sexual victimizations perpetrated by boyfriends, lovers, male friends, and men women meet at parties or other college or social-related activities on campus. Finally, *sexual harassment* is "any attempt to coerce an unwilling person into a sexual relationship, or to subject a person to unwanted sexual attention, or to punish a refusal to comply" (Brandenburg, 1982:322).

To understand behaviors constituting sexual victimizations (including sexual harassment), it is important to emphasize that victimizations can be classified as occurring along a continuum from coercion to force as seen in Figure I.

FIGURE 1
THE CONTINUUM OF SEXUAL VICTIMIZATION

coercion ◄ ─ ► force

Examples of *coercion* include a professor telling a student he will not pass her in the course if she does not perform a sexual favor for him, or a man who tells his date that he will not drive her home unless she has sex with him. Other forms of coercion include sexually victimizing someone in an altered state from alcohol or drug use. *Force,* on the other hand, includes physically pushing a woman down or using a weapon and actually making her have sex. Clearly, this is physical as well as sexual violence. Between coercion and force lay behaviors like *verbal threats* of violence, for example, "If you don't comply and have sex with me, then I will physically force you."

To assess the various forms of coercion and force in sexual victimizations, researchers have devised many categories of behaviors (Tables I and II). For example, Koss et al. (1985) developed four categories of male dating behavior: (1) *sexually nonaggressive* males participated only in mutually desired, noncoercive and nonabusive sex, (2) *sexually coercive* males used extreme verbal pressure such as false promises and threats to end the relationship if the woman would not have sexual intercourse, (3) *sexually abusive* males obtained sexual contact or attempted intercourse (where penetration did not occur) through force or threat of force, and (4) *sexually assaultive* males used the threat of harm or actual force to obtain oral, anal, or vaginal intercourse (Table I). Other research on college students also supports a continuum in the levels of sexual aggression in date rapes (DeKeseredy & Kelly, 1993; Ward et al., 1991; Rivera & Regoli, 1987; Rapaport & Burkhart, 1984; Koss & Oros, 1982).

TABLE I
RESEARCH EXAMPLES OF CONTINUUMS IN DATE RAPE*

Koss et al. (1985)	*DeKeseredy and Kelly (1993)*
sexually non-aggressive	unwanted sexual contact
sexually coercive	sexual coercion
sexually abusive	attempted rape
sexually assaultive	completed rape

*The categories are reported in terms of the least to the most serious levels.

The continuum of sexual aggression also applies to sexual harassment (Table II). Examples of categories of sexual harassment perpetrated by professors or instructors directed at students include: (1) *undue attention,* like being too eager to please or help; (2) *body language,* including leering or standing too close; (3) *verbal sexual advances,* like expressions of sexual attraction; (4) *invitations for dates;* (5) *physical advances,* including kissing, touching, and fondling breasts; and (6) *sexual bribery,* involving pressure to sexually comply to receive a good grade (Adams et al., 1983; Benson & Thomson, 1982). Another continuum of sexual harassment comprises (1) *gender harassment,* including general sexist remarks and behavior, (2) *seductive behavior,* like sanction-free sexual advances, (3) *sexual bribery,* soliciting sex by promise of reward, (4) *sexual coercion,* coercing sex through threat of punishment, and finally, (5) outright *sexual assault* (Fitzgerald, Weitzman et al., 1988). In one study, female college seniors reported experiencing harassing behaviors perpetrated by their instructors ranging from "vague to blatant," from invitations to dinner to invitations to a weekend in a mountain resort. Many students reported instructors would not accept no for an answer and would call repeatedly after being firmly rejected (Benson & Thomas, 1982).

The varying degrees of coercion in sexual harassment make it difficult to define both legally and personally (Paludi et al., 1990). While those categories along the continuum which involve force and punishment for failure to comply are more extreme, the less extreme categories can be

TABLE II
RESEARCH EXAMPLES OF CONTINUUMS IN SEXUAL HARASSMENT*

Adams et al. (1983)	Fitzgerald et al. (1988)
sexist comments	gender harassment
undue attention	seductive behavior
body language	sexual bribery
verbal sexual advance	sexual coercion
invitations for dates	sexual assault
physical advances	
explicit propositions	
sexual bribery	

*The categories are reported in terms of the least to the most serious levels.

very confusing and extremely disturbing. It is necessary to understand that coercion—as well as force—is a serious violation of a person's self-determination. Furthermore, understanding the continuum of sexually exploitive behaviors acknowledges that sexual aggression, even by boyfriends, fraternity members, male friends, and college professors, can occur in forms of extreme violence, as well as coercive violations. Viewing violence against women on a continuum facilitates understanding of the wide spectrum of violations, recognizes that the objectification of women underlies these victimizations, and increases appreciation of the impact these offenses have on students' lives (Leidig, 1992).

Finally, it is also important to mention the potentially damaging ramifications of consensual sexual relationships between students and faculty members. It has been well documented that intimate relationships between faculty members and students exist on college campuses (Fitzgerald et al., 1988; Glaser & Thorpe 1986; Skeen & Nielson, 1983). Many campuses are currently debating whether there should be policies against these relationships; the major argument against them is that relationships between faculty members and students are always asymmetric in nature, and that students have as much to lose by participating in these relationships as by refusal to cooperate. Moreover, it is sometimes difficult to determine whether student-faculty relationships are coercive. Women students who experienced consensual sexual relationships with male faculty members reported they later felt the actions of the professor were coercive, and the relationship had resulted in negative consequences for the students (Glaser & Thorpe, 1986). Because academic opportunities (and work in general) are characterized by vertical stratification and asymmetrical relations between teachers and students, supervisors and subordinates, individuals in positions of power can use their positions to receive sexual compliance for their students or subordinates. The interaction of gender and organizational power in an institutional structure increases the likelihood resistance will be minimal or nonexistent.

THE INCIDENCE AND CHARACTERISTICS OF AGGRESSION AGAINST COLLEGE WOMEN

Studies on courtship violence have found that about three out of five college students know of someone involved in a violent dating relationship, and about one in five have actually experienced violence in a dating relationship (Stets and Pirog-Good, 1987; Knutson & Mehm, 1986; Bogal-Allbritten & Allbritten, 1985; Matthews, 1984; Cate et al., 1982; Makepeace, 1981). As expected, women generally report higher courtship victimization rates than men (Flynn, 1990; Aizenman & Kelly, 1988). A study comparing battering in intimate relationships as documented in police reports found that physical violence and weapon use was more common in unmarried (boyfriend/girlfriend and ex-marital relationships) than married couples (Erez, 1986). Similarly, studies of college students found that cohabitating couples (unmarried heterosexual couples living together) report more violence and physical injury than heterosexual couples who date but do not live together or are married (Makepeace, 1989; Stets & Straus, 1989). The potential for violence and injury in intimate relationships is clearly not restricted to married couples.

The most frequent reasons given for courtship violence are jealousy, disagreements over drinking behaviors, and anger over sexual denial (Makepeace, 1981, 1986; Lane & Gwartney-Gibbs, 1985; Matthews, 1984). Thus, the nonsexual physical violence in courtship violence is often related to issues of sexuality and jealousy. It is not surprising, then, that many relationships where there is courtship violence often include sexual violence. For example, a study of unmarried college students found that injury was most common in rapes where the victim and offender were an estranged couple, "suggesting that some men use rape and violence during a rape to punish the victim for some grievance" (Felson & Krohn, 1990:222). Other research has confirmed that acquaintance rapes can be quite violent. In fact, one study on acquaintance rapes found that the better known the acquaintance, the more likely (1) the victim will suffer injuries and (2) attempts at rape will be completed (Belknap, 1989).

Date rape is largely invisible because acquaintance rapes have not been viewed as "real rapes" in our culture (Estrich, 1987). Self-report victimization studies of college women suggest that eight to fifteen percent have experienced *forced* intercourse, mostly as college students (DeKeseredy & Kelly, 1993; Reilly et al., 1992; Ward et al., 1991; Warshaw, 1988; Amick & Calhoun, 1987; Koss et al., 1987; Muehlenhard & Linton, 1987; Rivera & Regoli, 1987; Berger et al., 1986; Parrot, 1986; Lane & Gwartney-Gibbs, 1985; Korman & Leslie, 1982; Koss & Oros, 1982; Lott et al., 1982). Rates of self-reported coerced intercourse are much higher (Miller & Marshall, 1987).

There has been a recent attempt to downplay the seriousness and rates of date rape victimization (Roiphe, 1993). This work criticizes prior research establishing high rates of victimization, citing that the victims themselves often fail to identify their experiences as rape. This, however, is the essence of this prior work: that women have come to judge rape by some men's criteria and deny their forced sex experiences as rape simply because they were forced by acquaintances. Furthermore, this critique of feminist research (Roiphe, 1993) is based on selective and invalid interpretation of the data.

Notably, the research on self-reported sexual assaults by college *males,* while confirming the frequency of date rape, generally suggests that such victimizations are less common than women report (DeKeseredy & Kelly, 1993; Ward et al., 1991; Miller & Marshall, 1987). This might be due to few men committing rapes against many women and/or because male offenders are less likely than female victims to report a behavior as rape or force.

Regarding self-reported male behavior, one study found that over half of college men "thought it was somewhat justifiable to force kissing with tongue contact; [and] over a fifth thought it was somewhat justifiable to touch the woman's genitals against her wishes" (Muehlenhard et al., 1985:308). Another study of male psychology students found that 15 percent reported having forced intercourse at least once or twice, and 28 percent reported using directly coercive methods to obtain sex (Rapaport & Burkhart, 1984).

Some studies suggest that date rapes are more likely in the early stages of dating (Kanin & Purcell, 1977), and others in the middle stages of dating (Kanin, 1984). Most studies, however, claim that violence most frequently occurs where the couple has been seriously dating for some time (Lloyd et al., 1989; Makepeace, 1989; Aizenman & Kelly, 1988; Muehlenhard & Linton, 1987; Stets & Pirog-Good, 1987; Henton et al., 1983; Cate et al., 1982), and the longer the couple were dating before the violence occurred, the longer it takes the woman to leave the abusive man (Flynn, 1990). The discrepancies in these findings, on the relationship between the stage in dating and the level of violence, *might* be explained by the type of abuse noted, namely, nonsexual compared to sexual dating abuse. Perhaps sexual abuse in dating is more common in the earlier stages and nonsexual abuse in the later stages. At any rate, both kinds of violence may occur at any stage of an intimate "romantic" relationship, from the first date to after a divorce.

Researchers have attempted to explain both the sexual and nonsexual violence that begins or escalates in the later stages of a dating relationship. One explanation is that as the dating relationship becomes more serious and exclusive, it becomes more like marriage. "This shift in status seems to elicit expectations tied to gender, including the male's right to control his partner and the female's obligation to yield to his wishes" (Gamache 1991:73). Similarly, rapes first initiated in long-term dating relationships could be due to some men's (and women's) beliefs that men are entitled to sex after dating a woman over time (Berger et al., 1986; Weis & Borges, 1973).

Sexual harassment is also prevalent on college campuses. As noted previously, the form most commonly researched is that perpetrated by male faculty members or instructors toward female students. Studies of sexual harassment estimate that between 30 and 35 percent of female undergraduate and graduate students report sexual harassment by at least one faculty member over the course of their education (McKinney et al., 1988; Dziech & Weiner, 1984; Adams et al., 1983; Benson & Thomson, 1982). When the definitions of sexual harassment include sexist remarks and other forms of "gender harassment," the incidence in undergraduate populations nears 70 percent (Adams et al., 1983; Lott et al., 1982). Studies have also found that sexual harassment in academic settings is evenly distributed across departments on campus (Fitzgerald et al., 1988; Adams et al., 1983; Benson & Thomson, 1982).

Women college students report that sexual harassment often interferes with their education (McKinney et al., 1988; Adams et al., 1983; Benson & Thomson, 1982). Sexual harassment can make a student wonder what her true ability in a class is and it can threaten her self-confidence and commitment to academic pursuits (Benson & Thomson, 1982). Students may be reluctant to go to a professor's office or to request a letter of recommendation from a professor who has sexually harassed them. Thus, many students are placed in a situation where they must adopt strategies to minimize interactions with the potential for further harassment (Dziech & Weiner, 1984; Benson & Thomson, 1982). Sexual harassment thus not only impedes the victims' opportunities but can deter fellow women students from pursuing possibilities for study. Indeed, students report avoiding working with, or taking classes from, faculty members with a reputation for making sexual advances at students (McKinney et al., 1988; Adams et al., 1983).

Trying to politely communicate to a male professor that a female student is not interested in anything but a professional relationship places the "power dependent" student in an unenviable situation (Benson & Thomson, 1982). While she may understandably feel outraged and/or offended, she usually feels that it is best to handle the harassment as "low key" as possible. Not surprisingly, then, almost one-third of the students avoid direct complaints to the harasser. Even when the victim requests the harasser to stop, however, harassers do not necessarily discontinue their abuse (Benson & Thomson, 1982).

Finally, it is important to note that the research on campus sexual harassment has routinely left out the students' race in analyses of this problem, and thus failed to account for the role and dynamic of race in exploring harassment. It is likely that women of color are sexually harassed more often than their Anglo sisters, due to the interaction of racism and sexism (DeFour, 1990). For example, attitudes that African-American women are "sexually free," Asian women are docile and submissive, Hispanic women are "hot-blooded," and so on, greatly impact women of color's vulnerability to sexual harassment (DeFour, 1990). The research on date rape and courtship violence has also failed to adequately account for race. Future research needs to elucidate the effect of the student's race on the risk of victimization and the university and justice system responses to her allegations.

FACTORS RELATED TO THE AGGRESSION AGAINST WOMEN ON CAMPUS

The Climate

About one-third of college males have reported that they would rape women under some circumstances, if they knew that they would not get caught (Reilly et al., 1992; Check & Malamuth, 1985; Malamuth, 1981; Tieger, 1981). Research suggests that compared to women, men view sexually related behavior on the job and at school as more natural, less serious, and more to be expected (Lott et al., 1982). Given social science findings that male violence against women is related to "cultural attitudes, the power relationship between women and men, the social and economic status of women relative to men of their group, and the amount of other forms of violence in the society" (Scully 1990:48), the extent of campus violence against women is not surprising. Gang rapes are such an institutionalized activity in some fraternities that they are given names like "trains" and "spectrums" by fraternity brothers (Warshaw, 1988).

Fraternity practices and values in particular are conducive to coercive and violent sex and aggression against women. Fraternity brotherhood emphasizes a macho conception of men and masculinity and a narrow and stereotyped conception of women and femininity. The fraternity practices associated with these conceptions commodify women: use them as bait to attract new members or "take care" of the guys, and provide sexual access to women as a presumed benefit of fraternity membership. Excessive alcohol use, competitiveness between fraternities, and normative support for secrecy within fraternities further facilitate coercive sex and the treatment of rape as intrafraternity sport or contest. Women thus become the prey in the intrafraternity rivalry games (Martin & Hummer, 1989).

Reports have also noted that rarely are any sanctions placed on date or fraternity rapists, sexual harassers, or men who physically abuse their girlfriends (DeKeseredy et al., 1993; Lopez, 1992; Sanday, 1990; Warshaw, 1988; Adams et al., 1983). This failure to sanction violators is partly due to victims' unwillingness to report, but also to the university authorities' and the criminal justice system's reluctance to take action against offenders reported to them. These victimizations of women are often trivialized and joked about as the "sporting" parts of men's lives (Leidig, 1992).

One answer, then, as to why some men rape, abuse, and sexually harass women on campus is because they can. Recent research confirms that men who abuse women rarely receive negative consequences and are seldom shunned by their peers (Siegel & Raymond, 1992; Gamache, 1991; Martin & Hummer, 1989). In fact, some research has found that men who participate in courtship violence and date rape often receive peer support from their male friends, who may even encourage the abuse (Gwartney-Gibbs & Stockard, 1989; Martin & Hummer, 1989; DeKeseredy, 1988). Other studies found that although couples in physically abusive dating relationships most frequently attach *anger* and *confusion* as the meanings behind the abuse, approximately one-quarter believe abuse signifies "love" (Matthews, 1984; Cate et al., 1982).

Gender Differences and Stereotypes

Besides a climate which has historically allowed the subjugation and victimization of women, there are profound gender differences which promote courtship violence, date rape, and sexual harassment. First, studies report that men are more likely to sexualize behaviors than women (Shotland & Craig, 1988; Goodchilds & Zellman, 1984). Consequently, what women perceive as friendly behavior, men are more likely to perceive as sexual interest (Muehlenhard, 1989; Abbey, 1987). Similarly, both sexes report that a woman's flirting is often assumed by men to mean she desires sexual intercourse when she is attracted but unwilling to commit to that level of sexual intimacy (Miller & Marshall, 1987). Second, many myths still prevail that men have more sexual needs than women, men should initiate sex, men should be sexual, and women are responsible for controlling men's sexual behavior (Benson et al., 1992). As expected, men, particularly men who report being abusive, are more likely than women to believe rape myths and support sexual aggression (Reilly et al., 1992; Malamuth, 1989; Gilmartin-Zena, 1988; Warshaw, 1988; Dull & Giacoppasi, 1987; Greendlinger & Byrne, 1987; Muehlenhard & Linton, 1987; Giacoppasi & Dull, 1986; Wilson et al., 1983; Kanekar & Kolsawalla, 1980).

A third gender difference related to male aggression against women is that men who support and adhere to traditional sex role stereotypes (that women's roles and rights should be restricted) are more likely to support sexually assaultive behaviors or even self-report rapes (Muehlenhard, 1989; Muehlenhard & Linton, 1987; Hall et al., 1986; Costin, 1985; Check

& Malamuth, 1983). The "control myths" teach that men are inherently superior and women are inferior, while socialization practices teach men that they have expected sexual needs that correspond with female accessibility (Gamache, 1991; Scully, 1990:49). It appears that sexually coercive males act on a system of values wherein females are perceived as adversaries, and this value system is potentiated by the characterological dimensions of irresponsibility and poor socialization. Sexual encounters become the setting for the behavioral expression of these values and personality traits (Rapaport & Burkhart, 1984:220).

Boys and men are commonly socialized into, and receive reinforcement for, attitudes negatively stereotyping women. Moreover, some males and females are raised to believe that males are superior and females are inferior. Girls and women are often expected to act weak and passive, and even rewarded for these behaviors. These gender roles and stereotypes set up a climate for sexual harassment, date rape, and courtship violence. The gender differences promote males to commit these offenses while at the same time making it difficult for women to resist. Therefore, women who hold progressive attitudes about women's roles in society are likely to get out of abusive relationships sooner than those who hold traditional views (Flynn, 1990), emphasizing the importance of changing men's *and* women's attitudes. Finally, the gender stereotypes and rape myths prevalent in our culture often result in unduly placing the burden for these crimes on the victim.

In the organizational setting within which sexual harassment of female students occurs, related gender differences were found. Faculty men are less likely than faculty women to include consensual relationships in their definition of sexual harassment (Fitzgerald et al., 1988). Faculty men are also less likely than faculty women to view jokes, sexually teasing remarks and unwanted suggestive gestures or looks as harassment. Men are also significantly more likely than women to agree that attractive women have to expect sexual advances, that it is natural for men to make sexual advances to attractive women, and people who receive unwanted sexual attention have provoked it. Male faculty also are more likely than women to believe individuals can handle annoying sexual attention without involving the university. Men faculty thus perceive sexual harassment as a personal and not an organizational issue (Burickman, Pauludi & Rabinowitz, 1992).

Male Entitlement

Male entitlement is a common theme throughout the analysis of the causes of courtship violence, date rape, and sexual harassment. Whether it is the professor who believes he has the right to date or harass his students, the fraternity member who believes all women who attend parties are "fair game," or the boyfriend who "justifies" hitting his girlfriend because she talked with another man, male entitlement is a common thread in the victimization of women. Perhaps nowhere is this more evident than women students physically and sexually victimized by male athletes (Bohmer & Parrot, 1993; Eskenazi, 1990; Warshaw, 1988). These victims are often viewed as "groupies" who got what they "asked for," women who changed their minds after the "consensual" sex, or "gold diggers" trying to make money off athletes.

Altered States: The Effect of Alcohol and Drugs

Research on date rapes and fraternity gang rapes has found a strong link between alcohol/drug consumption and unwanted sexual experiences (Ward et al., 1991; Martin & Hummer, 1989; Pritchard, 1988; Warshaw, 1988; Muehlenhard & Linton, 1987; Lott et al., 1982) and courtship violence (Bogal-Allbritten & Allbritten, 1985). Moreover, there is considerable evidence that these rapists often *plan* before the date or party how to debilitate their victims through drugs and alcohol (Sanday, 1990; Martin & Hummer, 1989; Ehrhart & Sandler, 1985; Kanin, 1985).

Being in an altered state places a potential victim at increased risk of inability to resist the attacker, particularly if she is passed out. Additionally, while the public and criminal justice decision makers view the rapist as *less* responsible for raping if he was drunk, they view the rape victim as *more* responsible for being raped if she was drunk (Bromley & Territo, 1990; Lundberg-Love & Geffner, 1989; Warshaw, 1988; Ehrhart & Sandler, 1985; Goodchilds & Zellman, 1984; Richardson & Campbell, 1982).

THE DYNAMICS AND CONSEQUENCES OF VICTIMIZATION

Acquaintance victimizations pose unique problems for the victim, such as confusion surrounding coercion, the self-blame from trusting another person, and acknowledging "the depth and degree to which we tolerate male entitlement in our culture" (Fenstermaker, 1989:258). Often, women who have experienced victimization fail to define themselves as victims (Koss, 1990; Rabinowitz, 1990). First, there is a stigma attached to being a victim of these crimes in our culture. Victims often trivialize the experiences to protect their senses of vulnerability and integrity (Koss, 1990). Second, along with society, victims often blame themselves for their victimization of battering, rape, or sexual harassment (Koss, 1990; Berger et al., 1986). They often feel ashamed of their victimizations, particularly if they were attracted to their dates or professors before being raped, battered, or sexually harassed. A long period usually passes before a victim acknowledges her victimization. The women who resist and respond immediately are the exception: "Often the woman who speaks out is a person with a strong sense of integrity who can no longer ignore injustice" (Koss, 1990:77).

Women often do not report sexual harassment, date rapes, or courtship violence to formal authorities (e.g., university personnel or the police) and often not even to informal support persons (e.g., friends, family, and counselors) (DeKeseredy & Kelly, 1993; Benson et al., 1992; Ward et al., 1991; Belknap, 1989; Pirog-Good & Stets, 1989; Miller & Marshall, 1987). Many fear that they will not be taken seriously (Berger et al., 1986; U.S. Merit Systems Protection Board, 1981). Some students are hesitant to complain about sexual harassment because they are afraid that they will be held responsible for the victimization or are doubtful that any corrective action will be taken (Brandenburg, 1982).

These fears are not always unfounded. Offenders frequently go unpunished, whereas *victims* are negatively sanctioned in the media and/or on the campus or work site (Sanday, 1990; U.S. Merit Systems Protection Board, 1981). In fact, many victims of date and fraternity rapes and sexual harassment drop out of school while their offenders continue at the university (Sanday, 1990; Warshaw, 1988).

POLICY IMPLICATIONS

In the last decade, great headway has been made in raising awareness about the various kinds of victimizations of women on college campuses. Yet, there is still considerable ignorance of the harm these actions inflict on victims and denial about the magnitude of the problem. Furthermore, students, faculty, and staff are often unsure about resources available for the victims, as well as the policies and procedures regarding these acquaintance victimizations (Sullivan & Bybee, 1987; Adams et al., 1983;

Metha & Nigg, 1982). For too long, the focus on the victimization of college women revolved around preventing stranger rape (e.g., improving lighting and providing extra security locks), ignoring the far more common acquaintance victimizations (Steenbarger & Zimmer, 1992; Miller & Marshall, 1987). This section concludes with necessary steps for deterring the violence and violations of college women.

The first and most important action that college or university administration can take is to acknowledge that sexual harassment, date rape, and courtship violence are realities on campuses (Benson et al., 1992; Roark, 1989).

The second step is prevention. Enforcing policies and laws regarding acquaintance victimizations often results in accepting one person's word (and credibility) against another's, making prevention particularly important. Prevention can best be served by promoting education and awareness of the dynamics of sexual harassment, date rape, and courtship violence to students, faculty members, and staff (Bohmer & Parrot, 1993; Benson et al., 1992; Leidig, 1992; Steenbarger & Zimmer, 1992; Ward et al., 1991; Roark, 1989; Warshaw, 1988; Amick & Calhoun, 1987; Adams et al., 1983). Awareness may prevent potential offenders from committing these offenses and keep potential victims from experiencing them. Moreover, such knowledge will help those in the academic community to better understand, and thus respond appropriately to victims who approach them.

Third, it is important to make clear policy statements about sexual harassment, date rape, and courtship violence. The policy statements should identify: (1) definitions of sexual harassment, date rape, and courtship violence; (2) who is responsible for handling charges regarding victimizations on campus, both formally (e.g., the police or a grievance board) and informally (e.g., mediation through a counselor or ombudsman's office); and (3) the consequences for offenders of violating the policies (Bohmer & Parrot, 1993; Benson et al., 1992; Virginia State Council on Higher Education, 1992; Biaggio et al., 1990; Adams et al., 1983; Brandenburg, 1982; Metha & Nigg, 1982).

Fourth, the grievance boards or administrators in charge of processing the charges should ensure that action is taken as quickly, efficiently, confidentially, and carefully as possible.

Fifth, the university needs to widely disseminate the policies so everyone in the academic community (students, faculty members, and staff) has access to them (Bohmer & Parrot, 1993; Benson et al., 1992; Branden-burg, 1982; Metha & Nigg, 1982).

Sixth, there needs to be an ongoing evaluation of the effectiveness of the policies to ensure that those responsible for enforcement take these violations seriously (Bohmer & Parrot, 1993; Adams et al., 1983; Bran-denburg, 1982; Metha & Nigg, 1982).

Seventh, there must be victim advocate services available on campus to respond to the short- and long-term emotional, medical, and logistic filing complaint needs of these victims/survivors (Bohmer & Parrot, 1993; Benson et al., 1992; Leidig, 1992; Roark, 1989).

Finally, student victims need to know that they may take a sexual harassment grievance directly to the Office of Civil Rights in the U.S. Department of Education or press charges in a private lawsuit against offenders perpetrating sexual harassment, date rape, and courtship violence, whether a grievance procedure exists on their campus or not (Brandenburg, 1982). Perhaps this fact alone should convince university administrators that if they fail to adequately work toward prevention and inadequately respond once victimizations occur, that victims can appeal to the legal system outside the academic community.

It is encouraging to note that consistent with the policy recommenda-tions put forth in this chapter, the Higher Education Amendment of 1992 included a section to deter and respond to campus sexual offenses. Not only is this law a landmark in recognizing campus sexual victimization, but it is well thought out and provides funding for its stated goals of developing rape education/awareness, disciplinary boards, victim coun-seling and medical services, and dissemination of legal information and assistance to victims. This federal recognition of one of the victimiza-tions that college women frequently encounter is an important step in legitimizing the seriousness of campus rapes and should be funded. Hopefully, similar legislation will help combat sexual harassment and courtship violence on college campuses.

REFERENCES

Abbey, A. (1987) "Misperceptions of Friendly Behavior as Sexual Interest." *Psychology of Women Quarterly 11:*173–94.

Adams, J.W., J.L. Kottke, and J.S. Padgitt (1983) "Sexual Harassment of University Students." *Journal of College Student Personnel 24:*484–90.

Aizenman, M. and G. Kelley (1988) "Incidence of Violence and Acquaintance Rape in Dating Relationships Among College Males and Females." *Journal of College Student Development* 29:305–311.

Amick, A.E. and K.S. Calhoun (1987) "Resistance to Sexual Aggression: Personality, Attitudinal, and Situational Factors." *Archives of Sexual Behavior* 16:153–163.

Barrett, K. (1982) "Date Rape: A Campus Epidemic?" *Ms.,* September, pp. 49–51, 130.

Belknap, J. (forthcoming) *The Invisible Woman: Gender, Crime, and Justice.* Belmont, CA: Wadsworth.

—— (1989) "The Sexual Victimization of Unmarried Women by Nonrelative Acquaintances." In M.A. Pirog-Good and J.E. Stets (eds.), *Violence and Dating Relationships: Emerging Social Issues.* NY: Praeger, pp. 215–218.

Benson, D., C. Charlton, and F. Goodhart (1992) "Acquaintance Rape on Campus." *Journal of American College Health* 40:157–65.

Benson, D.J. and G.E. Thomson (1982) "Sexual Harassment on a University Campus." *Social Problems* 29:236–51.

Berger, R.J., P. Searles, R.G. Salem, and B.A. Pierce (1986) "Sexual Assault in a College Community." *Sociological Focus* 19:1–26.

Biaggio, M.K., D. Watts, and A. Brownell (1990) "Addressing Sexual Harassment: Strategies for Prevention and Change." In M.A. Paludi (ed.) *Ivory Power: Sexual Harassment on Campus.* Albany, NY: State University of New York Press, pp. 213–30.

Bogal-Allbritten, R.B. and W.L. Allbritten (1985) "The Hidden Victims: Courtship Violence Among College Students." *Journal of College Student Personnel* 26:201–204.

Bohmer, C. and A. Parrot (1993) *Sexual Assault on Campus.* New York: Lexington Books.

Brandenburg, J.B. (1982) "Sexual Harassment in the University: Guidelines for Establishing a Grievance Procedure." *Signs* 8:320–36.

Bromley, M.L. and L. Territo (1990) *College Crime Prevention and Personal Safety Awareness.* Springfield, IL: Charles C Thomas.

Burickman, R.B., M.A. Pauldi, and V.C. Rabinowitz (1992) "Sexual Harassment of Students: Victims of the College Students; Victims of the College Experience." In E.C. Viano (ed.), *Critical Issues in Victimology: International Perspectives.* New York, NY: Springer, pp. 153–165.

Cate, R.M., J.M. Henton, J. Koval, S.F. Christopher, and S. Lloyd (1982) "Premarital Abuse: A Social Psychological Perspective." *Journal of Family Issues* 3:79–90.

Check, J.V.P. and N.M. Malamuth (1983) "Sex Role Stereotyping and Reactions to Depictions of Stranger Versus Acquaintance Rape." *Journal of Personality and Social Psychology* 45:344–356.

Clark, A. (1987) *Women's Silence Men's Violence: Sexual Assault in England 1770–1845.* London: Pandora.

Costin, F. (1985) "Beliefs About Rape and Women's Social Roles." *Archives of Sexual Behavior* 14:319–325.

Currie, D.H. and B.D. MacLean (1993) "Woman Abuse in Dating Relationships: Rethinking Women's Safety on Campus." *Journal of Human Justice* 2(1):1–24.

DeFour, D.C. (1990) "The Interface of Racism and Sexism on College Campuses." In

M.A. Paludi (ed.), *Ivory Power: Sexual Harassment on Campus.* Albany, NY: State University of New York Press, pp. 45–52.

DeKeseredy, W.S. and K. Kelly (1993) "Woman Abuse in University and College Dating Relationships." *Journal of Human Justice* 2(1):25–52.

DeKeseredy, W.S., M.D. Schwartz, and K. Tait (1993) "Sexual Assault and Stranger Aggression on a Canadian Campus." *Sex Roles* 28:263–77.

DeKeseredy, W.S. (1988) *Woman Abuse in Dating Relationships: The Role of Male Peer Support.* Toronto: Canadian Scholars Press.

Dull, R.T. and D.J. Giacopassi (1987): "Demographic Correlates of Sexual and Dating Attitudes: A Study of Date Rape." *Criminal Justice and Behavior* 14:175–193.

Dziech, B.D. and L. Weiner (1984) *The Lecherous Professor.* Boston: Beacon.

Ehrhart, J.K. and B.R. Sandler (1985) "Campus Gang Rape: Party Games?" In Project on the Status of Education and Women (ed.), *Sexual Harassment: A Hidden Issue.* Washington, DC: National Association of Colleges, pp. 1–19.

Erez, E. (1986) "Intimacy, Violence, and the Police." *Human Relations* 39:265–81.

Eskenazi, G. (1990) "The Male Athlete and Sexual Assault." *The New York Times,* June 3, p. 45.

Estrich, S. (1987) *Real Rape.* Cambridge, Mass: Harvard University Press.

Felson, R.B. and M. Krohn (1990) "Motives for Rape." *Journal of Research in Crime and Delinquency* 27:222–42.

Fenstermaker, S. (1989) "Acquaintance Rape on Campus: Responsibility and Attributions of Crime." In M.A. Pirog-Good and J.E. Stets (eds.), *Violence and Dating Relationships: Emerging Social Issues.* New York: Praeger, pp. 257–272.

Fitzgerald, L.F., S. Shullman, N. Bailey, Y. Gold, and M. Ormerod (1990) "Sexual Harassment: The Definition and Measurement of a Construct." In M.A. Paludi (ed.), *Ivory Power: Sexual Harassment on Campus.* Albany, NY: State University of New York Press, pp. 21–44.

—— (1988) "The Incidence and Dimensions of Sexual Harassment in Academia and the Workplace." *Journal of Vocational Behavior* 32:152–175.

Fitzgerald, L.F., L.M. Weitzman, Y. Gold, and M. Ormerod (1988) "Academic Harassment: Sex and Denial in Scholarly Garb." *Psychology of Women Quarterly* 12:329–40.

Flynn, C.P. (1990) "Sex Roles and Women's Responses to Courtship Violence." *Journal of Family Violence* 5:83–94.

Gamache, D. (1991) "Domination and Control: The Social Context of Dating Violence." In B. Levy (ed.), *Dating Violence: Young Women in Danger.* Seattle, WA: Seal Press, pp. 69–83.

Giacopassi, D.J. and R.T. Dull (1986) "Gender and Racial Differences in the Acceptance of Rape Myths Within a College Population." *Sex Roles* 15(1):63–75.

Gilmartin-Zena, P. (1988) "Gender Differences in Students' Attitudes Toward Rape." *Sociological Focus* 21(2):279–292.

—— (1987) "Attitudes Toward Rape: Student Characteristics as Predictors." *Free Inquiry in Creative Sociology* 15(1):175–182.

Glaser, R.D. and J.S. Thorpe (1986) "Unethical Intimacy: A Survey of Sexual

Contact and Advances Between Psychology Educators and Female Graduate Students." *American Psychologist 41*(1):43–51.

Goodchilds, J.D. and G.L. Zellman (1984) "Sexual Signaling and Sexual Aggression in Adolescent Relationships." In N.M. Malamuth and E. Donnerstein (eds.), *Pornography and Sexual Aggression.* Orlando, FL: Academic Press, pp. 233–243.

Greendlinger, V. and D. Byrne (1987) "Coercive Sexual Fantasies of College Men as Predictors of Self-Reported Likelihood to Rape and Overt Sexual Aggression." *Journal of Sex Research 23*(1):1–11.

Gwartney-Gibbs, P. and J. Stockard (1989) "Courtship Aggression and Mixed-Sex Peer Groups." In M.A. Pirog-Good and J.E. Stets (eds.), *Violence and Dating Relationships: Emerging Social Issues.* New York: Praeger, pp. 185–204.

Hall, E.R., J.A. Howard, and S.L. Boezio (1986) "Tolerance of Rape: A Sexist or Antisocial Attitude?" *Psychology of Women Quarterly 10*(1):101–118.

Henton, J., R. Cate, J. Koval, S. Lloyd, and S. Christopher (1983) "Romance and Violence in Dating Relationships." *Journal of Family Issues 4*(3):467–82.

Higher Education Amendment of 1992 (1992) 20 USC 1, 145h. Public Law 102-325 [sec. 1150] July 23, 1992 Part D: Grants for Sexual Offenses Education.

Kanekar, S. and M.B. Kolsawalla (1980) "Responsibility of a Rape Victim in Relation to her Respectability, Attractiveness, and Provocativeness." *Journal of Social Psychology 112*(1):153–154.

Kanin, E.J. (1985) "Date Rapists: Differential Sexual Socialization and Relative Deprivation." *Archives of Sexual Behavior 14*(2):219–31.

—— (1984) "Date Rape: Unofficial Criminals and Victims." *Victimology 9*(1):95–108.

—— (1957) "Male Aggression in Dating-Courtship Relations." *American Journal of Sociology 63*(1):197–204.

Kanin, E.J. and S.R. Parcell (1977) "Sexual Aggression: A Second Look at the Offended Female." *Archives of Sexual Behavior 6*(1):67–76.

Knutson, J.F. and J.G. Mehm (1986) "Transgenerational Patterns of Coercion in Families and Intimate Relationships." In G. Russell (ed.), *Violence in Intimate Relationships.* New York: PMA Publishing Corporation, pp. 67–90.

Korman, S.K. and G.R. Leslie (1982) "The Relationship of Feminist Ideology and Date Expense Sharing to Perceptions of Sexual Aggression in Dating." *Journal of Sex Research 18*(1):114–129.

Koss, M.P. and C.J. Oros (1990) "Changed Lives: The Psychological Impact of Sexual Harassment." In M.A. Paludi (ed.), *Ivory Power: Sexual Harassment on Campus.* Albany, NY: State University of New York Press, pp. 77–92.

—— (1982) "Sexual Experiences Survey: A Research Instrument Investigating Sexual Aggression and Victimization." *Journal of Consulting and Clinical Psychology 50*(4):455–457.

Koss, M.P., C.A. Gidycz, and N. Wisniewski (1987) "The Scope of Rape: Incidence and Prevalence of Sexual Aggression and Victimization in a National Sample of Higher Education Students." *Journal of Consulting and Clinical Psychology 55*(2): 162–170.

Koss, M.P., K.E. Leonard, D.A. Beezley, and C.J. Oros (1985) "Nonstranger Sexual

Aggression: A Discriminant Analysis of Psychological Characteristics of Unde-tected Offenders." *Sex Roles* 12(5):981–992.

Lane, K.E. and P.A. Gwartney-Gibbs (1985) "Violence in the Context of Dating and Sex." *Journal of Family Issues* 6(1):45–49.

Leidig, M.W. (1992) "Continuum of Violence Against Women: Psychological and Physical Consequences." *Journal of American College Health* 40(2):149–55.

Levine-MacCombie, J. and M.P. Koss (1986) "Acquaintance Rape: Effective Avoid-ance Strategies." *Psychology of Women Quarterly* 10(2):311–320.

Lloyd, S., J.E. Koval, and R.M. Cate (1989) "The Help Seeking Behavior of Physi-cally and Sexually Abused College Students." In M.A. Pirog-Good and J.E. Stets (eds.), *Violence and Dating Relationships: Emerging Social Issues.* New York: Praeger, pp. 126–144.

Lott, B., M.E. Reilly, and D.R. Howard (1982) "Sexual Assault and Harassment: A Campus Community Case Study." *Signs* 8(3):296–319.

Lopez, P. (1992) "He Said, She Said: An Overview of Date Rape from Commission through Prosecution through Verdict." *Criminal Justice Journal* 13(3):275–302.

Lundberg-Love, P. and R. Geffner (1989) "Date Rape: Prevalence, Risk Factors, and a Proposed Model." In M.A. Pirog-Good and J.E. Stets (eds.), *Violence and Dating Relationships: Emerging Social Issues.* New York: Praeger, pp. 169–184.

Makepeace, J.M. (1989) "Dating, Living Together, and Courtship Violence." In M.A. Pirog-Good and J.E. Stets (eds.), *Violence and Dating Relationships: Emerging Social Issues.* New York: Praeger, pp. 94–107.

—— (1986) "Gender Differences in Courtship Violence Victimization." *Family Rela-tions* 35(3):383–88.

—— (1983) "Life Events and Courtship Violence." *Family Relations* 32(1):101–109.

—— (1981) "Courtship Violence Among College Students." *Family Relations* 30(1): 97–102.

Malamuth, N.M. (1989) "Predictors of Naturalistic Sexual Aggression." In M.A. Pirog-Good and J.E. Stets (eds.), *Violence and Dating Relationships: Emerging Social Issues.* New York: Praeger, pp. 219–240.

—— (1981) "Rape Proclivity Among Males." *Journal of Social Issues* 37(1):138–157.

Martin, P.Y. and R.A. Hummer (1989) "Fraternities and Rape on Campus." *Gender and Society* 3(4):457–473.

Matthews, W.J. (1984) "Violence in College Couples." *College Student Journal* 18(2): 150–58.

McKinney, K., C.V. Olson, and A. Satterfield (1988) "Graduate Students' Experi-ences with and Responses to Sexual Harassment." *Journal of Interpersonal Violence* 3(4):319–25.

Metha, A. and J. Nigg (1982) "Sexual Harassment: Implications of a Study at Arizona State University." *Women's Studies Quarterly* 10(1):24–26.

Miller, B. and J.C. Marshall (1987) "Coercive Sex on the University Campus." *Journal of College Student Personnel* 28(1):38–47.

Muehlenhard, C.L. and M.A. Linton (1989) "Misinterpreted Dating Behaviors and the Risk of Rape." In M.A. Pirog-Good and J.E. Stets (eds.), *Violence and Dating Relationships: Emerging Social Issues.* New York: Praeger, pp. 241–256.

—— (1987) "Date Rape and Sexual Aggression in Dating Situations: Incidence and Risk Factors." *Journal of Counseling Psychology* 34(2):186–196.

Muehlenhard, C.L., D.E. Friedman, and C.M. Thomas (1985) "Is Date Rape Justifiable? The Effects of Dating Activity, Who Initiated, Who Paid, and Men's Attitudes toward Women." *Psychology of Women Quarterly* 43(2):186–196.

Paludi, M.A., M. Grossman, C.A. Scott, J. Kindermann, S. Matula, J. Oswald, J. Dovan, and D. Mulcahy (1990) "Myths and Realities: Sexual Harassment on Campus." In M.A. Paludi (ed.), *Ivory Power: Sexual Harassment on Campus.* Albany, NY: State University of New York Press, pp. 1–14.

Parrot, A. (1986) *Acquaintance Rape and Sexual Assault Prevention Training Manual* (2 ed). Ithaca, NY: Department of Human Service Studies, Cornell University.

Pirog-Good, M.A. and J.E. Stets (1989) "The Help-Seeking Behavior of Physically and Sexually Abused College Students." In M.A. Pirog-Good and J.E. Stets (eds.), *Violence and Dating Relationships: Emerging Social Issues.* New York: Praeger, pp. 108–125.

Pritchard, C. (1988) *Avoiding Rape On and Off Campus.* Wenonah, NJ: State College.

Project on the Status and Education of Women (1978) *Sexual Harassment: A Hidden Issue.* Washington, DC: Association of American Colleges.

Rabinowitz, V.C. (1990) "Coping with Sexual Harassment." In M.A. Paludi (ed.), *Ivory Power: Sexual Harassment on Campus.* Albany, NY: State University of New York Press, pp. 15–35.

Rapaport, K. and B.R. Burkhart (1984) "Personality and Attitudinal Characteristics of Sexually Coercive College Males." *Journal of Abnormal Psychology* 93(2):216–221.

Reilly, M.E., B. Lott, D. Caldwell, and L. DeLuca (1992) "Tolerance for Sexual Harassment Related to Self-Reported Sexual Victimization." *Gender and Society* 6(1):122–138.

Richardson, D. and J.L. Campbell (1982) "The Effect of Alcohol on Attributions of Blame for Rape." *Personality and Social Psychology Bulletin* 8(4):468–76.

Rivera, G.F. and R.M. Regoli (1987) "Sexual Victimization Experiences of Sorority Women." *Sociology and Social Research* 72(1):39–42.

Roark, M.L. (1989) "Sexual Violence." In D. Siegel and C. Raymond (eds.), *Responding to Violence on Campus.* New York: Jossey-Bass, pp. 41–52.

—— (1987) "Preventing Violence on College Campuses." *Journal of Counseling and Development* 65(3):367–370.

Roiphe, K. (1993) *The Morning After: Sex, Fear, and Feminism on Campus.* Boston: Little, Brown and Company.

Scully, D. (1990) *Understanding Sexual Violence.* Boston: Unwin Hyman.

Schwartz, M.D. (1991) "Humanist Sociology and Date Rape on College Campus." *Humanity and Society* 15(3):304–16.

Shotland, R.L. and J.M. Craig (1988) "Can Men and Women Differentiate between Friendly and Sexually Interested Behavior?" *Social Psychology Quarterly* 51(1):66–73.

Smith, M.D. (1988) "Professor Beware: The Law and Sexual Harassment in 1988." *Capstone Journal of Education* 8(1):75–83.

Steenbarger, B.N. and C.G. Zimmer (1992) "Violence on Campus: The Changing Face of College Health." *Journal of American College Health* 40(2):147–148.

Stets, J.E. and M.A. Straus (1989) "The Marriage License as a Hitting License: A Comparison of Assaults in Dating, Cohabitating, and Married Couples." In M.A. Pirog-Good and J.E. Stets (eds.), *Violence and Dating Relationships: Emerging Social Issues.* New York: Praeger, pp. 33–54.

Stets, J. and M. Pirog-Good (1987) "Violence in Dating Relationships." *Social Psychology Quarterly 50*(2):237–46.

Sullivan, M. and D.I. Bybee (1987) "Female Students and Sexual Harassment: What Factors Predict Reporting Behavior." *Journal of the National Association for Women Deans, Administrators, and Counselors 50*(1):11–16.

Tieger, T. (1981) "Self-Rated Likelihood of Raping and Social Perception of Rape." *Journal of Research in Personality 15*(1):147–58.

Till, F.J. (1980) *Sexual Harassment: A Report on the Sexual Harassment of Students.* Washington, DC: National Advisory Council on Women's Educational Programs.

U.S. Merit Systems Protection Board (1981) *Sexual Harassment in the Federal Workplace: Is it a Problem?* Washington, DC: U.S. Government Printing Office.

Virginia State Council on Higher Education (1992) *Sexual Assault on Virginia's Campuses.* Richmond, VA: Senate Document No. 17.

Ward, S.K., K. Chapman, S. White and K. Williams (1991) "Acquaintance Rape and the College Social Scene." *Family Relations 40*(1):65–71.

Warshaw, R. (1988) *I Never Called It Rape.* New York: Ms. Magazine/Sarah Lazin Books.

Weis, K. and S.S. Borges (1973) "Victimology and Rape: The Base of the Legitimate Victim." *Issues in Criminology 8*(1):71–115.

Wilson, K., R. Faison, G.M. Britton (1983) "Cultural Aspects of Male Aggression." *Deviant Behavior 4*(2):241–55.

Chapter 9

FEAR OF CRIME AND PERCEIVED RISK OF VICTIMIZATION IN AN URBAN UNIVERSITY SETTING

BONNIE S. FISHER, JOHN J. SLOAN, III AND DEBORAH L. WILKINS[1]

INTRODUCTION

College students, their parents, faculty and staff, and campus administrators have become increasingly aware of and concerned with campus crime and security-related issues on campus during the last ten years (Bromley, 1995; Fisher & Sloan, 1993). Much of this concern stems from: (1) the media presenting a steady stream of reports on serious crimes occurring at college campuses (Lederman, 1993, 1994; Matthews, 1993); (2) recent court decisions holding colleges and universities liable for "foreseeable" victimizations (Smith, 1995); and (3) grassroots movements by family members and friends of victimized students lobbying state and federal legislatures and campus administrators for more security measures and crime prevention programs on campuses (Cohen, 1994).

These concerns prompted Congress to pass the Student Right-to-Know and Campus Security Act of 1990 (20 USC 1092) requiring colleges and universities "to prepare, publish, and distribute" an annual report that, at a minimum, describes campus security policies and reports campus crime statistics for six FBI Index offenses and three violations (House Report 101–883, Section 201-205, 1990; Seng, 1995; Seng & Koehler, 1993). Recently, several state legislatures have also passed legislation requiring colleges and universities to compile and publicly report campus crime statistics and security procedures (Griffaton, 1995).

Despite recent concern about campus crime and security, two important responses to crime on campuses—perceived *risk* of victimization and fear of victimization—have received limited attention by researchers (see Brantingham, Brantingham & Seagrave, 1995). Scholars understand much about perceived risk and fear of victimization in residential and commercial settings and their effects on both people and the community (LaGrange

179

& Ferraro, 1992; Fisher, 1991; Lab, 1988; Skogan, 1990; Warr & Stafford, 1983; Skogan & Maxfield, 1981). However, researchers know and understand far less about fear of victimization and perceived risk of victimization in a college or university context. Few published studies have examined the levels or the causes of individual-level fear of victimization in a college campus context (see Brantingham et al., 1995; Day, 1994; Fisher & Nasar, 1992a, 1992b, 1992c). To our knowledge, no published research has yet examined the perception of *risk* of victimization among students, faculty, or staff in a college or university context.

This chapter examines perceived risk and fear of on-campus victimization by students, faculty and staff at a large, urban university campus located in the Southeast. We have three major goals for the chapter. First, we review previous work on fear and perceived risk, especially the dominant theoretical models used to predict or explain perceived risk and fear of victimization. We then link this body of work to the campus setting by arguing the campus is a community in much the same way as neighborhoods or residential areas are communities. Next, we test whether perceived risk and fear of victimization among campus community members are influenced by the same variables identified in prior work as influencing risk and fear in other contexts. Finally, based on our analyses, we offer recommendations to campus administrators about how they might reduce perceived risk and fear of victimization on their campuses.

PERCEIVED RISK AND FEAR OF VICTIMIZATION AND THEIR CORRELATES: WHAT DO WE KNOW?

Perceived risk and fear of victimization have been the focus of many studies (LaGrange, Ferraro & Supanic, 1992; LaGrange & Ferraro, 1989; Taylor & Hale, 1986). As a result, not only has our understanding of the meaning of the concepts of perceived risk (a cognitive assessment of the probability of victimization) and fear of victimization (an emotional response to perceived danger) improved, but our knowledge about the correlates and causes of risk and fear has significantly advanced as well (LaGrange, Ferraro & Supanic, 1992; Skogan, 1990; Rohe & Burby, 1988; Gates & Rohe, 1987; Stafford & Galle, 1984; Warr & Stafford, 1983; Skogan & Maxfield, 1981).

Five major models of perceived risk and fear of victimization have dominated recent research in this area. These models include: social and physical vulnerability, victimization (direct and vicarious), physical and social disorders, community integration, and formal social control. We now review general findings from previous research and examine each set of explanatory variables.

Social and Physical Vulnerability

The social and physical vulnerability model of risk and fear emphasizes the importance of demographic indicators to both perceptions of risk and onset of fear (Day, 1994; Rohe & Burby, 1988). Skogan and Maxfield (1981:77–78) defined two independent dimensions of personal vulnerability: physical and social. By physical vulnerability they meant "openness to attack, powerlessness to resist attack, and exposure to significant physical and emotional consequences if attacked." Indicators of physical vulnerability included gender (female) and age (elderly). Skogan and Maxfield (1981:73) defined social vulnerability as when people are "frequently exposed to the threat of victimization because of whom they are, and when the social and economic consequences of victimization weigh more heavily [on] them." Primary characteristics of social vulnerability include minority status (African American) and membership in lower socioeconomic groups (poverty).

Much empirical support has been generated about the importance of demographic indicators of vulnerability in predicting fear of victimization. The most consistent finding has been that, despite having lower rates of victimization, women significantly fear victimization more than men (Smith & Hill, 1991; LaGrange & Ferraro, 1989; Gordon & Rigor, 1989; Box, Hale & Andrews, 1988; Gates & Rohe, 1987; Stafford & Galle, 1984; Warr & Stafford, 1983; Skogan & Maxfield, 1981).

Researchers have reported contradictory findings about the relationship between age and fear, perhaps the result of various measures used. Studies that measured fear of crime in unidimensional terms (e.g., "afraid of being out alone in your neighborhood at night") have found a direct relationship between age and fear of crime (Smith & Hill, 1991; Ortega & Myles, 1987; Hill, Howell & Driver, 1985; Stafford & Galle, 1984; Jeffords, 1983; Ollenburger, 1981; Skogan & Maxfield, 1981; Clemente & Kleiman, 1977; Conklin, 1975). However, when researchers measured fear by asking respondents about their fear of victimization from diverse *types* of crime, LaGrange and Ferraro (1989) found older people (65 years and older) had lower levels of fear than younger adults (18 to 29 years old). Although they found an inverse relationship between age and fear of *personal* crime, they found no significant relationship between age and fear of *property* crime. Additionally, they also reported levels of perceived *risk* of property victimization generally increased with age, but only to a point when perceived risk decreased.

Several studies suggest race is a strong predictor of fear of crime. These studies suggest, based on neighborhood-level analyses, that African Americans are not only more likely to be afraid than whites but are also more likely than whites to be crime victims (Skogan & Maxfield, 1981; Clemente & Kleiman, 1977; Erskine, 1974). However, Ortega and Myles (1987), based on a national sample of people, suggested whites are more afraid of crime than African Americans. Stinchcombe, Adams, Heimer, Scheppele, Smith and Taylor (1980) have also suggested that fear of crime among whites is higher than among African Americans because whites are afraid of African Americans, not of crime. LaGrange and Ferraro (1989) reported that while African Americans have higher levels of perceived *risk* of personal and property crime, their levels of *fear* did not differ significantly from whites.

In sum, the social and physical vulnerability model incorporates personal characteristics of vulnerability as determinants of perceived risk and fear of victimization. Although some research findings contradict one other about the relationship of personal vulnerability with fear or risk, their effects must be considered when estimating statistical models of risk and fear of victimization.

Victimization Model

The victimization model emphasizes the importance of direct or vicarious victimization experiences to the onset of risk and fear. People who have been victimized are expected to perceive a higher risk of future victimization and to be more fearful than those who have not been victimized (Taylor & Hale, 1986). Additionally, the model hypothesizes that people who either know crime victims or who have heard about criminal events (vicarious victimization) have higher levels of either fear or perceived risk than people who do not know crime victims (Skogan & Maxfield, 1981).

Several studies have identified prior victimization as a strong correlate of risk and fear (LaGrange & Ferraro, 1992; Smith & Hill, 1991; Ollenburger, 1981; Skogan & Maxfield, 1981). Skogan and Maxfield

(1981:67) found that "while victims are more fearful than non-victims, few people . . . have been victimized in any recent period."

Other research that examined the relationship between prior victimization and fear has concluded that prior victimization is either a weak predictor of fear of crime (Hindelang, Gottfredson & Garafalo, 1978; Garofalo, 1979) or is not related to fear of crime (LaGrange & Ferraro, 1992; Hill, Howell & Driver, 1985). LaGrange and Ferraro (1992) reported, however, that past victimization was a significant predictor of perceived *risk* of victimization.

Fear of victimization is also related to kind of victimization suffered (personal compared to property). Smith and Hill (1991) found that, after controlling for social background characteristics, victims of property crime, and victims of *both* property and personal crimes, reported significantly higher levels of fear than non-victims. Surprisingly, they also reported that experience with personal crime alone was not associated with higher levels of fear (Smith & Hill, 1991:234). One possible explanation for this last finding was that the relative infrequency of personal victimization among the sample may have attenuated the effect. Finally, although not extensive, there is some evidence suggesting that vicarious victimization and fear of crime are directly related to each other (Lab, 1988; Ollenberger, 1981; Skogan & Maxfield, 1981). Thus, the victimization model as a predictor of perceived risk and fear of victimization appears, at best, to have contradictory support.

Social and Physical Disorders

The social and physical disorders model incorporates the breakdown of local social cohesion and social control with the onset of perceived risk and fear of victimization (Skogan, 1990; Gates & Rohe, 1987; Wilson & Kelling, 1982). Social disorder, according to Skogan (1990:4), "is a matter of behavior: you see it happening (public drinking or prostitution), experience it (catcalling or sexual harassment), or notice direct evidence of it (graffiti or vandalism)." Physical disorder, on the other hand, "involves visual signs of negligence and unchecked decay: abandoned or ill-kept buildings, broken streetlights, trash-filled lots."

This model is based on arguments made by Wilson and Kelling (1982) and Skogan (1990) which suggest that perceived social and physical incivilities, or symbols of disorder, are directly linked to both crime and to fear of crime. People may perceive the likelihood of victimization as

high and become fearful because they perceive an environment characterized with much incivility to be threatening, and especially threatening
to their physical safety.

Much support has been found for the disorders thesis (Perkins, Meeks
& Taylor, 1992; Skogan & Maxfield, 1981). Prior research has consistently
found strong relationships among fear of crime, incivility, and other
neighborhood problems (Perkins, Wandersman, Rich & Taylor, 1993;
Greenberg, 1986; Kennedy & Silverman, 1985).

Neighborhood Integration Model

The neighborhood integration model is grounded in the traditions of
urban sociology and social disorganization theory that suggest neighborhood integration is a causal building block to understanding people's
assessment of their life space and to understanding a variety of social
pathologies, including fear and crime (Merry, 1981; Hunter, 1974; Wirth,
1938). Integration has two major dimensions: a residential component—a
commitment to the neighborhood in terms of living in an area for a long
time—and a social component—knowing people in the neighborhood
and differentiating who belongs from whom does not. This model posits
negative relationships between social and residential integration and
fear (Merry, 1981; Skogan & Maxfield, 1981).

A variety of studies, using various methodologies, have found mixed
support for the neighborhood integration model; few, if any, studies
have examined the relationship between neighborhood integration and
perceived risk. Merry's (1981) study of a small ethnically diverse neighborhood suggested that knowing people in the neighborhood contributed to a feeling of safety. Taylor, Gottfredson and Brower (1984) found
residents' ability to distinguish between strangers and people who belonged
on the block, length of residence on the block, and feelings of responsibility for what goes on in the block were related to fear levels. Skogan and
Maxfield's (1981) analysis of survey data from a sample of respondents in
three major cities provided no evidence that community integration had
any significant indirect benefits on fear of crime. They reported the
relationship between crime conditions and fear was virtually the same
for those reporting varying levels of community integration.

Formal Social Control Model

The formal social control model emphasizes confidence in the police as a force accelerating or muting the development of fear of victimization (Box, Hale & Andrews, 1988). It suggests if people believe the police are effective and efficient in addressing crimes and apprehending criminals, they are less likely to feel fearful. Recent arguments propose that the style of policing (community oriented compared to incident oriented) significantly reduces fear of crime in both residential and commercial settings (Moore & Trojanowicz, 1988; Brown & Wycoff, 1987; Cordner, Marenin & Murphy, 1986; Pate, 1986; Trojanowicz, 1982).

Many studies also show that citizen attitudes toward police more generally (i.e., formal social control mechanisms) are related to fear of crime (see Stacey 1990 for review; Box, Hale & Andrews, 1988; Carter, 1985; Smith, 1983; Benson, 1981; Conklin, 1975). Other studies report no relationship between fear and global attitudes toward the police (Zamble & Annesley, 1987; Thomas & Hyman, 1977; Smith & Hawkins, 1973). Thus, there is some support for the formal social control model: style of policing and confidence in the police, as well as more global attitudes toward the police, seem to cause fear of crime. This model, however, has not been formally tested as an explanation for perceived risk.

REASONS CAMPUS COMMUNITY MEMBERS MAY PERCEIVE RISK OR FEEL FEARFUL

For several reasons, the college campus offers an interesting context in which to study the dynamics of perceived risk and fear of victimization. Although its population is moderately transitory, a college or university campus also has many constant and familiar activities and routines. Students go to classes, study in the library, live in the dormitories, attend various entertainment or cultural events, or enjoy a party or two. Faculty members teach, do research, or enjoy entertainment or cultural events on campus (see Wooldredge, Cullen & Latessa, 1995). Staff maintain the daily operations of the institution. Many campuses are "open" 24 hours a day, seven days a week, with much property like computer, laser printers, CD players, and stereo equipment.

Typically, a college campus is not thought of as representing a community in the same way we think about a city embodying a community. Mansour and Sloan (1992), however, have argued that college campuses *are* communities by suggesting college campuses have the three basic components of a community, including a fixed geographic location, common ties among people, and social interaction (Poplin, 1972; Dobriner, 1969). For example, a campus is a distinct geographic location because it persists as a physical place and takes up space (i.e., acreage). It has geographic "markers" (e.g., logo identification signs, entry gates, class-room buildings, laboratories and libraries) which alert people to its physical boundaries. It has common ties among its people (students, faculty, or staff) based on friendship, social, and educational networks that develop on campus. Social interaction is found in the day-to-day activities occurring inside its borders; faculty teaching in their class-rooms or having office hours, students interacting in classrooms, dining halls, libraries and other common spaces, and staff speaking with faculty, students, administrators and other staff members in and around aca-demic and administrative departments across campus.

We are not saying, however, a college campus is a community in the same sense a town or city is a community. Some cities (e.g., Chicago) contain "communities in communities," for example, suburbs or isolated ethnic neighborhoods (Poplin, 1972). Similarly, some campuses (particu-larly those in urban areas) may also be examples of "communities in communities," or they may constitute a special *kind* of community set apart from the larger community in which the campus is located. Clearly, there are striking differences between a college campus and a city or town in terms of the characteristics of the population, the political environment, stratification system, and the diversity of activity engaged in by the population. Further, the scope of life on a college campus is much narrower than that found in a city or a town.

If the campus is a community, what might enhance or reduce per-ceived risk and fear of victimization among its members (students, staff, and faculty)? Depending on the group (students, faculty, or staff), some members of the campus community are transitory which could reduce their integration into the community. Students, for example, although enrolled in classes each term, are usually on campus only during the day. In their first year, they may live in one dormitory, the next year they may move to another dorm or move off campus. Because of these patterns, they may never really know their neighbors although they are on cam-pus for four or five years of study. Additionally, some students enroll on a part-time basis and take only night or weekend classes. This, too, may reduce integration into the campus community.

Faculty are less transitory than students. Each term, they may be assigned diverse classes in several classrooms (some with familiar and some with unfamiliar faces). Professors and instructors work in their departmental offices, laboratories, or in the library at varying hours and days of the week. At different times in the academic calendar, faculty go on leave or sabbatical. Untenured faculty members find jobs elsewhere after a short period. Visiting professors or instructors arrive and stay for varying lengths of time. Generally, while students and faculty members are on campus for a nine-month period, both may have little attachment to the campus other than as a temporary place of learning and employment.

Probably the least temporary members of the campus community are staff who typically have jobs entailing working in the same office or department a set number of hours, five days per week, for 12 months. Compared to other campus members, in general, they probably have the longest tenure at the institution.

The transitory extent of membership in the campus community could limit interaction of community members and undermine either the development of social ties and cohesion among them or emotional attachment to the institution. As a result, some members could feel at risk of becoming a victim or might be reluctant to walk around the campus, in part because they do not know who "officially" is part of the campus environment. Interestingly, who should "officially" be there could be people that community members should fear: research has found most campus perpetrators are students currently enrolled in classes (Siegel & Raymond, 1992).

On the other hand, faculty and staff interact with others in departments housed in the same building. As a result, there are opportunities to interact with and know which people "officially" belong there. Other interactions go on throughout the campus, for example, in classrooms or college-level committees among faculty members and students from diverse departments. Students eventually select majors and become "part of" a department for a few years by taking required classes for a major. They interact with professors in their chosen major and vice versa. Professors are socialized into becoming members of a department, their respective college, and the university. A common mission—to promote education—may help develop social and psychological ties among the campus members (Boyer, 1990). Thus, community members may perceive little risk of victimization and not feel fearful while on campus.

Campuses are typically park-like and easily accessible day and night. This openness may create high levels of perceived risk of victimization and fear of victimization among campus community members, especially the physically vulnerable (e.g., women and older community members).

Typically, campuses have fewer people on them at night, and on some nights, those present may be actively celebrating the end of the school week. Women or older members of the community on campus at night for classes, employment, research, or meetings may perceive they are more at risk of becoming a victim and, as a result, feel more afraid than men and younger people. Those who study or take classes at night or who do research or teach at night on campus may not perceive a higher risk or be more fearful. On the one hand, working or attending classes at night on campus could create a sense of familiarity resulting in less perceived risk or less reluctance to walk around at night because of fear. Frequently, there is less activity on campus at night in part because there are fewer campus community members present (e.g., fewer classes are offered, offices close at 5 p.m., or maintenance schedules are reduced). On the other hand, members of the community never on campus at night or who spend only a few nights per week on campus may feel uneasy with the environment and experience higher levels of perceived risk or feel more fearful.

Some campuses are divided into specific parts having distinct functions; this setting may also contribute to increased levels of perceived risk and feelings of fear. For example, it is not uncommon for campuses to have an area housing classrooms and offices for the liberal arts community and another area housing the medical (or other professional) school community. Community members in each area may have different experiences and routines that contribute to fear and risk. The liberal arts area is typically full of faculty members and students coming and going to class or to office hours on a routine schedule, while the medical school area typically has many patients coming and going on an irregular schedule. The familiar routine in the liberal arts area of campus may reduce perceived risk of victimization and fear among its members than in the transitory medical area.

Campuses usually do not *appear* dangerous for several reasons. First, the physical image of a campus is important in attracting students and employees. Therefore, campus administrators take much pride in the upkeep of the buildings and grounds. Even when campuses are adjacent to a community plagued with social and physical disorders (e.g., the University of Chicago or Yale), the campus does not bear these signs of crime. Second, most faculty and staff have little reason to be aware of campus crime since some research suggests it usually occurs between the hours of 1 a.m. and 4 a.m. (Siegel & Raymond, 1992). Yet criminal victimization may be a common part of college life. For example, close to 40% of the undergraduates in a national study by Towson State University's Campus Violence Prevention Center reported having been victimized during their university experiences (Siegel & Raymond, 1992). Bausell, Bausell & Siegel (1991) found the most commonly reported victimizations among students were (in descending frequency): theft, fights/physical assaults, sexual assaults (like date or acquaintance rape), and robbery. Finally, a study of undergraduates at Towson State University found that 88% of the students surveyed knew a victim of violence on campus (Siegel & Raymond, 1992). This contradicts other research showing that most crime committed on campus is property related (Sloan, 1994; Bromley, 1992).

Although physical and social disorders, like abandoned vehicles buildings with broken windows, or trash strewn on streets or walkways, are not typical characteristics of college campuses, the civility of a campus community can still be threatened. Drug and alcohol use among students are well-documented realities. Seigel and Raymond (1992) reported that almost one-third of the undergraduates in their sample reported consuming alcohol at least once a week and over 60% reported drinking it more often than once a month. Few members of the sample (about 11%) reported complete abstinence from alcohol. Additionally, over 35% of the sample members reported using illicit drugs.

Most colleges and universities have campus police or campus security department or hire a private security to patrol campus (see Lanier, 1995; Peak, 1995; Sloan, 1992). Uniformed officers patrol the campus in cars, on foot, on bicycles, or even on horses throughout the day. As a result, most campus community members are exposed to their presence daily and may even cordially interact with the officers on patrol. On the one hand, seeing the officers may make community members feel less risk and be less fearful. Other community members, however, may believe the presence of the officers indicates possible danger, causing them to feel at risk and incite fear. Still others may view the campus police as "pseudo" police officers and may question their effectiveness (Sloan, 1992). Several studies have shown fear of crime and attitudes toward the police (formal social control mechanisms) are related (see Stacey, 1990). To the extent campus community members perceive formal control mechanisms (like the police) have failed, they may evidence higher or lower levels of fear or perceived risk.

College or university campuses appear to have the sociological, geographic, and psychological characteristics of communities. As a result, many dynamics that generate fear and perceived risk of victimization in other community contexts (e.g., residential neighborhoods) may also occur on campus. But the campus may also have characteristics not typically found in a community; these could reduce perceived risk and fear. However, because of limited research on fear of crime and perceptions of risk in a campus setting, the specifics of fear and risk-generating processes on campus are uncertain. Following, we review published studies that examine fear and perceived risk in a campus context.

PERCEPTIONS OF RISK AND FEAR OF VICTIMIZATION IN THE CAMPUS SETTING: PREVIOUS RESEARCH

Most studies of campus crime have focused on two areas: institutional-level or community-level correlates of campus crime rates (Fernandez & Lizotte, 1995; Sloan, 1992, 1994; Fox & Hellman, 1985; McPheters, 1978), or sexual assault and date rape (Belknap & Erez, 1995; Day, 1994). Few studies have examined fear of victimization among students, faculty or staff on college and university campuses (Wooldrege, Cullen & Latessa, 1992) and no published studies have examined perceived risk.

Very few studies have examined fear among students; to our knowledge, none has examined fear or perceived risk among faculty or staff (Brantingham et al., 1995; Fisher & Nasar, 1992a). The few studies that examine fear and risk among students suggest a consistent pattern—while their victimization levels are low, students are fearful. For example, as previously noted, close to 40% of students in one study reported they had been victims of crime during their college tenure (Siegel & Raymond, 1992). Sigler and Koehler (1993) surveyed students at the University of Alabama-Tuscaloosa and reported the risk of becoming a victim on that campus was about one chance in three. Yet surveys have repeatedly found that students are fearful. For example, in a 1986 survey of over 500 students on 100 campuses nationwide, 38% of the students reported worrying about crime on or near their campuses (cited in Smith, 1988). Fisher and Nasar (1992b, 1992c), in their study at the primary campus of The Ohio

State University, found that over 30% of the students reported they feared walking around the campus at night.

As the vulnerability model predicts, female students had higher fear levels than male students while on campus. Fisher and Nasar (1992c) found female students were more fearful than male students on campus, especially at night. Brantingham et al. (1995) also found this pattern between female and male students about feelings of safety during the day and at night at Simon Fraser University, but fear did not vary by time spent on campus at night. This supports Fisher and Nasar's conclusion that fear of victimization was not related to familiarity (as measured by the number of times walking past a specific building in a typical week) with a precise area on campus.

Limited research has examined the explanatory power of the victimization model. Fisher and Nasar (1992a) reported no relationship between students' victimization experiences and their fear of victimization. Kirk (1988) found that vicarious victimization experiences of students had no effect on their fear levels. Day (1994) argued that a sexual assault victimization on campus may be related to perceived risk and fear of victimization, but no research has examined this hypothesis.

In a study at the University of Cincinnati, Wooldredge, Cullen and Latessa (1992) found that 27% of the faculty members in their sample reported suffering property victimizations while about 5% reported enduring personal crime victimizations. However, faculty members did not perceive the campus as "dangerous"; a majority agreed they felt safe on the campus.

To our knowledge, no published studies have tested if the components described in the physical disorders model predict or explain perceived risk and fear of victimization in a campus context. Unfortunately, little is understood about the effects of the lack of informal social control or how the breakdown of social cohesion on campus effects campus community members' fear levels.

Prior research on fear and perceived risk has suggested five possible models to explain why people are afraid and how their perceived levels of risk may be generated. While these models have identified key variables, the models have either not been fully tested in a college or university context or, if they have been tested, have limited their focus to students. We do not know, for example, the extent prior on-campus victimization is related to perceived risk of victimization among faculty or staff members. Additionally, while evidence based on student surveys provides some support for the vulnerability model, the research is limited, and we do not know the extent this model might explain fear and risk among faculty and staff. Further, to our knowledge, no published research has examined the social and physical disorder model, the neighborhood integration model, or the formal social control model in a campus context.

METHODOLOGY

The data we report are from a larger study of campus victimization, fear of crime, crime prevention activities, and crime-related attitudes of faculty, staff, and students at the University of Alabama-Birmingham (UAB) begun in 1992. UAB is a large, doctoral-granting institution whose campus occupies nearly 80 city blocks near downtown Birmingham, a city of nearly 250,000 people. In June of 1992, when data collection began, nearly 14,000 undergraduate, graduate, and professional students were enrolled at UAB. Additionally, there were 12,926 non-student personnel working for the university.

The UAB campus is about equally divided into two discrete areas: the "Medical Center" and "Liberal Arts" sides of campus. The Medical Center contains a Veterans Administration Hospital; the Schools of Medicine, Dentistry, and Optometry; four multiple-level parking decks; the Schools of Nursing, Public Health, and Health Related Professions; two teaching hospitals, a psychiatric hospital, and the Alabama Eye Foundation Hospital; the University Computer Center; and a library. The Liberal Arts side of campus contains the Schools of Natural Science and Mathematics, Social and Behavioral Sciences, Arts and Humanities, Engineering, and Business; four high-rise residence halls; low-rise, university-owned apartments for graduate and professional students; a recreational facility; six multi-story classroom buildings; several small office buildings housing some of the academic departments; research laboratories; the University Student Center; a library; many parking lots; and the headquarters of the UAB Police Department.

The Medical Center is an extremely busy setting. Thousands of people visit its facilities each day and many thousands more work there, resulting in significant traffic congestion. Additionally, there is significant pedestrian traffic as medical center personnel and visitors walk to and from buildings in the complex. The Liberal Arts side of campus has less traffic congestion but, like the Medical Center, experiences significant pedestrian traffic as students walk from parking lots to classrooms, the library, or to other facilities. Many public streets crisscross the campus; as a result, the campus is easily accessible from all directions.

The campus is surrounded by four distinct neighborhoods. West of campus is an older, working-class, racially mixed neighborhood consisting of modest single-family dwellings and small apartment houses. South of campus is a racially mixed, upper-middle-class residential area, consisting of large (and sometimes ornate) single-family dwellings built before the 1930s. This area is currently undergoing rapid gentrification, new housing construction is also occurring, and some of the largest homes have been converted to townhouses. To the east, the campus borders a large public housing project consisting of low-income apartments. North of campus is a business district containing small warehouses, light industry, small businesses, and many restaurants.

In July of 1992, using computerized records available from UAB, we selected a stratified random sample (Babbie, 1989) of 2,383 members of the UAB community: 1,050 faculty and staff and 1,333 students. We sent copies of a "UAB Campus Crime Survey" to students at their home address, and faculty and staff received copies of the survey using campus mail. We enclosed a stamped, self-addressed envelope with each survey. Additionally, we enclosed a letter from the Vice-President for Administration urging them to complete the survey.[2] The survey was divided into seven sections designed to measure general attitudes about campus crime, risk and fear, campus victimization experiences, perceptions of how big a problem are crime and crime-related issues on the UAB campus, areas of campus where respondents felt were unsafe to walk during the day and at night (and the reason for their fear), crime prevention activities practiced, attitudes toward the UAB police, and demographics.

From the 2,383 surveys originally sent to sample members, 684 usable surveys were returned.[3] Surveys were returned from 330 students, 209 staff, and 137 faculty. The response rate for the sample was 29%; there was, however, variation in response rates across the groups: 33.8% for employees (faculty and staff) and 24.7% for students.

Description of the Variables

Sample members responded to two statements that measured fear of crime: "I am reluctant to walk alone on the UAB campus during the day," and "I am reluctant to walk alone on the UAB campus at night." Perceived risk of victimization was measured by the statement "It is *very likely* I will be the victim of a crime while on the UAB campus." A four-point Likert-type response set was used for the three statements: "strongly agree," "agree," "disagree," and "strongly disagree."

Measures of vulnerability included the respondent's gender, race, and age. We also asked respondents to estimate during the preceding 12 months the average number of nights they spent on campus (responses ranged from "none" to "five or more nights" on campus).

Victimization measures involved two questions. First, we asked respondents whether they had *ever* been the victim of a crime while on the UAB campus. Second, we asked respondents about their *recent* victimization experiences on the UAB campus during the preceding 12 months. We asked about victimizations involving larceny (with and without contact), robbery, sexual assault, simple assault, burglary of an office or dorm room during which personal property was stolen, burglary during which UAB property was stolen, automobile theft, automobile burglary, date rape, and bicycle theft. The question "Have you heard or read about *any* crime occurring on the UAB campus during the past month?" was our measure of vicarious victimization of the sample members.[4]

Perceptions of crime and disorder on campus were measured by asking respondents to rank how big a problem on the UAB campus were 15 crime-related problems. Three scales were created from the following crimes: (1) burglary, theft of UAB property, theft of personal property, automobile theft, automobile burglary, vandalism (property crimes scale), (2) murder, stranger rape, robbery, assaults, date rape (violent crime scale), and (3) selling drugs on campus, using illegal drugs on campus, underage drinking, and homosexual activities in public restrooms (public order scale).

Community integration involved two measures. First, we asked where on campus respondents had spent most of their time during the past year. Second, we asked respondents to identify their status: student, faculty member, or staff.

To measure attitudes about and perceptions of the police, we presented respondents a series of 12 statements about the UAB police department and its officers. Similar to the perceived risk and fear of victimization statements, a four-point Likert response set was used (strongly agree, agree, disagree, strongly disagree). From these statements, we created three scales of attitudes toward the police: attitudes about the police educating the community on crime prevention (police education scale), attitudes about the global performance of the UAB police (police performance scale), and attitudes about the patrol practices (foot, bicycle, and mounted) of the police (police patrol scale).

ANALYSES AND RESULTS

Table I presents a summary of the characteristics of the sample members. The majority of sample consisted of women (66%), whites (78%), and those between 25–35 years old (38%). Students comprised about one-half (49%) of the sample, staff comprised close to a third (31%) of the sample, and faculty members comprised only one-fifth (20%) of the sample. Nearly all the sample members reported spending most of their time in one of two places: the Medical Center (50%) or the Liberal Arts (43%) side of campus. Nearly 85% of the sample reported, on average, they spent at least one night per week on campus during the preceding year.

About one-fourth (24%) of the sample members indicated they had *ever* been the victim of a crime while on the UAB campus. Among sample members who reported at least one victimization during the preceding year, the most prevalent victimization involved property crimes (15%). About 2% of the respondents reported they had been the victim of a violent crime; even fewer (1%) reported they had been the victim of a sexual assault or a rape. About 1% of the respondents reported they had been victims of *both* property and violent crime; About 6% reported they had been victims multiple times. Finally, turning to the vicarious victimization experiences of sample members, about 64% reported having "heard or read about" a crime occurring on the UAB campus in the past month (see Note 3).

Social and Physical Vulnerability and Perceived Risk and Fear

Turning first to the social and physical vulnerability model, Table II shows respondent gender is important to understanding perceived risk and fear of victimization in a campus setting. Women were two to three times as likely as men to place themselves in the "agree" and "strongly agree" response categories for the fear question. Women were also significantly more likely than men to perceive themselves to be likely victims of crime while on campus, and they were more fearful than men both during the day and at night.

TABLE I
CHARACTERISTICS OF THE SAMPLE

	Percent	(n)
Gender:		
Female	65.8	(447)
Male	34.2	(232)
Race:		
White	77.9	(450)
Non-White	22.1	(128)
Age (in years):		
18–24	22.8	(131)
25–35	37.8	(217)
36–49	32.6	(187)
50+	6.8	(39)
Community Standing:		
Faculty	20.3	(137)
Staff	30.9	(209)
Students	48.8	(330)
Where Spend Most Time:		
Medical Campus	50.3	(323)
Liberal Arts Campus	43.1	(277)
Other	6.4	(42)
Number of Nights On Campus:		
None	16.4	(111)
1–2	39.3	(266)
3–4	27.4	(185)
5+	16.9	(114)
Victimization Experiences:		
Ever victimized	23.6	(160)
Victimized At Least Once		
Last Year:		
Property	14.8	(101)
Violent	1.6	(11)
Both Property and Violent	1.2	(8)
Sexual	1.0	(7)
Repeat Victimization[1]	6.3	(43)
Heard About A Crime:[2]	63.5	(275)

[1]Respondents victimized twice or more by the same type of crime.
[2]Not asked of all respondents (see: Methodology section).

Race was not significantly related to perceived risk or fear. Similar percentages of whites and non-whites reported they were likely to be victims and were fearful, although whites were more fearful than non-whites during the day and at night. Age and the number of nights on

TABLE II
PERCENT REPORTING "STRONGLY AGREE" OR "AGREE"
AMONG SOCIALLY AND PHYSICALLY VULNERABLE

Vulnerability Characteristic	Perceived Risk		Fear During the Day		Fear At Night	
	%	(n)	%	(n)	%	(n)
Gender:						
Female	27.3	(117)***	16.6	(73)	86.1	(379)***
Male	14.5	(33)	5.7	(13)	44.5	(102)
Race:						
White	23.1	(101)	13.3	(59)	73.1	(324)
Non-White	25.0	(32)	9.5	(12)	68.8	(88)
Age:						
18–24	26.4	(32)	14.6	(19)	71.3	(92)
25–35	23.5	(50)	11.2	(24)	74.8	(160)
36–49	21.3	(39)	11.3	(21)	71.9	(133)
50+	20.0	(7)	10.8	(4)	57.9	(22)
Number of Nights on Campus:						
None	18.9	(20)	14.0	(15)	77.8	(84)
1–2	20.5	(53)	12.6	(33)	73.4	(193)
3–4	23.4	(46)	11.4	(21)	70.8	(131)
5+	29.1	(32)	12.4	(14)	66.1	(74)

* $p < .05$ ** $p < .01$ *** $p < .001$
Significance represents the results of a chi-square test of independence.

campus were not significantly related to perceived risk and fear. Older respondents were less likely to perceive themselves at risk and less likely to be fearful, especially at night, than younger respondents. The more nights respondents spent on campus, they less likely they were to see themselves at risk or feel fearful, especially at night.

Victimization and Perceived Risk and Fear

The victimization model argues that direct and vicarious victimization are related to perceived risk of victimization and fear of victimization. Table III displays the relationships between victimization experiences, perceived risk, and fear of victimization. Sample members victimized during the past year, regardless of the crime type, had higher levels of perceived risk. The greatest difference in perceived risk among victims and non-victims was found when we contrasted victims of violence and victims of *both* violence and property to non-victims. Apparently, prior victimization is associated with a high perceived risk of future victimization.

TABLE III
PERCENT REPORTING "STRONGLY AGREE" OR "AGREE" AMONG VICTIMS AND NONVICTIMS

Type Victimization Past Year	Perceived Risk		Fear During the Day		Fear At Night	
	%	(n)	%	(n)	%	(n)
Sexual Assault	57.1	(4)*	57.1	(4)***	85.7	(7)
Non-Victim	22.6	(148)	12.3	(82)	72.0	(480)
Property	44.9	(44)***	14.3	(14)	78.8	(78)
Non-Victim	19.1	(108)	12.5	(72)	71.0	(408)
Violent[1]	63.6	(7)***	36.4	(4)**	90.9	(10)
Non-Victim	22.3	(145)	12.4	(82)	71.8	(476)
Both Property and Violent	61.1	(22)***	17.1	(6)	75.0	(27)
Non-Victim	20.8	(130)	12.6	(80)	71.9	(459)
Ever a Victim						
Yes	42.9	(66)***	14.0	(22)	76.6	(121)
No	16.8	(85)	12.5	(64)	70.8	(363)
Vicarious Victimization						
Yes	27.0	(72)	12.7	(35)	73.5	(200)
No	20.0	(31)	10.3	(16)	71.3	(112)

* p < .05 ** p < .01 *** p < .001
Significance represents the results of a chi-square test of independence.
[1]Does not include sexual assault victimizations.

Type of victimization was related to fear of victimization during the day. For example, victims of sexual assault and violent crime were almost three to five times more likely to feel fearful during the day than non-victims. Surprisingly, however, victims were not significantly more fearful at night than non-victims.

Respondents who had *ever* been a victim (regardless of when the victimization occurred) on campus were two-and-one-half times more likely to perceive themselves at risk than non-victims, but did not feel significantly more fear during the day or at night than non-victims.

Vicarious victimization, however, was not related either to perceived risk or fear of victimization. Respondents aware of a campus crime occurring in the preceding month did not perceive more risk or feel more fearful than those who did not know about a crime incident.

Perceptions of Crime and Disorders and Perceived Risk and Fear

The disorders model posits a relationship between risk and fear of victimization and perceived disorders, including crime. Table IV indicates that respondents who "strongly agreed" or "agreed" that they were likely victims, or reluctant to walk on campus during the day or at night, reported that property crime, violent crime, and public order were much bigger problems on campus than those who "strongly disagreed" or "disagreed."

The mean for each of the three scales is significantly larger for those who perceive themselves at risk and fearful on campus during the day and at night compared to those who did not see themselves at risk and do not feel fearful.

TABLE IV
PERCEPTIONS OF CRIME AND DISORDERS AND
PERCEIVED RISK AND FEAR OF VICTIMIZATION

Risk and Fear Measures	Property Crime Scale		Violent Crime Scale		Public Order Scale	
	Mean	(n)	Mean	(n)	Mean	(n)
Perceived Risk:[1]						
0	3.14	(419)***	2.51	(484)***	2.77	(480)**
1	3.89	(143)	3.13	(144)	3.11	(140)
Fear During the Day:						
0	3.26	(560)***	2.56	(552)***	2.79	(545)***
1	3.75	(80)	3.32	(80)	3.20	(78)
Fear At Night:						
0	2.94	(179)***	2.29	(174)***	2.70	(175)*
1	3.48	(463)	2.81	(460)	2.91	(450)

* $p < .05$ ** $p < .01$ *** $p < .001$
Significance represents the results of a chi-square test of independence.
[1]Coding was "0" for responses "disagree", or "strongly disagree", and "1" for "agree" or "strongly agree."

Community Integration and Perceived Risk and Fear

Many scholars argue that community integration is an important influence on perceptions of risk and fear of victimization. Table V presents a comparison of perceived risk and fear levels among students, faculty and staff, and those who spent most of their time in the Medical Center or the Liberal Arts side of campus.

Students, faculty and staff, and those who spent most of their time either at the Medical Center or the Liberal Arts campus did not significantly differ in their perceived risk or fear during the day. Staff were significantly more likely to be fearful at night than faculty members and students. Interestingly, a larger percentage of the respondents who spent most of their time on the Liberal Arts campus were more fearful during the day than those spending most of their time at the Medical Center, while a larger percentage of respondents who spent their time at the Medical Center where more fearful at night compared to those spending their time on the Liberal Arts campus.

TABLE V

**PERCENT REPORTING "STRONGLY AGREE" OR "AGREE"
WITH COMMUNITY INTEGRATION MEASURES**

	Perceived Risk		Fear During the Day		Fear at Night	
Community Integration	%	*(n)*	%	*(n)*	%	*(n)*
Community Standing:						
Students	23.1	(75)	15.3	(30)	71.4	(232)**
Staff	23.0	(46)	11.2	(23)	78.6	(162)
Faculty	22.1	(29)	9.0	(12)	63.5	(87)
Where Spent Most Time On Campus:						
Medical Campus	24.7	(77)	10.1	(32)*	76.9	(246)**
Liberal Arts Campus	22.5	(61)	16.1	(44)	67.8	(185)

* $p < .05$ ** $p < .01$ *** $p < .001$
Significance represents the results of a chi-square test of independence.

Formal Social Control and Perceived Risk and Fear

Table VI presents the results of our analysis of the relationship between attitudes toward the UAB police and perceived risk and fear of victimization. In general, Table VI reports a relationship between attitudes toward formal social control and both perceived risk and fear of victimization.

Those respondents who perceived a high risk of becoming a victim, as well as those who reported feeling fearful during the day or at night, had a less positive attitude toward the performance of the campus police than those who did not perceive a risk or feel fearful. This attitude did not carry over to attitudes about the police educating the community about crime prevention or about police patrol practices. Those who perceived a risk and felt fearful rated the educational and patrol efforts of the police higher than those who did not perceive a risk and did not feel fearful.

TABLE VI
ATTITUDES TOWARD THE CAMPUS POLICE AND
PERCEIVED RISK AND FEAR OF VICTIMIZATION

Risk and Fear Measures	Police Education Scale		Police Performance Scale		Police Patrol Scale	
	Mean	(n)	Mean	(n)	Mean	(n)
Perceived Risk:[1]						
0	3.05	(432)**	3.05	(445)***	3.01	(473)*
1	3.35	(126)	2.86	(125)	3.27	(138)
Fear During the Day:						
0	3.08	(484)***	3.03	(502)***	3.03	(540)***
1	3.40	(75)	2.85	(72)	3.36	(76)
Fear At Night:						
0	2.88	(155)***	3.07	(165)***	2.90	(176)*
1	3.22	(406)	2.98	(410)	3.14	(441)

* p < .05 ** p < .01 *** p < .001
Significance represents the results of a chi-square test of independence.
[1]Coding was "0" for responses "disagree" or "strongly disagree", and "1" for "agree" or "strongly agree."

CONCLUSIONS AND IMPLICATIONS

This chapter has examined perceived risk and fear of victimization by faculty, staff, and students at a large urban university. It reviewed the extant literature on perceived risk of victimization and fear of victimization, described various models of risk and fear, and discussed research which has tested these models in a non-campus context. It also discussed how a college campus can be conceived as a community and described why members of a campus community might perceive risk and feel fearful on campus. It then presented the results of tests of current models of fear and perceived risk in a campus community setting, specifically a large, urban university in the Southeast.

Clearly, this study is exploratory. It examined perceived risk and fear at one large, urban campus containing a medical complex adjacent to the Liberal Arts side of campus; this is probably not representative of college campuses more generally. It did, however, examine risk and fear among three groups of people: faculty, staff, and students. As a result, it extended prior research on fear of crime which only focused on students. The study also generated some implications for campus administrators.

While we found mixed support for the models, the results may reflect the complex dynamics that come together to create perceived risk and fear of victimization on campus. Some of these dynamics, for example, physical and social vulnerability, and vicarious victimization, may be less important in a campus context than in other contexts. But some, such as gender, appear important regardless of context. Other dynamics, for example, perceived crime and disorders, attitudes toward formal social control, and certain types of victimization experiences may be important across different types of contexts such or work (for faculty and staff) and school (for students).

If campus administrators hope to reduce fear and perceived risk of victimization, they must understand that the *perceptions* of faculty, staff, and students are related to both risk and fear. We found, for example, that perceived crime and disorders on campus were strongly related to perceived risk and fear. These perceptions may be created by sight, word of mouth, or by reading media accounts of campus crime. If, for example, the *perception* among faculty, staff, and students is "crime is a big problem," administrators should expect faculty, staff, and students to have high levels of perceived risk and fear of victimization.

Additionally, administrators must work to reduce the perceived risk and fear of victimization among women on campus. Like other researchers, we found gender was strongly related to both perceived risk and fear of victimization. Reducing fear among women (regardless if they are faculty, staff, or students) may be accomplished by educating women that, generally, they are far less likely than men to be the victims of crime, by offering women self-defense classes, or offering crime prevention classes. In cooperation with campus security officials, campus administrators can easily develop, implement, and evaluate the effectiveness of these programs (see Fisher & Sloan, 1993).

Administrators must also be aware of the relationship between where faculty, staff, and students spend their time and levels of perceived risk and fear. We found, for example, the campus area where sample members spent their time was related to fear of victimization during the day and at night. What may be occurring is a combination of the effects of perceived disorders *and* where people spend their time. For example, if a student spends most of his or her time on the liberal arts side of campus, he or she could develop the perception that (1) this *area* of campus is dangerous (because of what I see going on or hear about), or (2) the student may feel, because I do not spend time in other areas of campus and have not seen or heard first hand about what goes on, *these* areas are more dangerous than where I spend most of my time. These possible combinations must be further explored to untangle their unique contributions to generating risk and fear. Nonetheless, using various methods (e.g., surveys or meetings with members of the campus community), administrators can determine whether there are "hot spots" of crime and "fear spots" on their campuses and take proper actions to reduce the causes of both crime and fear on their campuses.

One of our strongest results involved the relationship between prior victimization and perceived risk (and, to a lesser extent, between victimization and fear). Administrators can implement programs and policies to reduce the likelihood of *future* victimization. Another action that administrators can take (and the courts are more frequently imposing this duty) is to provide warning or taking other steps to alert people to places where victimizations have occurred and take steps to change the characteristics of the location which provide opportunities for victimization. Successful situational crime prevention strategies are well documented in contexts other than the campus, and administrators could learn from these case studies (Clarke, 1992). Administrators might also consider creating assistance programs for campus crime victims that campus police or security departments would operate (see Belknap & Erez, 1995). These programs would offer support to campus victims and could help reduce perceived risk, fear and possible future victimizations. These programs might also produce positive attitudes toward the campus police or security; we found that attitudes toward the police, in turn, were related to both perceived risk and fear.

This chapter lays a foundation for future research. Clearly, further investigation of perceived risk and fear of victimization in a campus setting is necessary. For example, are there differences in levels of perceived risk and fear across various campus settings (e.g., urban, rural, suburban)? Does using diverse measures of risk and fear result in the same findings as those reported above? What would multivariate modeling of the dynamics of perceived risk and fear show? These are but some of the areas ripe for further study. As campus crime, security, and related issues continue to generate widespread interest, greater understanding of the dynamics of perceived risk and fear of victimization should be forthcoming.

NOTES

(1) This project was made possible by a grant from the Office of the Vice-President for Administration, the University of Alabama-Birmingham. We thank John Walker, Pauline Howland, and Joyce Iannuzzi for their assistance. Points of view are the authors and do not necessarily reflect those of the University of Alabama-Birmingham.

(2) UAB maintains 14 different "classifications" for its employees. We limited our sample selection to employees with the following designations: full-time regular, part-time regular, University Hospital residents, alternate staff (e.g., "floating" nurses), employees "on" for 7 days, and employees on a "3-1-2" shift. Our sample of faculty and staff is therefore taken from 10,729 non-student employees.

(3) Measuring vicarious victimization of sample members was not originally a part of this study. However, at approximately the same time we were drawing the sample, a rape occurred in one of the dormitories on the UAB campus. The incident received widespread attention by campus and local media. To control for the possible confounding effects of this incident on sample members' attitudes, we constructed three versions of the crime survey. Each version of the survey was randomly assigned to sample members—about one-third of the sample received each version of the survey. Two of the versions included a two-part contingency question sequence asking respondents if they had heard or read about any crime which had been committed on the UAB campus during the past month; if they responded yes to this question, they were then asked what type of crime they had heard about. The third version of the survey did not contain the two questions. Additionally, we varied placement of the two questions in the surveys. Four-hundred thirty-three sample members completed surveys containing these questions.

REFERENCES

Babbie, E. (1989) *The Practice of Social Research* (5th ed.) Belmont, CA: Wadsworth Publishing Co.

Bausell, C., B. Bausell, and D. Siegel (1991) *The Links Among Drugs, Alcohol and Campus Crime.* Towson, MD: Campus Violence Prevention Center, Towson State University.

Bausell, C. and C. Maloy. (1990) *The Links Among Drugs, Alcohol, and Campus Crime: A Research Report.* Baltimore, MD: Towson State University Center for the Study and Prevention of Campus Violence.

Belknap, J. and E. Erez (1995) "The Victimization of Women on College Campuses: Courtship Violence, Date Rape, and Sexual Harassment." In B.S. Fisher and J.J. Sloan, III (eds.) *Campus Crime: Legal, Social, and Policy Perspectives.* Springfield, IL: Charles C Thomas.

Benson, P. (1981) "Political Alienation and Public Satisfaction with Police Services." *Pacific Sociological Review* 24(1):45–64.

Box, S., C. Hale, and G. Andrews (1988) "Explaining Fear of Crime." *British Journal of Criminology* 28(4):340–356.

Boyer, E. (1990) *Campus Life: In Search of Community.* Princeton, NJ: Carnegie Foundation for the Advancement of Teaching.

Brantingham, P., P.J. Brantingham, and N. Seagrave (1995) "Crime and Fear of Crime at a Canadian University." In B.S. Fisher and J.J. Sloan, III (eds.) *Campus Crime: Legal, Social, and Policy Perspectives.* Springfield, IL: Charles C Thomas.

Bromley, M.L. (1995) "Securing the Campus: Political and Economic Factors Affecting Decision Makers." In B.S. Fisher and J.J. Sloan, III (eds.) *Campus Crime: Legal, Social, and Policy Perspectives.* Springfield, IL: Charles C Thomas.

—— (1992) "Campus and Community Crime Rate Comparisons: A Statewide Study." *Journal of Security Administration* 15(2):49–64.

Brown, L.P. and M.A. Wycoff (1987) "Policing Houston: Reducing Fear and Improving Service." *Crime and Delinquency* 33(1):71–89.

Carter, D. (1985) "Hispanic Perception of Police Performance: An Empirical Assessment." *Journal of Criminal Justice* 13(4):487–500.

Clarke, R.V. (1992) *Situational Crime Prevention: Successful Case Studies.* Albany, NY: Harrow and Heston Publishers.

Clemente, F. and M.B. Kleiman (1977) "Fear of Crime in the United States: A Multivariate Analysis." *Social Forces* 56(2):519–531.

Cohen, G. (1994) "A False Sense of Security." *U: The National College Magazine,* May, pp. 18–19.

Conklin, J. (1975) *The Impact of Crime.* New York: MacMillan.

Cordner, G., O. Marenin and J. Murphy (1986) "Police Responsiveness to Community Norms: Guidance and Autonomy." *American Journal of Police* 11(1):83–107.

Day, K. (1994) "Women's Fear of Sexual Assault on Campus: A Review of Its Causes and Recommendations For Campus." Paper presented at Environmental Design and Research Association Annual Conference, San Antonio, Texas, April 1994.

Dobriner, W.M. (1969) *Social Structures and Systems: A Sociological Overview.* Pacific Palisades, CA: Goodyear.

Erskine, H. (1974) "The Polls: Fear of Violence and Crime." *Public Opinion Quarterly* 38(1):131–135.

Fernandez, A. and A.J. Lizotte (1995) "Campus Crime and Community Crime: An Analysis of Reciprocal Relationships." In B.S. Fisher and J.J. Sloan, III (eds.) *Campus Crime: Legal, Social, and Policy Perspectives.* Springfield, IL: Charles C Thomas.

Fisher, B.S. and J.J. Sloan (1993) "University Responses to the Campus Security Act of 1990: Evaluating Programs Designed to Reduce Campus Crime." *Journal of Security Administration* 16(1):67–79.

Fisher, B.S. and J.L. Nasar (1992c) "Students' Fear of Crime and Its Relation to Physical Features of the Campus." *Journal of Security Administration* 15(2):65–75.

—— (1992b) "Hot Spots of Fear: The Convergence of Prospect, Concealment, and Escape." Department of Political Science Working Paper Series, #1. University of Cincinnati.

—— (1992a) "Fear of Crime in Relation to Three Exterior Site Features." *Environment and Behavior* 24(1):35–65.

Fisher, B.S. (1991) "A Small Neighborhood Business Area is Hurting: Crime, Fear of Crime and Disorders Take Their Toll." *Crime and Delinquency* 37(4):363–373.

Garofalo, J. (1979) "Victimization and Fear of Crime." *Journal of Research in Crime and Delinquency* 16(1):80–97.

Gates, L. and W. Rohe (1987) "Fear and Reactions to Crime: A Revised Model." *Urban Affairs Quarterly* 22(3):425–453.

Gordon, M.T. and S. Riger. (1989) *The Female Fear.* New York: Free Press.

Griffaton, M.C. (1994) "State Level Initiatives and Campus Crime." In B.S. Fisher and J.J. Sloan, III (eds.) *Campus Crime: Legal, Social, and Policy Perspectives.* Springfield, IL: Charles C Thomas.

—— (1993) "Forewarned is Forearmed: The Crime Awareness and Campus Security Act of 1990 and the Future of Institutional Liability for Student Victimization." *Case Western Reserve Law Review* 43(1):525–590.

Greenberg, M.A. (1986) "The Bureau of Criminal Deterrence." *Campus Law Enforcement Journal* 16(1):12–14.

Hindelang, M.J., M.R. Gottfredson, and J. Garofalo (1978) *The Victims of Personal Crime: An Empirical Foundation for a Theory of Personal Victimization.* Cambridge, MA: Ballinger.

Hill, G.D., F.M. Howell, and E.T. Driver (1985) "Gender, Fear, and Protective Handgun Ownership." *Criminology* 23(3):541–552.

Hunter, A. (1974) *Symbolic Communities: The Persistence and Change of Chicago's Local Communities.* Chicago: University of Chicago Press.

Jeffords, C.R. (1983) "The Situational Relationship Between Age and Fear of Crime." *International Journal of Aging and Human Development* 17(2):103–111.

Kennedy, L.W. and R.A. Silverman (1985) "Perception of Social Diversity and Fear of Crime." *Environment and Behavior* 17(1):275–295.

Kirk, N. (1988) "Factors Affecting Perceptions of Safety in a Campus Environment." In L.R. Habe, A. Hacker, and D. Sherrod (eds.) *People's Needs/Planet Management: Paths to Coexistence.* Washington, DC: EDRA.

Lab, S. (1988) *Crime Prevention: Approaches, Practices, and Evaluations.* Cincinnati, OH: Anderson.

LaGrange, R.L., K.F. Ferraro and M. Supancic (1992) "Perceived Risk and Fear of Crime: Role of Social and Physical Incivilities." *Journal of Research in Crime and Delinquency* 29(3):311–334.

LaGrange, R. and K. Ferraro (1989) "Assessing Age and Gender Differences in Perceived Risk and Fear of Crime." *Criminology* 27(4):697–719.

Lanier, M.M. (1994) "Campus Policing on University Campuses: Tradition, Tactics, and Outlooks." In B.S. Fisher and J.J. Sloan, III (eds.) *Campus Crime: Legal, Social, and Policy Perspectives.* Springfield, IL: Charles C Thomas.

Lederman, D. (1993) "Colleges Report 7500 Violent Crimes on Their Campuses in First Annual Statements Required Under Federal Law." *The Chronicle of Higher Education.* January 20, pp. A32–A43.

Lee, G.R. (1982) "Sex Differences in Fear of Crime Among Older People." *Research on Aging* 4(3):284–298.

Mansour, N. and J.J. Sloan (1992) "Campus Crime and Campus Communities:

Theoretical and Empirical Linkages." Paper presented at the Annual Meetings of the Academy of Criminal Justice Sciences, Pittsburgh.

Matthews, A. (1993) "The Ivory Tower Becomes an Armed Camp." *New York Times Magazine,* March 7, pp. 38–47.

Merry, S.E. (1981) *Urban Danger: Life in a Neighborhood of Strangers.* Philadelphia, PA: Temple University Press.

Moore, M.H. and R.C. Trojanowicz (1988) "Policing and the Fear of Crime." *Perspectives on Policing.* Washington, DC: U.S. Department of Justice.

Ollenburger, J.C. (1981) "Criminal Victimization and Fear of Crime." *Research on Aging 3*(1):101–118.

Ortega, S.T. and J.L. Myles (1987) "Race and Gender Effects on Fear of Crime: An Interactive Model with Age." *Criminology 25*(1):133–152.

Pate, A. (1986) *Reducing Fear of Crime in Houston and Newark: A Summary Report.* Washington, DC: Police Foundation.

Peak, K.J. (1995) "The Professionalization of Campus Law Enforcement: The 1990s and Beyond." In B.S. Fisher and J.J. Sloan, III (eds.) *Campus Crime: Legal, Social, and Policy Perspectives.* Springfield, IL: Charles C Thomas.

Perkins, D.D., J.W. Meeks and R.B. Taylor (1992) "The Physical Environment of Street Blocks and Resident Perceptions of Crime and Disorder: Implications for Theory and Measurement." *Journal of Environmental Psychology 12*(1):21–34.

Perkins, D.D., A. Wandersman, R.C. Rich, and R.B. Taylor (1993) "The Physical Environment of Street Crime: Defensible Space, Territoriality and Incivilities." *Journal of Environmental Psychology 13*(1):29–49.

Poplin, D.E. (1972) *Communities: A Survey of Theories and Methods of Research.* New York: MacMillan.

Raddatz, A. (1988) *Crime on Campus: Institutional Tort Liability for the Criminal Acts of Third Parties.* Washington, DC: National Association of College and University Attorneys.

Rohe, W.M. and R.J. Burby (1988) "Fear of Crime in Public Housing." *Environment and Behavior 20*(5):700–720.

Seng, M.J. (1994) "The Crime Awareness and Campus Security Act: Some Observations, Critical Comments, and Recommendations." In B.S. Fisher and J.J. Sloan, III (eds.) *Campus Crime: Legal, Social, and Policy Perspectives.* Springfield, IL: Charles C Thomas.

Seng, M.J. and N.S. Koehler (1993) "The Crime Awareness and Campus Security Act: A Critical Analysis." *Journal of Crime and Justice 16*(1):97–110.

Sherrill, J.M. and D.G. Siegel (1989) *Responding to Violence on Campuses.* San Francisco, CA: Jossey-Bass Higher Education Series.

Siegel, D.G. and C. Raymond (1992) "An Ecological Approach to Violent Crime on Campus." *Journal of Security Administration 15*(2):19–29.

Sigler, and N.S. Koehler (1993) "Victimization and Crime on Campus." *International Review of Victimology 2*(1):331–343.

Skogan, W.G. (1990) *Disorder and Decline: Crime and the Spiral of Decay in American Neighborhoods.* New York: Free Press.

—— (1986) "Fear of Crime and Neighborhood Change." In A.J. Reiss and M.R.

Tonry (eds.) *Communities and Crime.* Chicago: University of Chicago Press, pp. 203–229.

Skogan, W.G. and M.G. Maxfield (1981) *Coping with Crime: Individual and Neighborhood Differences.* Beverly Hills, CA: Sage.

Sloan, J.J. (1994) "The Correlates of Campus Crime: An Analysis of Reported Crimes on College and University Campuses." *Journal of Criminal Justice 22*(1):51–61.

—— (1992) "Campus Crime and Campus Communities: An Analysis of Crimes Known to Campus Police and Security." *Journal of Security Administration 15*(2):31–46.

Smith, L.N. and G.D. Hill (1991) "Victimization and Fear of Crime." *Criminal Justice and Behavior 18*(2):217–239.

Smith, P. and R. Hawkins (1973) "Victimization, Types of Citizen-Police Contacts, and Attitudes Toward the Police." *Law and Society Review 1*(1):135–151.

Stacey, H.S. (1990) "Attitudes Toward the Police: A Study of Members of the Campus Community." Unpublished master's thesis, University of Cincinnati.

Stafford, M. and O. Galle (1984) "Victimization Rates, Exposure to Risk and Fear of Crime." *Criminology 22*(2):173–185.

Stinchcombe, A.L., R. Adams, C. Heimer, K. Scheppele, T. Smith, and G. Taylor (1980) *Crime and Punishment: Changing Attitudes in America.* San Francisco: Jossey-Bass.

Student Right-to-Know and Campus Security Act (1990) Public Law No. 101–542 (1990) amended by Public Law No. 102–26, 10(e) (1991) 20 USC 1092(f).

Taylor, R.B. and J. Covington (1993) "Community Structural Change and Fear of Crime." *Social Problems 40*(3):374–395.

Taylor, R.B. and M. Hale (1986) "Testing Alternative Models of Fear of Crime." *The Journal of Criminal Law and Criminology 77*(1):151–189.

Taylor, R.B., S.P. Gottfredson and S. Brower (1984) "Block Crime and Fear: Defensible Space, Local Social Ties, and Territorial Functioning." *Journal of Research in Crime and Delinquency 21*(2):303–331.

Thomas, C. and J. Hyman (1977) "Perceptions of Crime, Fear of Victimization, and Public Perceptions of Police Performance." *Journal of Police Science and Administration 3*(4):305–317.

Trojanowicz, R.C. (1983) "The University and the Police." *The Police Chief 50:*40–41.

United States House of Representatives (1990) *House Report* 101–883, Section 201–205.

Warr, M. (1990) "Dangerous Situations: Social Context and Fear of Victimization." *Social Forces 68*(4):891–907.

—— (1985) "Fear of Rape Among Urban Women." *Social Problems 32*(2):238–50.

—— (1984) "Fear of Victimization: Why are Women and the Elderly More Afraid?" *Social Science Quarterly 65*(3):681–702.

Warr, M. and J. Stafford (1983) "Fear of Victimization: A Look at the Proximate Causes." *Social Forces 61*(4):1033–1043.

Wilson, J.Q. and G. Kelling (1982) "The Police and Neighborhood Safety: Broken Windows." *Atlantic Monthly 127:*29–38.

Wirth, L. (1938) "Urbanism as a Way of Life." *American Journal of Sociology 49*(1):46–63.

Wooldredge, J.D., F.T. Cullen, and E.J. Latessa (1995) "Individual Demographics Versus Routine Activities: Predicting the Likelihood of Faculty Victimization."

In B.S. Fisher and J.J. Sloan, III (eds.) *Campus Crime: Legal, Social, and Policy Perspectives.* Springfield, IL: Charles C Thomas.

—— (1992) "Victimization in the Workplace: A Test of Routine Activities Theory." *Justice Quarterly* 9(2):325–335.

Zamble, E. and P. Annesley (1987) "Some Determinants of Public Attitudes Toward the Police." *Journal of Police Science and Administration* 15(2):285–290.

PART III
THE SECURITY CONTEXT
OF CAMPUS CRIME

INTRODUCTION TO PART III
THE SECURITY CONTEXT OF CAMPUS CRIME

Campus administrators, when addressing the problem of crime on their campuses, face a variety of security issues. These issues generally involve developing programs and strategies to help prevent crime, as well as responding to crime as it occurs. These programs and strategies, however, are shaped by both political and economic forces at work on and off the campus. Additionally, administrative policies may have different goals (e.g., reduce current levels of crime or prevent future victimization).

This final section of the book examines security issues confronting campus policymakers. In Chapter 10, Max Bromley describes the political and economic forces shaping campus security policy. Using a case study of security program development and implementation at the University of South Florida, Bromley chronicles how state-level political and economic forces affected these programs. He also uses this case study as a model to illustrate how other campuses might address their security problems.

Chapter 11, "The Professionalization of Campus Law Enforcement: Comparing Campus and Municipal Law Enforcement Agencies," by Kenneth Peak, briefly describes the evolution of campus police agencies in this country, their adoption of a professional model of policing, and the similarities and differences between campus and municipal police departments.

In Chapter 12, Mark Lanier examines the prospects of using community-based policing on college and university campuses. He describes the philosophy of community policing, examines the strengths and weaknesses of community policing in a campus context, and presents examples of universities currently using community policing.

Thus, the chapters address both global security concerns (factors shaping campus security policy) as well as more practical concerns (the professionalization of campus law enforcement and use of community policing on campus).

Chapter 10

SECURING THE CAMPUS: POLITICAL AND ECONOMIC FORCES AFFECTING DECISION MAKERS

MAX L. BROMLEY

INTRODUCTION

Criminal acts committed on college campuses have long been a part of the history of higher education. According to Baldwin (1971), there is evidence that as far back as the Middle Ages, crimes were committed on university campuses in Bologna, Italy and Paris, France. Gelber (1972) noted that during the 200-year history of higher education in America, there has been concern about criminal activity on campus and how to provide security for faculty members and students. In the 1990s, it appears many post-secondary institutions are seeing alarming increases in the frequency and the seriousness of crime on their campuses. There is also evidence suggesting that today the nature of crime on college campuses is similar to the nature of crime in communities more generally (Fernandez & Lizotte, 1995; Sloan, 1994; Bromley, 1992; Fox & Hellman, 1985). The problem of crime presents a constant challenge to campus policymakers.

During the last two decades college campus communities have recognized that their campuses are not immune from criminal acts like murder, rape, and armed robbery. College faculty, students, administrators, and legislators have become increasingly concerned about the frequency and magnitude of criminal acts in the collegiate setting.

National and local media have focused on campus crime issues. For example, Hahn (1990) has described the relative safety of college campuses; Ordovensky (1990) has analyzed crimes committed on campus as well as the level of security of those campuses; Mathews (1993) has noted the serious nature of campus crime; and Lederman (1993, 1994) has analyzed college crime data collected in response to the mandates of the Student Right-to-Know and Campus Security Act of 1990 (see Seng, 1995).

Bordner and Petersen (1983) have said that "the university is like a city, as far as crime is concerned." Nichols (1986), a campus police chief who contributes to campus crime research, has noted that during the 1980s civil disorders on campus became less a security issue than concerns about serious criminal incidents. According to McBride (1991:269), "while it is unclear whether campus crime has actually increased, there is an ongoing debate on campus safety because of numerous violent felony crimes which gained media attention."

College and university presidents are concerned that student enrollments could be adversely affected by negative press surrounding serious campus crime. This concern becomes more important as post-secondary institutions compete for students since students and their parents are increasingly aware of campus crime issues.

As might be expected, there is considerable pressure on campus security officials to make accurate assessments of security needs and to take the appropriate steps to enhance campus safety. These decisions are frequently made in the context of a politically charged atmosphere and many of them have economic ramifications.

Using a case study of a university in Florida, this chapter describes, illustrates, and analyzes the political and economic forces affecting campus policymakers as they address campus security needs. The chapter concludes by presenting the implications of this analysis and makes suggestions for future policy directions.

BACKGROUND

Boyer (1990) has recognized the need to make college campuses more hospitable and, presumably, places where fewer serious crimes are likely to occur. The importance of developing guidelines for campus security standards has been recognized by several state and national organizations; several of these organizations have developed campus security standards. For example, in 1984, the Association of Independent Colleges and Universities (AICU) developed standards for post-secondary institutions in Massachusetts. In 1985, the American Council on Education (ACE) developed and published guidelines for its members, while in 1989, the National Association of State Universities and Land Grant Colleges (NASULGC) published a set of steps to be followed for achieving a safe campus environment. Following the passage of the Campus Security Act of 1990, the National Association of Student Personnel Administrators

(NASPA) and the National Association of College and University Business Officers (NACUBO) in 1991 issued to their members self-regulation guidelines for campus security policies. For each of the organizations listed, formulation of sound policy is an essential ingredient in the effort to effectively address campus crime.

The next section of the chapter describes several significant campus security policy issues confronting executives at today's post-secondary educational institution.

POLICY ISSUES

A major policy concern for campus administrators reflects the need to provide a safe campus while allowing the public access to grounds and facilities. It is a challenge to simultaneously allow the freedom of movement required in the pursuit of academic endeavors while still providing reasonably safe campus grounds and facilities. In general, most college campuses (particularly public institutions) are open to nearly anyone at all hours of the day. While private colleges may be more restrictive about accessibility, policy decisions about security must still be made.

Decisions about the scheduling and location of evening classes may be made in a framework of security considerations and explicit questions should be addressed. For example, if evening classes are planned on campus, are they scheduled in busy areas of campus? Is it possible to provide security or police patrol in the classroom buildings selected? Should the college provide an escort service for the safety of its students, faculty members, and staff during the evening hours?

Permitting access to campus buildings after normal working hours is also a policy decision. Likewise, a series of questions also need to be studied. For example, when should facilities be locked? Who should be granted after-hours access to these buildings? Does the campus have a key control policy that clearly provides for accountability? Campus decision makers should also be concerned with building access policies and the appropriate application of trespass laws. Ultimately, a balance must be struck between, on the one hand, allowing open access to a campus and, on the other, prohibiting people from interfering with the normal educational process by committing crimes. In any event, if access is restricted, it must be done to enhance campus security and cannot result in the unlawful denial of the individual rights. The American Council of Education (1985) has summarized this policy:

[W]hether to restrict access to campus buildings by visitors or to monitor such access should take into account the security risks existing in the neighborhood of the building, the effect of restrictions on the academic value of the facility, the physical layout of the building, the hours during which significant numbers of campus community members are present in the building, and the degree permitting outsiders access to such buildings furthers institutional interests.

A second policy issue is the establishment of security standards for campus grounds and for the physical design of buildings. For example, campus decision makers must realize the importance of adequately maintaining shrubbery and trees present on many college campuses. Failure to keep foliage closely trimmed may afford a would-be assailant a place of concealment. Shrub and tree placement should be examined from a security and from an aesthetics viewpoint. Plant growth along pedestrian walkways should likewise be maintained on a regular schedule. Tree limbs should not be allowed use as ladders to gain after-hours access to dormitories or campus buildings.

Decision makers also need to consider establishing a policy that requires the plans for proposed new facilities and major building renovation projects to be reviewed with security considerations. This type of review is typically done for fire safety and can be accomplished for security purposes as well. According to Greenburg, Rohe and Williams (1982), criminologists and planners have joined forces to physically design urban environments that reduce criminal opportunities. For example, this crime prevention through environmental design approach has been a long-term part of the community planning process in Sarasota, Florida. Campus administrators can also benefit from this approach to campus safety enhancement. Before construction projects begin, plans for security devices like additional lighting, closed-circuit television monitors, and alarms can be incorporated into either new building construction or major renovation projects. Clearly a policy that requires the architect, construction personnel, and security officials to confer is an important decision, and such a collaborative effort should reduce the opportunities for crimes to occur on the campus.

Another policy issue to consider is the need to provide education programs about crime problems for campus community members. It is impossible for the campus security/police department to prevent all criminal acts at an institution. However, policies can be established that encourage the development of proactive public education programs for students, faculty, and staff members at the college.

Educational programs can be developed in the post-secondary institutional setting that will inform community members about their potential risk of victimization from crimes like rape, assault, robbery, and theft. Examples might include newsletters, seminars, slide shows, video production, and brochures used to disseminate appropriate information to the campus community. The policy can require the involvement of campus personnel outside the police or security department to assist in crime prevention efforts. For example, bookstore or credit union cashiers can be required to attend robbery prevention workshops; custodians can be trained to identify and report suspicious people seen in campus buildings; or maintenance personnel can report areas that need additional lighting or other security devices. The decision to seek the active involvement in crime prevention efforts from people throughout the campus community is a policy-level decision.

A related policy that is an important part of public education and crime prevention efforts is the requirement to notify members of the campus community when serious criminal incidents have occurred on or adjacent to campus so they might take additional security precautions. Thus, liaison with off-campus law enforcement agencies is also important because they will typically have information about off-campus criminal acts. Campus officials must also inform members of the campus community how to report criminal acts or related emergencies.

ECONOMIC ISSUES

Economic issues related to campus crime must be understood in the context of present economic trends in higher education in the United States. The state of the national economy has had a significant influence on higher education everywhere. Cage and Blumenstyx (1990) highlighted examples of states whose higher educational institutions have been negatively affected by recent economic downturns. In many of these states, a reduction in collected state tax revenues led to midyear budget reductions for higher education. As a result, it was not unusual for support services (like campus security) to feel the impact as colleges struggled to protect academic programming. These budget reductions, according to Jaschik (1990), have occurred at a time in which the growth rate of state spending for higher education is at its lowest point in thirty years.

At a time when the national economy is negatively influencing funding for post-secondary education, Congress passed the Student Right-to-Know and Campus Security Act of 1990. This law requires that all post-secondary institutions gather and publish statistics related to serious crimes occurring on their campuses (see Seng, 1995; Seng & Koehler, 1993). In addition, each institution must publish a variety of security policies. Therefore, a dilemma is created for campus administrators when the general economy is down and yet newly enacted legislation forces them to allocate more resources to security.

There are potential economic ramifications for colleges and universities as they publish crime information. For example, campus crime data are typically published as raw numbers. This could result in people comparing either the total crimes (i.e., total burglaries, robberies, rapes, assaults, and so forth), or the number of specific crimes (e.g., *all* rapes or *all* burglaries) reported at one campus with those reported at other campuses. People would then draw conclusions about how "safe" one campus is compared to another.

Generally, when people compare the number of crimes reported at one campus with the number of crimes reported at another, they do not have complete information about variables that affect campus crime rates. Therefore, some campuses may experience negative public responses which could translate into reduced enrollment and economic losses.

The question remains whether some institutions will experience a drop in enrollment after publication of their crime statistics. In addition, the number of private donors or graduates visiting the campus and ultimately contributing financially may also decrease at some institutions if they are perceived as "dangerous." Colleges and universities that depend heavily on night-student enrollments could also be negatively affected by the reporting of campus crimes committed at night. While most institutions may experience few fiscal consequences from the publication of their crime statistics, other, less financially sound institutions may have some difficulty.

An economic effect has also been created by newly enacted state campus crime laws that require colleges and universities to take steps *beyond* those mandated by federal legislation (Tuttle, 1991). For example, one of the provisions of the Florida Post-Secondary Education Security Information Act (1989) requires that each public and private college and university to conduct an annual assessment of physical plant safety. In this example, if security systems like locks, alarms, or video cameras need updating in a campus residence hall or other facility, there will be costs to absorb. Likewise, if a decision is made to use a night clerk to monitor access points in a dormitory, his or her salary must be absorbed by the campus budget.

A small college (like Atlantic Christian College in Wolfson, North Carolina) may be hit the hardest by the economic effects of campus crime legislation. Atlantic Christian, with an enrollment of only 1,250 students, has already invested $25,000 in additional security measures because of state and federal campus crime legislation (College Security Report, 1990). Given the level of national publicity surrounding the campus crime and the federal statutory requirement to publish crime statistics and security policies, there is little question that all colleges, large and small, public and private, will experience some economic effects of the legislation.

The budgetary effects of campus crime legislation will vary among institutions for several reasons. The first has to do with the quality of an institution's security program. This would include elements like the adequacy of police or security personnel, crime prevention programming efforts, security devices (e.g., emergency telephones, alarms, and other hardware), and current levels of policymaker commitment to the security program. Once evaluated, some institutions will find they have enormous security deficiencies that must be upgraded. On the other hand, colleges and universities having well-developed security programs will experience less economic strain because of legislative mandates. Any change required to meet the legislative intent of campus crime laws will either cost money or, at a minimum, require a reallocation of existing institutional-level resources. However, it is improbable that state legislatures will allocate additional fiscal resources to help post-secondary institutions comply with legislative requirements.

A final reason for variation in the fiscal effects of campus crime legislation on post-secondary institutions is because most states do not have campus crime laws. In states that do not have campus crime statutes, post-secondary institutions need to comply only with federal legislation. As a result, the budgetary impact on institutions in those states should be less than on institutions that must comply with both state and federal legislative requirements.

The above points are illustrated in the following case study. The study helps illustrate the political and economic forces that influenced campus security decision makers in one of this country's largest university systems.

CAMPUS SECURITY DECISION MAKING: A CASE STUDY

Political and economic interests in Florida have heavily contributed to campus security decision making in the State University System. Following the lead of Pennsylvania, which in 1988 passed the first state-level campus security law, the Florida legislature enacted the Florida Post-Secondary Education Security Information Act in 1989. The act requires institutions to prepare an annual report that includes three years of crime statistics and an annual assessment of campus safety. The legislature also directed Florida's Post-Secondary Education Planning Commission to review the status of campus security and submit a report to the state board of education and to the state legislature by March of 1990 (Green, 1989).

A committee appointed by the state's Post-Secondary Education Planning Commission collected data on campus security policies and procedures among member institutions. They also hired a team of consultants to prepare a report based on information gained by site visits at various institutions throughout the state. The committee worked closely with representatives of groups like the State Board of Education, student organizations and other institutional groups, and the Florida Department of Law Enforcement.

The final report had both policy and economic ramifications for institutions in the state university system. At the same time concerned groups reviewed the report, five University of Florida students were brutally murdered in their off-campus apartments. Despite the fact that none of the homicides occurred on the University of Florida campus, the media were sharply focusing on the serious issue of campus crime. The chancellor of the board of regents, a long-time supporter of campus policing efforts, was determined to take the steps necessary to enhance campus security at the universities in the state university system.

After the murders, the chancellor sent a personal representative to meet with police chiefs from the nine-member universities to discuss their concerns and resource needs. A report summarizing those needs was subsequently sent to the chancellor, who then prepared a request to the state legislature for a special three-year budget allocation to enhance campus security at member institutions.

The legislature accepted the request and appropriated 100 percent of the funds necessary for the first year of a three-year effort. This decision was made in a year that saw cuts in nearly every member institution's budgets as well as employee layoffs. Clearly, legislators felt the political climate would support their decision and, ultimately, fully funded the second- and third-year requests.

The initiative led by the chancellor and supported by the legislature was not only bold political action but was also a significant statement of economic support during a recessionary period. For example, police departments at the nine-member schools were allocated 103 new positions and were given over $4 million to pay for them. This significant budgetary enhancement was expected to upgrade campus law enforcement resources to levels paralleling those of local police agencies in communities adjacent to the universities.

As a member school in the state university system, the University of South Florida (USF) could significantly improve its crime prevention and security programs because of the infusion of state-level resources. The remainder of this section describes the effect of these resources on USF security programs and policies.

Institutional Impact

At the University of South Florida, different groups and individuals have been actively involved in decisions about campus crime policies. For example, the office of the vice-president for student affairs supported several crime prevention programs. In November 1990, the National Association of Student Personnel Administrators (NASPA) produced a teleconference on effective approaches to campus security as part of their series, entitled "Enhancing Campus Community." Because of this program, representatives from the University Student Center at USF approached the University Police Department and requested assistance in developing a one-half-day workshop to include the teleconference as well as a live local component. The vice-president's office not only provided logistical support but also provided budgetary support by funding the teleconferences.

The decision was made by university police and student affairs sponsors to include people on the local panel to discuss campus crime issues.

The panel ultimately included faculty member representatives, as well as representatives from student government and student affairs, and the university police. The office of student affairs and security and police representatives from several colleges and universities throughout the state were invited and attended the program. During the workshop, a variety of campus crime policy issues were discussed and participants left with information that could be used to influence decision making at their respective institutions.

The student government at USF actively supported campus security efforts. They provided financial support for campus crime prevention efforts in several ways. For example, they have funded an on-campus escort program that operates seven days a week at night and spent $70,000 to purchase and install 18 emergency "blue-light" telephones on campus. The student government also established a security budget that pays for the services of off-duty university police officers required to work at student-sponsored special events like concerts and parties.

A group external to the University of South Florida that has been involved in campus crime issues includes the managers of off-campus student apartments. Many USF students live in apartment complexes that surround the campus. Following the Gainesville slayings, all of which occurred in off-campus apartment complexes, local apartment managers were flooded with requests from students to install additional security measures in their apartments. The university police department and apartment managers subsequently established a cooperative program to provide crime prevention information and education to students living off campus. Because of student demands, some of the apartment managers felt an economic impact because they had to purchase additional security hardware. Clearly, it was in the best political (and economic) interests of local apartment managers to become concerned about the crime concerns of students living in their buildings.

Additionally, the off-campus security demands of students have been partly met by the USF student government which operates an off-campus student housing office. The office provides assistance to students seeking off-campus apartments, gives them an off-campus security guide offering crime prevention tips, and helps them evaluate the relative safety of an apartment complex.

How apartment managers will respond to this guide remains unclear. However, as students compare apartment complexes based on the type and level of security provided, some managers may lose money as students become reluctant to live in apartments judged "unsafe." Managers, who have increased the security of their complexes through additional hardware or the provision of security patrols, have used "enhanced apartment security" as an advertising item to attract more renters. In a highly competitive student rental market, security features may become a key part of the economic success or failure of marginal apartment complexes.

IMPLICATIONS AND CONCLUSIONS

There is no question that the issue of campus crime will have continuing implications for American college and university policymakers during and beyond the 1990s. Although some campus executives probably prefer the issue not be present, there is little reason to think concern over campus crime will soon diminish.

The policies that have been derived because of campus crime issues will be decided, at least in part, in a political context. No campus policymaker can afford to deny that reality. Currently, the economic impact associated with campus crime has been felt by a few post-secondary educational institutions; soon, many more will be affected.

National organizations like the American Council on Education, National Association of College and University Business Officers, the International Association of Campus Law Enforcement Administrators, and the National Association of Student Personnel Administrators will continue to provide direction to address campus crime issues. However, responding to the general issue of campus crime requires leadership, particularly at the institutional level. There can be no substitute for leadership if effective policy decisions are to be made. Campus administrators must assume a proactive role in conducting institutional self-evaluations on topics like: campus police or security department services, building access policy, dormitory security, the relative safety of campus and its surrounding community, the need for security devices (e.g., video cameras and alarms), and the status of crime prevention and education programs.

Reasonable policy decisions can be made based on an evaluation of these and related components of campus crime. Top-level administrators will then assume more responsibility for assuring that security policies are in place and that resources are identified to support the necessary programs for their accomplishments.

Senior campus administrators must come to the realization that although the campus security or police department are crucial to providing protection for the institution, other departments must also provide support. For example, the provost, the chief student affairs officer, the physical plant director, the student residence life administrator, the general counsel, and the vice-president for business should assume a role in security-related issues. The development of a campus-wide "team approach" to campus crime problems is essential. This team, with the assistance of the campus security or police department, could develop an institutional-level plan to reduce the opportunity for serious campus crimes to occur. This plan could also be used as the basis for an institutional response to a security-related lawsuit. Instituting an interdepartmental approach to address the issue of campus crime diminishes the notion that campus security is the sole responsibility of one department. In addition, such an approach should demonstrate a strong sense of institution-wide commitment to campus crime issues.

It is difficult to project which political and economic forces may affect campus security decision makers in the future. We can be reasonably sure that state legislatures and Congress will continue to be interested in campus crime issues as they affect their voting constituents. Continued political interest will generate pressure on college presidents and others involved in campus security decision making to evaluate and enhance existing programs. Improving the level of campus security will always have an economic effect on the institution; while the general level of resources on college campuses is limited, campus security as a budget item will, in all likelihood, continue to increase. The provision of 24-hour campus police services is expensive. However, on most campuses, these services are a necessity. Complying with the provisions of federal campus security legislation will increase security costs at many institutions. In states that have passed campus security laws, additional costs may be incurred because of legislative mandates (see Griffaton, 1995).

There has been no time in recent history that the issue of campus crime has had such a high profile at the local, state, and national levels. It is currently unclear if policies can be established to effectively confront the problem. This presents both a challenge and an opportunity for decision makers in higher education.

NOTES

(1) I thank Dr. Leonard Territo for his helpful comments and suggestions for this chapter.

(2) The International Association of Campus Law Enforcement Administrators (ICLEA) has published a document *Departmental Self-Study: A Guide for Campus Law Enforcement Administrators* which provides useful information for campus administrators wanting to conduct a self-study of their security arrangements.

REFERENCES

American Council on Education (1985) *Guidelines for Achieving Reasonable Campus Security.* Washington, DC: ACE.

Baldwin, J.W. (1971) *The Scholastic Culture of the Middle Ages: 1000–1300.* Lexington, KY: DC Heath and Company.

Bordner, D.C. and D.M. Petersen (1983) *Campus Policing: The Nature of University Work.* Lanham, MD: University Press of America.

Boyer, E.L. (1990) *Campus Life: In Search of Community.* Princeton, NJ: Carnegie Foundation.

Cage, M.C. and G. Blumenstyk (1990) "State Budget Deficits Force Many Public Colleges to Postpone Faculty Raises and Freeze Projects." *The Chronicle of Higher Education,* October 3, pp. A1–A26.

College Security Report (1990), February 2, p. 2.

Fernandez, A. and A.J. Lizotte (1995) "An Analysis of the Relationship Between Campus Crime and Community Crime: Reciprocal Effects?" In B.S. Fisher and J.J. Sloan, III (eds.) *Campus Crime: Legal, Social and Policy Perspectives.* Springfield, IL: Charles C Thomas.

Florida Post-Secondary Education Security Information Act (1989). Chap. 89 sec. 142, Laws of Florida.

Fox, J.A. and D.A. Hellman (1985) "Location and Other Correlates of Campus Crime." *Journal of Criminal Justice 13*(4):429–444.

Gelber, S. (1972) *The Role of Campus Security in the College Setting.* Washington, DC: U.S. Department of Justice.

Green, L. (1989). Memorandum. September 28.

Greenburg, S.W., W.M. Rohe, and J.R. Williams (1982) *Safe and Secure Neighborhoods: Physical Characteristics and Informal Territorial Control in High and Low Crime Neighborhoods.* Washington, DC: U.S. Department of Justice.

Griffaton, M. (1994) "State-Level Initiatives on Campus Crime." In B.S. Fisher and J.J. Sloan, III (eds.), *Campus Crime: Legal, Social and Policy Perspectives.* Springfield, IL: Charles C Thomas.

Hahn, C.A. (1990) "Special Report." *U. The National College Newspaper,* Spring, p. 6.

Jaschik, S. (1990) "State Spending $4.8 Billion on Colleges This Year: Growth Rate at a 30-Year Low." *The Chronicle of Higher Education,* October 24, pp. A1–A26.

Lederman, D. (1994) "Crime on the Campuses." *The Chronicle of Higher Education,* February 2, pp. A71–A41.

—— (1993). "Colleges Report 7,500 Violent Crimes on Their Campuses in First Annual Statements Required Under Federal Law." *The Chronicle of Higher Education,* January 20, pp. A32–A43.

Mathews, A. (1993) "The Campus Crime War." *The New York Times Magazine,* March 7, pp. 38–47.

McBride, R.B. (1991) "Critical Issues in Campus Policing." In J.W. Bizzack (ed.), *Issues in Policing: New Perspectives.* Lexington, KY: Autumn House, pp. 268–276.

National Association of Student Personnel Administrators (1991) *Complying with the Campus Security Act of 1990.* Washington, DC: NASPA.

Nichols, D. (1986) *The Administration of Public Safety.* Springfield, IL: Charles C Thomas.

Ordovensky, P. (1990) "Students Easy 'Prey' on Campus." *USA Today,* December 3, p. 1A.

Sloan, J.J. (1994) "The Correlates of Campus Crime: An Analysis of Reported Crimes on University Campuses." *Journal of Criminal Justice 22*(1):51–62.

Student Right to Know and Campus Security Act of 1990 (1990) 20 USC 1001, Public Law 101-542.

The Student Press Law Center (1991) *Access to Campus Crime Reports.* Washington, DC: Student Press Law Center.

Tuttle, D.F. (1991) "Campus Crime Disclosure Legislation." *Campus Law Enforcement Journal 21*(1):19–21.

Chapter 11

THE PROFESSIONALIZATION OF CAMPUS LAW ENFORCEMENT: COMPARING CAMPUS AND MUNICIPAL LAW ENFORCEMENT AGENCIES

KENNETH J. PEAK

INTRODUCTION

In recent years, concern about crime and disorder on college and university campuses has crystallized. The media provides a steady stream of reports about murders, rapes, assaults, and other serious crimes occurring on campus. The parents and friends of crime victims have organized "grass roots" movements to demand that campus administrators take steps to make college campuses safer. State and federal legislatures have passed campus crime laws forcing institutions to begin disseminating information about crime on their campuses (see Griffaton, 1995; Seng, 1995). The courts have begun holding institutions liable for criminal victimizations on their grounds (Smith, 1995).

Most of these efforts center on making college campuses "safer"; as a result, the spotlight has turned to campus law enforcement and its efforts to provide law enforcement and service to members of the campus community.

What is interesting, however, is that few social science researchers have rigorously examined the workings of campus police or campus safety departments. Before 1983, according to Bordner and Petersen (1983), few studies of campus policing had ever been published (e.g., Jacobs & O'Meara, 1980; Scott, 1976; Gelber, 1972; Etheridge, 1958). The small quantity of studies done on campus policing can be divided into two areas: research on attitudes toward the campus police, especially students' attitudes (Stacey, 1990; Trojanowicz, Carter, & Trojanowicz, 1988; Miller & Pan, 1987; Cordner, Marenin & Murphy, 1986) and research on the characteristics of departments and officers (Sloan, 1992; Peak, 1988; Jacobs & O'Meara, 1980; Abramson, 1974; Adams & Rogers, 1971).

As a consequence, police researchers know little about the development of campus policing at colleges and universities in this country. Elsewhere (Peak, 1988), I have argued campus police agencies "have become an integral part of the fabric of America's post-secondary educational institutions" and have "carved a niche following the genesis of many such units during the turbulent 1960s." Since many campuses are using campus police agencies, combined with the attention currently paid to the problems of campus crime and security, more information is needed about these rapidly developing agencies. Campus police, like other types and levels of police organizations, have a distinctive set of issues and problems.

The primary focus of this chapter is with the professionalization of campus law enforcement. Primarily, I trace the development of campus law enforcement during this century, explore the professionalization of campus policing, and compare and contrast campus with municipal policing.

THE EVOLUTION OF THE CAMPUS POLICE

Humble Beginnings

This first section of the chapter briefly reviews the creation and evolution of campus policing, which began in 1894 when Yale University hired two New Haven officers to patrol its campus (Bordner & Petersen, 1983). It describes how campus policing developed from a system of "watchmen" into a system of "professional" law enforcers.

Sloan (1992), Bordner and Petersen (1983), and Jacobs and O'Meara (1980) traced the origins of campus law enforcement. During the early 1900s, there was little need for campus law enforcement organizations because educational institutions handled most problems internally and depended on local police agencies only to assist with criminal violations that occurred on campus. This early period saw heavy reliance on a "watchman" system, primarily using retirees to protect university property from fire, water, vandalism, or other damage (Bordner & Petersen, 1983).

Securing the campus remained largely unchanged until the 1950s when, faced with unprecedented growth in student enrollment and size, post-secondary institutions created specialized "campus security departments" and began hiring retired municipal police officers as "directors of campus security." While signifying an important shift in the administration of campus security, the duties of the security "officers" remained largely custodial during this decade. The "officers" had no more power to control people's behavior than did ordinary citizens and the doctrine of *in loco parentis* continued to guide the actions of most campus security organizations (Sloan, 1992).

The late 1960s signaled the most important stage in the evolution of campus policing. As campus unrest grew, universities relied heavily on municipal police forces to handle crime and disorder on campus. But in case after case, the consequences of calling in city police to confront campus disorder were disastrous; the presence of the police often exacerbated conflict and polarized the campus (Skolnick, 1975). As campus disorder increased, post-secondary administrators realized that unless they took measures to keep order on campus, outside police agencies would do it for them. The idea of security forces on campus which might better corresponded with college norms and values naturally appealed to university administrators (Powell, 1971).

Thus, the late 1960s and early 1970s witnessed the birth of what Sloan (1992) calls the "modern campus police department." During this period, campus administrators attempted to upgrade the image of campus officers as old, overweight, and interested only in issuing parking tickets to campus officers as sworn law enforcement professionals (Webb, 1975; Sloan, 1992). The 1980s and early 1990s have seen campus police agencies (1) become increasingly autonomous, (2) develop a strong similarity to urban police departments in their administration, structure, and operations, (3) elevate educational and training standards for personnel, (4) develop a dedicated career path for employees, and (5) become part of the fabric of American post-secondary education (Sloan, 1992; Peak, 1988).

Thus, the past 25 years have been particularly significant in the development of campus policing. There has been a major shift in the characteristics of campus police organizations and officers. Presently, the use of campus police has become an unmistakable trend on American college and university campuses. Yet, little scholarly attention has been given by social scientists to this institutional change.

THE PROFESSIONALIZATION OF CAMPUS LAW ENFORCEMENT

The Professional Model of Policing

The history of campus law enforcement in this country involves the evolution of a "professional" model of campus law enforcement. To recognize this, it is important to first understand the "professional model" of policing that helped reform municipal policing (Walker, 1977; Douthit, 1975). Below, I explore this model and relate it to changes in campus law enforcement.

Several reform efforts of municipal police occurred during this century. The most important of these, the development of a "professional model" of policing, was created by chiefs of police and not forced on the departments by outsiders. To understand the state of campus policing in this country, this model must first be understood because many characteristics of the model have been incorporated into campus policing.

In his analysis of the history of American policing, Uchida (1993) described the professional model as the product of efforts by August Vollmer and O.W. Wilson to change the nature and function of American police. The "professionalization" of the police occurred during the period 1910–1960 and involved the following changes.

First, efforts were undertaken to make police officers "experts," that is, to apply knowledge about crime and criminals to their task and insuring they were the only people qualified to do the job. Second, increasing the autonomy of urban police departments was a crucial part of this reform. Reformers realized that for too long, urban police departments had been heavily influenced by local political "machines" and politicians. By increasing departmental autonomy, each department could make its own set of rules and regulate its own personnel. Finally, reformers sought to make departments administratively efficient. This involved having departments carry out their mandate to enforce the law using modern technology (e.g., motorized patrol and radio communications) and business-like practices.

August Vollmer's emphasis on enhancing the quality of police personnel was closely tied to the professional model. He was among the first to institute I.Q. tests, psychiatric evaluations, and neurological tests for prospective officers. Additionally, he helped pioneer the use of automobiles for patrol use and was among the first to use scientific techniques to study departmental efficiency.

Technological changes in policing were crucial to the professional model. Shifting officers from foot patrol to motorized patrol allowed more effective coverage of patrol areas and rapid response time to service calls. Two-way radios increased supervisory capacity. Supervisors now could instantly monitor the location of their officers. Telephone use was important for creating links between the police and public.

The Professional Model and Campus Law Enforcement

Returning to the evolution of campus law enforcement, its professionalization is evident. Since the 1960s, campus law enforcement has increasingly adopted many characteristics of the professional model. For example, many campus police departments now require the same level of training for recruits as required by municipal police departments (e.g., completion of police academy training and in-service training). Peak (1988), for example, reported agency directors in his sample expected to expand in-service training for their officers in the future. Sloan (1992) found that most agencies in his sample were designated "campus *police* departments."

To upgrade the quality of the officers, campus agencies use psychological testing, seek college-educated recruits, and complete background checks of recruits. Campus officers, like their municipal counterparts, have become "experts," applying the knowledge and the tools of their occupation to their tasks and have become "qualified" to do the job.

Campus police agencies have also become increasingly autonomous. According to Bordner and Petersen (1983), campus security was traditionally housed in the physical plant of the institution, however, this has changed. Sloan (1992) and Peak (1988) found that campus police agencies no longer were housed in the physical plant; instead, they were under the institutional direction of a vice-president for administration or under the direct supervision of the university chancellor. The agencies have budgets, recruitment standards, disciplinary codes, and administration. Thus, campus agencies have become comparatively autonomous, have developed "their own rules" and regulate their personnel.

Finally, campus law enforcement has used technological change and innovation to increase its efficiency. Use of motorized patrol, two-way radios, dispatch, and other technological innovations is common.

Thus, in recent years campus policing has taken on many characteristics of the professional model which has dominated municipal policing in this country for years. Campus officers receive rigorous training, use advanced technology, and work in fairly autonomous agencies. They engage in the typical activities common to municipal police: law enforcement, order maintenance, and service. Thus, the past thirty years has seen campus law enforcement emerge from a patchwork of divergent roles into a full-fledged professional orientation.

A REFLECTION OF THE LOCAL POLICE?

Similarities to Local Police

Because of the movement to professionalize campus policing, members of the campus community may not perceive members of campus police departments as "security guards" or "door-shakers" (Miller & Pan, 1987). Jacobs and O'Meara (1980) have argued campus police forces increasingly resemble their municipal counterparts and that three decades of steady growth and professionalization have enabled them to evolve into counterparts of their municipal cousins. Below, I examine this contention by comparing the characteristics of modern campus policing and municipal policing.

Like local police forces, the campus police are organized hierarchically using paramilitary ranks. One national survey (Peak, 1988) and a smaller survey of 10 departments at post-secondary institutions in the Southeast and Midwest (Sloan, 1992) found similarities in the rank structure of campus police and municipal or county police, without appearing "top-heavy." For example, Peak (1988) found only 38% of the agencies in his survey had deputy chiefs and only 23% of the agencies had captains. Investigator or detective designations were used at 34% of the agencies, and 17% of the agencies used corporals. The most commonly used designation of rank by campus police agencies included lieutenant (46%), sergeant (70%), and patrol officer (83%).[1]

Jacobs and O'Meara (1980) observed that campus officers use sophisticated equipment and surveillance technology and rely on roving patrol in marked squad cars. Police uniforms and rank systems, vehicles, investigative techniques, and crime prevention programs parallel those of the public police. They added that it is not uncommon for campus police officers to purchase their uniforms and badges from the same wholesalers who supply the municipal officers. Rifles, riot helmets, mace, and other specialized equipment are now commonly found in the campus police arsenal. Two-way mirrors, motion monitors, closed-circuit televisions, and intricate alarm systems enable them to regulate and monitor building ingress and egress. Calls to university police may be tape-recorded, and crime reporting is computerized (Jacobs & O'Meara, 1980). In some locations, municipal police departments even perform dispatch duties for the campus police unit.

Campus police officers are sometimes deputized, thereby giving them quasi-legal status. Jacobs and O'Meara (1980) added that campus police agencies have committed themselves to the professional model by recruiting campus police administrators from the ranks of municipal police departments. Peak (1988) found that 39% percent of the administrators at agencies in his survey had a background as municipal police officers. Additionally, many campus departments have developed pre-service and in-service training programs, and there has been continuous growth in the professional association of campus police officers and administrators (i.e., International Association of Campus Law Enforcement Administrators).

Further, some campus police administrators have joined municipal police chiefs and county sheriffs in seeking accreditation by the independent Commission on Accreditation for Law Enforcement Agencies. The accreditation process is a time-consuming and costly undertaking which requires the campus agency to comply with more than 800 standards—including the presumption that officers will be armed. For many administrators, accreditation of the campus agency is desirable for two reasons. First, it raises the level of professionalism in the department. Second, accreditation increases respect for the department in the eyes of other agencies because receiving accreditation is difficult. Finally, like their municipal counterparts, Peak (1988) found that 22% of the campus police agencies surveyed used auxiliary police personnel, including the use of students as part-time officers.

In general, close cooperation occurs among public and campus police agencies (especially the sharing of intelligence, investigations, and training information). Peak (1988) reported that 78% of campus police administrators in his sample had self-reported "excellent" or "very good" relations with other local police agencies.

Given these circumstances, Sloan (1992), and Jacobs and O'Meara (1980) concluded that as campus police departments have grown and become professionalized, they have become more like city police departments. Their organization, training, patrol and investigation tactics are patterned after those of municipal police agencies. However, Jacobs and O'Meara (1980) questioned whether expanding the role and function of university police has contributed to a safer campus environment. They maintained that the same trend found in larger society is now on campuses: increases in crime have paralleled increases in the size, sophistication, and authority of campus police agencies.

This does not mean, Jacobs and O'Meara (1980) asserted, that the campus police are ineffective; but it may indicate that, beyond a specific level, increases in personnel and expenditures have only minimal effect on the incidence of crime. Further, Jacobs and O'Meara (1980:293) have argued the establishment of a large and professional police department on campus may disturb the intellectual, social, and moral development of the university environment:

> Increasingly professionalized and bureaucratized police forces will not strengthen the problem solving capacities of colleges and universities. Indeed, it is more likely that they will weaken the individual's sense of responsibility for the vitality of the community. Student, faculty, and employee involvement in issues of crime and deviancy should be emphasized. Security forces should articulate with the special norms and institutional patterns of the university.

Confronting Crime

A central component of both campus and municipal law enforcement is confronting crime. To further understand the professionalization of campus law enforcement, the extent and nature of campus crime must be considered. While crime on campus per se is not the focus of this chapter, it is necessary to briefly consider violent and property crimes on campuses to provide a partial context in which campus officers operate. Following is a comparison of campus crimes reported to the Federal Bureau of Investigation (FBI) in 1988 and 1992. The figures below are illustrative and should be viewed with caution. One reason for this caution is because only about 10% of all post-secondary institutions in the United States report their crime figures to the FBI. Additionally, many institutions do not continuously report their figures—they report one year, then do not report for several years, then start reporting again. For example, there were approximately 30 more post-secondary campuses reporting crimes to the FBI in 1992 than in 1988 (U.S. Department of

Justice, 1993). Finally, some departments may misclassify offenses, for example, classifying a burglary as a theft or a rape as an assault.

In 1988, there were 1,990 violent crimes reported to the FBI by campus police/safety departments (U.S. Department of Justice, 1989), compared with 3,257 violent crimes reported in 1992 (U.S. Department of Justice, 1993), a 64 percent increase. There were 107,759 property crimes reported by campus police/safety departments in 1988 (U.S. Department of Justice 1989), compared with 134,312 such offenses in 1992 (U.S. Department of Justice, 1993), or a 20 percent increase. In sum, there were 109,749 violent and property crimes reported on college campuses in 1988, and 137,569 violent and property crimes reported in 1992, or a 25 percent increase. Keeping in mind the limitations of these data, a significant increase occurred in the number of campus crimes during this four-year period.

Although the prevalence and incidence of crime on university campuses is much less than is found in surrounding communities (Fernandez & Lizotte, 1995; Bromley, 1992), increases like these have contributed to the continued evolution and professionalization of campus law enforcement. Campus police departments have continued to apply technological advances to fight crime. Institutions have hired more officers or increased the budgets of their security departments. They have developed new "philosophies" (e.g., community-based or problem-oriented approaches) and tactics (e.g., foot patrol, bicycle patrol, mounted patrol) used to address crime problems (see Lanier, 1995; Benson, 1993; Riseling, 1993). When crime increases, the spotlight normally turns to the campus police and what they are doing about it.

Other Areas of Comparison

In a survey of 10 large Midwestern and Southeastern universities, Sloan (1992) documented other similarities between the campus police and their municipal counterparts. He noted the trend of larger institutions to have "police" departments and their considerable specialization, autonomy from other police agencies, and wide jurisdictional boundaries. Sloan found campus officer characteristics were similar to those of municipal officers: disproportionately white and male. Other similarities included most officers did not have four-year college degrees, earned about the same annual income, exercised wide discretion, and the role perceptions of both types of officers tended toward law enforcement, compared to a community service orientation.

Sloan (1992) also examined campus officer perceptions of their role and areas where they and municipal officers differ. He found that campus officer perceptions of their role mirrored those characteristics typically found with urban police (Peak, 1993; Broderick, 1987). Both types of police perceived that law enforcement was their primary role, while both give "lip service" to providing service to the community. Sloan (1992) also surmised the biggest differences between campus and municipal officers may be in years of experience on the job (40% of the campus officers in his survey had at least 10 years experience on the job) and the shift worked (nearly 50% of campus officers worked the day shift). Sloan, like Jacobs and O'Meara (1980), had little difficulty concluding today's campus officers have taken on the appearance and most duties of municipal officers (both wear distinctive uniforms and carry assorted authority symbols like badges and handcuffs).

KEY DIFFERENCES BETWEEN CAMPUS AND MUNICIPAL POLICE

The Campus Police: "Wearing Three Hats"

Despite attempts at professionalizing the campus police, one area where they still differ from their municipal counterparts is with achieving a universal role. For many engaged in campus policing, the role of campus police organizations and officers is undefined. Some officers feel they are second-rate police functionaries because they must "wear three hats": law enforcer, security guard, and door-shaker. While many post-secondary institutions hire separate personnel for these functions and thus do not create this role conflict, for too many officers it is still a problem.

Another historically-related problem concerns the image of campus police departments. While many departments enjoy respect from their campus constituencies, others are still attempting to shed the stereotype of "security guards" or "rent-a-cops" (Trojanowicz et al., 1988; Cordner et al., 1986). Although many departments have overcome this stereotype, doing so is not easy because of turnover in the composition of the campus community and because of people formerly hired by many campus police agencies: retirees from other jobs. Bordner and Petersen (1983:87) illustrate how the role conflict felt by campus officers is associated with the image problem by quoting an officer who works at an institution using a quarter system:

> We have to establish who we are four times a year and that's hard. A lot of people misunderstand who we are and what we are here for. They think of us as security servants. Every three months a new batch of people come in here and we have to teach that new batch what we are all about.

Traditionally, the image the campus police department wished to project determined whether the officers wore a uniform and how they were equipped. Today, depending on their role, campus officers may wear a plain, unadorned uniform, or the uniform components may include added accoutrements like a weapon, PR-24 baton, two-way radio, handcuffs, mace (or pepper spray) and other trappings. The patrol vehicle can range from a modest scooter to a patrol car complete with police markings (e.g., flashers, siren, police department logo), a cage separating the front and rear seats, on-board communication and computer systems, a shotgun prominently displayed near the dashboard, and a full range of other equipment (e.g., flares, riot gear, and bullet-proof vest) stored in the trunk. An example of how daunting some campus officers are today occurred recently when a police chief from a small campus in the East was visiting a large institution in the West. After arriving and observing one of the campus officers whose uniform displayed all manner of police equipment, he commented that "It looked [as if] we were going to war."

The tools of municipal police departments, when observed on postsecondary campuses, may seem anomalous in an environment where the discovery and transmission of knowledge are paramount. However, if the department has a full-fledged "law enforcement orientation," is responding to a crime crisis, or is located where off-campus criminals prey on the institution, its members and their property, a stronger police presence, role, and function is likely found.

Jurisdiction and Authority

There are several areas of similarity between campus and municipal police. However, one substantial difference between campus police and municipal, county, and other state police organizations concerns jurisdiction. Questions over jurisdiction typically include: What is the "proper" jurisdiction of the campus police? Should jurisdiction extend to any state property or to only campus properties? Should it be limited to the radius of the campus? If so, what is the proper radius? One mile? Five hundred yards? Or should jurisdiction extend only to the middle of the streets bordering the campus? Should the campus police be allowed to respond to an incident in an area that is "adjacent to campus" if a student is involved? What about outlying campus properties (e.g., farms, other administrative or instructional buildings)? What if an officer detects criminal behavior while en route to patrol those locations (e.g., an intoxicated driver observed on the highway)? How should campus police react if another police agency requests backup for a problem located a few blocks away from their normal jurisdiction?

These questions and situations arise daily for campus police organizations. Addressing them is obviously not simple. They demonstrate, however, the patchwork nature of campus police jurisdiction from one institution to another (Sloan, 1992). Many states grant campus police and security officers sworn status but limit their authority to the campus per se or to official university business off campus. These officers (generally) are allowed to exercise police powers if they leave their campuses in a valid chase, under the "hot pursuit" doctrine (Sloan, 1992; Smith, 1988). Again, the public's perception of the campus police is involved, as that may dictate how the state legislature views necessary and logical jurisdiction.

Peak (1988) found that only 10 percent of the responding agencies in his sample had jurisdiction anywhere in the state; 46 percent could act only on campus property; 15 percent had jurisdiction on campus and while en route to other campus properties; and 13 percent had jurisdiction inside a 10-mile radius of campus. Seventeen percent reported their officers were deputized to extend their jurisdiction when necessary. However, one-fourth of the responding agencies did not have full police powers. Thus, at some post-secondary institutions, the campus police have no more authority than private citizens, while at others, they are "sworn" and have full powers of arrest, search, and seizure.

While possible for anyone to make a "citizen's arrest," restraining campus police authority may result in a weakened public image—campus police limited to the same arrest power as citizens will often not be respected or taken seriously by students, potential offenders, other police agencies, or the public.

The extent of police powers available to campus officers can be a double-edged sword. With full arrest powers, they can effectively address serious criminal offenses and enjoy some protection by the privileges and immunities state laws often extend to good-faith actions by police officers. However, they may also face additional types of liability because of their status, like situations involving the negligent use of firearms, the treatment of offenders while in custody, and improper arrest, search, and seizure. Security officers not having full police authority may be able to seize evidence and receive confessions that later may be used in court, where as a fully empowered police officer would be barred from using them (Smith, 1988).

An additional issue involving jurisdiction is how campus officers should respond to off-campus problems. For example, when students are victims off campus, added pressure is put on campus authorities to "do something." Additionally, it is commonly believed that the most crime-prone area around many post-secondary institutions is the area on the campus fringe where students live and socialize (Brantingham, Brantingham & Seagrave, 1995; Campus Security Report, 1993).

Several campuses have taken measures to address off-campus problems. For example, as part of the community-oriented and problem-solving philosophy, Yale's police walk foot patrol between the hours 6 p.m. and 2 a.m. Yale's officers are fully empowered to patrol the streets of New Haven, and they maintain a substation close to campus.

Another distinctive off-campus program is at The Ohio State University, where a Community Crime Patrol project uses 22 patrollers (most of whom are students) to walk in two-person teams each night, equipped with radios, protective vests, flashlights, and whistles. They observe and report criminal activities, find lost children, help motorists in distress, and recover stolen vehicles (Campus Security Report, 1993).

Handling Suspects

Another area where municipal and campus police have strong role differences concerns the handling of offenders. Beyond occasional pressure not to arrest the "wrong" person, local police normally have no problem with arrest decisions. On college campuses, officers learn that arrests should be low key, and the range of options in possible arrest situations can be broad. For example, institutions can refer all cases (i.e., students arrested for either misdemeanor or felony offenses) to civil authorities for prosecution. Conversely, the campus may have an "in-house" policy of processing these matters using the campus disciplinary process.

Many misdemeanors committed on campus are harmless "pranks," and treated in-house. Campus administrators view felonies as another matter.

Although there have not been any comprehensive studies about how campus police treat offenders, Sloan (1992) found officers exercised discretion when confronting situations involving enforcement, service, and order maintenance. Bordner and Petersen (1983:209) found that 94 percent of campus police officers felt that students and others "should suffer the consequences of their actions." Because the attitudes of university and campus police administrators affect officer decision making, institutional policies about student conduct may illustrate the administration's proprietary attitude, which may translate into differential enforcement by officers. Conflicting policies, in turn, can create a dilemma for the officer who may not know "when to be aggressive and when not to" (Bordner & Petersen, 1983:215).

Many campus police administrators apparently agree that a student should not escape legal responsibility for committing a felony by virtue of having paid his or her tuition. As reported by Denney (1992), one campus police director from a Midwestern campus described it in these terms:

> [M]ore and more universities have come to treat crime on campus more like crime in the surrounding community and less like in-house "incidents." The doctrine of the university acting *in loco parentis* has all but disappeared. As a result, students are coming more and more to expect to be treated the same as any other member of society. A 19-year-old student who shoplifts from the campus bookstore should expect the same treatment as a 19-year-old auto mechanic who shoplifts from that . . . bookstore. It is . . . fundamentally wrong for the student to be taken to the dean's office and receive a one-year academic probation while the auto mechanic goes to jail. (p. 6)

Another reason some post-secondary institutions still prefer to keep their crime problems in-house is because of concern over their image. Critics of this practice argue the institutions may look for loopholes in the Student Right-to-Know and Campus Security Act of 1990 (20 USC 1092) and avoid having their crime information published (see Seng, 1994a; Seng, 1995; Seng & Koehler, 1993). Campus policymakers must reevaluate this strategy because it, too, sends the wrong message to campus officers.

SUMMARY AND CONCLUSIONS

This analysis of campus policing, including a discussion of the professional development of campus law enforcement, and a comparison of the characteristics of campus and municipal departments and officers, found areas of overlap as well as clear contrasts. One obvious conclusion is that campus policing has followed the professional model and continues to evolve at many post-secondary institutions, continuing a thirty-year trend. Considering their proliferation across the country, campus police agencies have "carved a niche" and become a substantive component of post-secondary education in this country.

Campus police departments have adopted much of the technology associated with policing more generally (Peak, 1989). For example, increased use of forensics, enhanced weaponry, and use of non-lethal weapons (e.g., pepper spray, stun guns, Tasers, and weapons firing plastic bullets) and use of computer-assisted technology (both in patrol cars and at the station) is common. Departments have also upgraded officer training (including requiring certification of officers) and begun to seek agency accreditation. Civil liability issues have also received increased attention (Peak, 1989).

At the same time, agencies are beginning to shift their focus away from the traditional "crime-fighting" role. There is mounting evidence that campus agencies are changing their philosophies (in much the same way urban police departments have begun to change theirs) to a more service-related approach (see Lanier, 1995; Peak, 1989). This shift will include greater accountability to members of the campus community, more educated and less bureaucratic executives, and a reduction in the paramilitaristic structure of the agency (Peak, 1989).

Additionally, campus police are moving toward using student and civilian personnel to accomplish non-enforcement or service-related tasks currently assigned sworn personnel. Besides the cost-effectiveness of this approach, it will free sworn personnel for more important tasks involving patrol, service, or training (Peak, 1989).

The milieu of campus law enforcement is fairly unique; it involves a comparatively small geographic area and a community of highly educated people. On the other hand, the community is moderately transitory: students graduate and are replaced by new ones; faculty members leave the institution and take new jobs or go on sabbatical; and staff may change their shifts or move to new departments. This environment presents the campus police the opportunity to experiment with innovations in both philosophy and tactics.

College and university campuses have, to some degree, become models of the larger society, which too has strengthened its police forces because of a myriad of social problems. Once seemingly idyllic post-secondary campuses are today too often beset with behaviors, events, and problems requiring a stronger hand of authority. University administrators have recognized these issues and, combined with the need to provide a safer environment for campus clientele (and defend against lawsuits alleging negligence), have opted to provide this presence. We may hope that campus officers strive to remain true to their roots and "walk softly," maintaining their service orientation and eschewing the harder image and specialization (e.g., special weapons and tactics teams) of their municipal and county cousins. However, the reality is that today's campus officers must nevertheless be prepared to confront many necessities that may arise. Their role has indeed changed, and it must continue doing so to conform to the complex milieu in which they function.

Like their municipal counterparts, campus police officers and agencies continue to evolve, moving forward from the professional model into a new era of policing. As the twenty-first century approaches, change will be the one constant when discussing campus police officers and agencies.

NOTES

(1) Of course, the relative lack of assistant chief, captain, and detective/investigator positions may be more a function of agency size than a conscious desire to avoid the use of these ranks.

REFERENCES

Abramson, S.A. (1974) "A Survey of Campus Police Departments." *The Police Chief* 41(1):54–56.

Adams, G.B. and P.G. Rogers (1971) *Campus Policing: The State of the Art.* Los Angeles, CA: University of Southern California.

Benson, B.L. (1993) "Community Policing Works at Michigan State University." *Journal of Security Administration* 16(1):43–52.

Bordner, D.C. and D.M. Petersen (1983) *Campus Policing: The Nature of University Police Work.* Lanham, MD: University Press of America.

Brantingham, P., P. Brantingham, and J. Seagrave (1995) "Crime and Fear of Crime at a Canadian University." In B.S. Fisher and J.J. Sloan, III (eds.) *Campus Crime: Legal, Social and Policy Perspectives.* Springfield, IL: Charles C Thomas.

Broderick, J.J. (1987) *Police in a Time of Change* (2ed). Prospect Heights, IL: Waveland.

Campus Security Report (1993) Port Washington, NY: Rusting Publications.

Cordner, G., O. Marenin, and J. Murphy, (1983) "Police Responsiveness to Community Norms: Guidance and Autonomy." *American Journal of Police 11*(1):83–107.

Denney, J.R. (1992) "Policing a College Campus." Paper presented at the Annual Meetings of the Society for Campus and University Planners.

Douthit, N. (1975) "August Vollmer: Berkley's First Chief of Police and the Emergence of Police Professionalism." *California Historical Quarterly 54*(1):101–124.

Etheridge, R.F. (1958) "A Study of Campus Protective and Enforcement Agencies at Selected Universities." Unpublished doctoral dissertation, Michigan State University.

Fernandez, A. and A.J. Lizotte (1994) "An Analysis of the Relationship Between Campus Crime and Community Crime: Reciprocal Effects?" In B.S. Fisher and J.J. Sloan, III (eds.) *Campus Crime: Legal, Social and Policy Perspectives.* Springfield, IL: Charles C Thomas.

Gelber, S. (1972) *The Role of Campus Security in the College Setting.* Washington, DC: U.S. Government Printing Office.

Jacobs, J.B. and V.A. O'Meara (1980) "Security Forces and the Transformation of the American University. *College and University 31*(2):283–297.

Lanier, M.M. (1994) "Community Policing on University Campuses: Tradition, Practice, and Outlook." In B.S. Fisher and J.J. Sloan, III (eds.) *Campus Crime: Legal, Social and Policy Perspectives.* Springfield, IL: Charles C Thomas.

Miller, J.L. and M. Pan (1987) "Student Perceptions of Campus Police: The Effect of Personal Characteristics and Police Contacts." *American Journal of Police 6*(1):27–44.

Peak, K.J. (1993) *Policing America: Methods, Issues, Challenges.* Englewood Cliffs, N.J.: Regents/Prentice-Hall.

—— (1989) "Campus Law Enforcement in Flux: Changing Times and Future Expectations." *Campus Law Enforcement Journal 19*(6):21–25.

—— (1988) "Campus Law Enforcement: A National Survey of Administration and Operation." *Campus Law Enforcement Journal 19*(5):33–35.

Powell, J.W. (1971) "The History and Proper Role of Campus Security." *Security World 8*(1):19–25.

Riseling, S. (1993) "Problem-Oriented Policing at the University of Wisconsin." *Journal of Security Administration 16*(1):31–42.

Scott, E.J. (1976) "College and University Police Agencies." Police services study report 10. Workshop in Political Theory and Policy Analysis, Indiana University.

Seng, M.J. (1994b) "The Crime Awareness and Campus Security Act: Some Observations, Critical Comments, and Recommendations." In B.S. Fisher and J.J. Sloan, III (eds.), *Campus Crime: Legal, Social, and Policy Perspectives.* Springfield, IL: Charles C Thomas.

—— (1994a) "The University's Response to Campus Crime: A Study of Compliance with the Crime Awareness and Campus Security Act." Paper presented at the 1994 Annual Meetings of the Academy of Criminal Justice Sciences, Chicago.

Seng, M.J. and Koehler, N.S. (1993) "The Crime Awareness and Campus Security Act: A Critical Analysis." *Journal of Crime and Justice 16*(1):97–110.

Skolnick, J. (1969) *Politics of Protest.* Washington, DC: U.S. Government Printing Office.

Sloan, J.J. (1992) "The Modern Campus Police: An Analysis of Their Evolution, Structure, and Function." *American Journal of Police 11*(1):85–104.

Smith, M.C. (1988) *Coping with Crime on Campus.* New York: Macmillan.

Stacey, H.S. (1990) "Attitudes Towards the Police: A Study of Members of the Campus Community." Unpublished master's thesis, University of Cincinnati.

Trojanowicz, R.C., B. Benson, and S. Trojanowicz (1988) *Community Policing: University Input into Campus Police Policy-Making.* East Lansing, MI: National Neighborhood Foot Patrol Center.

Uchida, C.D. (1993) "The Development of the American Police: An Historical Overview." In R.D. Dunham and G.A. Alport (eds.) *Critical Issues in Policing.* Prospect Heights, IL: Waveland Press, pp. 16–32.

United States Department of Justice, Federal Bureau of Investigation (1993) *Crime in the United States: The Uniform Crime Reports 1992.* Washington, DC: U.S. Government Printing Office.

—— (1989) *Crime in the United States: The Uniform Crime Reports, 1988.* Washington, DC: U.S. Government Printing Office.

Walker, S. (1977) *A Critical History of Police Reform: The Emergence of Professionalism.* Lexington, MA: DC Heath and Company.

Webb, J. (1975) "The Well-Trained, Professional University Police Officer: Fact or Fiction?" *FBI Law Enforcement Bulletin 44*(1):26–31.

Witham, D.C. (1985) *The American Law Enforcement Chief Executive: A Management Profile.* Washington, DC: Police Executive Research Forum.

Chapter 12

COMMUNITY POLICING ON UNIVERSITY CAMPUSES: TRADITION, PRACTICE, AND OUTLOOK

MARK M. LANIER

INTRODUCTION

Community policing is the latest police reform movement. It seeks to maintain the benefits associated with a "professional" police force and establish symbiotic relations with community members. After a promising start, this approach to crime control is used by ever-increasing numbers of police departments and communities. However, when the community comprises a college or university campus, a distinct situation occurs. Campus police and campus community members differ from police and residents found in other settings.

This chapter describes the possibilities and the problems of community-based policing in a university setting. First, I present a comprehensive definition of community policing. Next, I articulate an apparent need for community policing on campuses. Following this needs assessment, I describe the historical similarities in the development of campus police services and community policing. Fourth, I provide a discussion of various police models. Included in this section is a brief summary of the major criticisms and problems associated with community policing. In the next section, I present examples how community police officers have been used on small, medium and large campuses. I conclude by considering future trends concerning crime and campus policing. Here, I emphasize the relationship between the increasing diversity of college students and proactive police activities.

WHAT IS COMMUNITY POLICING?

Prominent "liberals" (e.g., Currie, 1985) and "conservatives" (e.g., Wilson, 1983a, 1983b) have endorsed community policing. Despite this broad ideological endorsement, there is confusion over the definition of community policing (Bayley, 1988; Greene & Mastrofski, 1988). Therefore, it is crucial to begin my discussion by explicitly defining what is meant by "community policing."

Wilson and Kelling (1982) articulated a theoretical justification for community policing when they presented their "Broken Windows" thesis. According to this thesis, if the physical and social conditions of a community are allowed to erode, crime will inevitably increase. The analogy Wilson and Kelling provided was if a broken window is allowed to remain unrepaired, other windows will soon be broken, graffiti will appear, and disorder will increase. This perspective postulates that a lack of care is equated with increasing crime rates in a community.

Defining Community Policing

Because community policing is the focus of this chapter, I first present an inclusive definition of "community policing." One comprehensive definition of community policing (CP) offered by Trojanowicz and Carter (1988) suggests it is "[A] proactive, decentralized approach, designed to reduce crime, disorder, and by extension, fear of crime, by intensely involving the same officer in the same community on a long-term basis." In addition, it is crucial to recognize the importance of community participants, since police rely on active solicitation and involvement of community members to reduce fear and criminal offenses. In fact, according to Sparrow (1988:1), both community policing advocates and officers "perceive the community as an agent and partner in promoting security rather than as a passive audience". Regardless of the methods, reducing crime is the explicit objective of law enforcement agencies. Crime reduction is achieved using techniques associated with community policing by reducing *disorder* (i.e., a breach of the civil peace, either social or physical), by reducing *fear of crime*, and by creating a sense of *cohesion* among law-abiding citizens ("cohesion" involves a mutual attraction or need which connects community members).

Understanding community policing is the first step toward deciding if it is the best community or police response to crime. Several characteristics of campuses and campus police appear congruent with the theory and tactics associated with community policing. However, campus policymakers must first consider the need for community policing.

IS THERE A NEED FOR
COMMUNITY POLICING ON CAMPUSES?

At least three hundred municipal departments in the United States use community policing, including six of the largest departments (Trojanowicz & Bucqueroux, 1990). President Clinton is poised to authorize federal funding for an additional 100,000 police officers, all of whom will practice community policing. Obviously, community policing is the latest movement in police reform. However, is there a legitimate need for college campuses to jump on the community policing bandwagon?

University campuses are distinct environments, in part, because there is no one type of campus. There is wide diversity among college campuses: at one extreme is the small commuter school with no students residing on campus; at the other extreme is the large research university whose campus may house thousands of students. There is also variation in the location (e.g., urban or rural) and control (e.g., public or private) of campuses. Further, the same university may have more than one type of campus. For example, Auburn University, a large state university in Alabama, has one large campus located in a rural area (Auburn, Alabama) and a second smaller campus located in a large metropolitan area (Montgomery, Alabama).

Policing several types of campuses requires a flexible police strategy. By definition, community policing is the most flexible policing strategy. The director of public safety at the University of Cincinnati recently noted that his department "is [mandating] a community policing approach to law enforcement that will treat each university campus as a separate community with [distinctive] problems" (University Currents, 1994:1).

Beyond the physical environment, most campuses reflect racial, ethnic, age, religious, and temperamental diversity.[1] Recent demographic trends indicate that by the year 2020, most children in six states will be African American, Asian, or Latino (Schwartz & Exter, 1989). These children will become the university students of the near future. However, these trends are currently felt in states like California, where Caucasians are no longer the dominant numerical group on some campuses. For example, Caucasians make up only 35 percent of the 28,000 students at Pasadena City College (Mullendore, 1991). Moreover, the "graying" of American society will soon mean more older students will be enrolled in college, further changing the traditional demographic profile of college students.

Thus, the dynamics of campus environments will increasingly reflect changing national-level demographic trends. Only community policing can incorporate and harness this diversity to the mutual benefit of law enforcement and law-abiding citizens (Trojanowicz & Carter, 1990). Compared to traditional, reactively based policing, proactive police tactics provide more flexibility and better problem-solving potential (Eck & Spelman, 1989). This flexibility is necessary to adapt to a continuously changing campus environment. Finally, community policing is flexible enough to address variation in the form and the extent of crime on diverse campuses in this country.

There is a growing awareness of, and concern with, campus crime, despite the fact there are no accurate estimates of how much crime there is on college campuses. The *Security Newsletter* (1985), for example, reported a study of the 81 largest American universities that found 34.8 major crimes per 10,000 students. However, Sloan (1994) and Bromley (1992) report lower rates.

This concern, coupled with a glaring lack of crime data, led to the passage of the Crime Awareness and Campus Security Act of 1990 (Seng, 1995; Seng & Koehler, 1993). A summary of first annual reports from schools complying with the act revealed that during 1992, at least 7,500 violent crimes were reported to police at American colleges and universities (see Lederman, 1993). If accurate, these numbers indicate campus communities are generally safer than other communities having similar demographic profiles (Fernandez & Lizotte, 1995; *Security Newsletter*, 1985).

Interestingly, there is evidence that college campuses with small student bodies have higher ratios of security personnel (*Security Newsletter*, 1985). This means that large universities would rely on someone outside law enforcement to assist with crime-related problems on their campuses. Practitioners, politicians, academicians, and social commentators have argued that community policing is the "best" response to campus crime (Jackson, 1992; Kelling & Stewart, 1989). The genesis of the campus police provides the basis of support for this position.

HISTORICAL DEVELOPMENTS IN CAMPUS AND COMMUNITY POLICING

Historical forces which influenced the development and the practices of modern campus police agencies make the college campus appear more conducive to community policing than has been the case with municipalities.

During the past twenty years, U.S. cities have generally witnessed a series of events that resulted in serious and critical examinations of police practices, especially an over-reliance on reactive policing. This criticism was partly because of police responses during the 1960s to social unrest and increases in crime. Consequently, a strategy evolved that focused on proactive, or police-initiated, community-focused crime reduction tactics (Riechers & Roberg, 1990; Manning, 1984, 1988, 1989; Greene & Mastrofski, 1988; Brown & Wycoff, 1987; Friedmann, 1987; Greene, 1987; Munro, 1987). Interestingly, similar upheavals occurring on college campuses were responsible for the development of modern campus police agencies. According to Sloan (1992:87):

> The late 1960s signaled the last major shift in the evolution of campus policing. As campus unrest grew and the specter of urban police on college campuses loomed, college administrators confronted a dilemma. . . . One possible solution was to create their own police departments. Thus, the late 1960s and early 1970s saw the birth of the "modern" campus police departments.

A second historical catalyst for changing municipal police strategies was the publication of results from the Kansas City Preventive Patrol Experiment (Kelling, Pate, Dieckman & Brown, 1974). These findings raised serious questions about police tactics like saturation and reactive patrol strategies. At the same time, researchers and social commentators noted that police over-reliance on rapid response and radio dispatch resulted in large segments of American society becoming alienated from the police. Because officers were only responding to calls or cruising in patrol cars (i.e., engaging in "preventive patrol"), officers had few opportunities to interact with people beyond traffic stops or stressful crime-related incidents; additionally, inadequate police attention was focused on crime prevention activities.

In contrast with major municipal police forces, campus police agencies have traditionally relied on a crime preventive and service approach to policing. For example, Gelber (1972) found that campus police overemphasized service-related duties compared to enforcement duties. Bordner and Peterson (1983) also concluded that university police officers were much more service and crime prevention oriented and less focused on enforcement components of policing. Additionally, because campus police have relied more on foot patrol they have greater interaction with students, faculty, and staff. These realities could make community policing efforts on campuses successful undertakings.

There are additional reasons suggesting why campus police agencies may be better positioned to establish community policing than municipal agencies.

Projections

Compared to municipal police departments, campus police agencies are in a favorable position to effectively initiate proactive policing for several reasons. First, according to Jackson (1992), campus police have routinely relied on proactive preventive measures (e.g., foot patrol). In addition, compared to municipal police, campus officers may have greater input and control over the physical environment of the campus which can enhance crime prevention efforts. According to Esposito and Stormer (1988:28):

> [I]n contrast to cities and municipalities, campuses [can] exercise a much greater level of control over their physical and social environment. Usually four operational departments—housing, physical plant, student services, and law enforcement—exercise the most influence over these two significant areas.

Second, in contrast to major municipal departments, campus police interact more with their "clients": students, faculty, and staff members who constitute the campus community. For example, campus police have successfully used students (both paid and volunteers) to perform a variety of police-related functions on campus, a promising component of any campus-based community policing effort (Brug, 1984).

Third, because they work in a higher education environment, campus police and community members should be not only more flexible and innovative than police officers and residents of a municipality but should also be exposed to the most current philosophical and pragmatic police practices. Greenberg (1987), for example, has suggested that "the same kind of energy or drive that . . . motivate[s] campus community enthusiasm for human rights and other social concerns could be harnessed for the sake of public safety" (p. 41).

A COMPARATIVE ANALYSIS OF CURRENT POLICE MODELS

Campus police departments are both similar to and differ from municipal police departments (Sloan, 1992; Bordner & Peterson, 1983). For example, Eric Jackson (1992), chief of the University of North Texas

Police Department, developed a schematic (Table I) which compares and contrasts five common elements of traditional law enforcement, campus policing, and community policing. The schematic shows how the police mandate, police authority, police role, police-community relations, and political ingredients of policing operate to place campus police in a promising position to establish community policing.

Table I shows there is variation in the "police mandate" among the three models. Traditionalists, for example, stress crime control, one of the core premises of the "professional model" of policing (see Trojanowicz & Bucqueroux, 1990:31). Community policing and campus policing also seek crime control; however, they emphasize order maintenance and increased peace and security as the best means of doing so. Traditionalists, on the other hand, rely on deterrence and the apprehension of suspects to control crime.

The mandate for a "traditional" department also implies *reactive* policing in which response time is a primary measure of department efficiency. By contrast, a community policing model emphasizes *prevention,* yet still recognizes the need for crisis response. Like the community policing model, campus agencies are also concerned with prevention.

Turning to the source of police authority, Table I shows that the source of police authority in a traditional model is based *solely* on the application of law and mandated procedures (e.g., arrest policy and procedure). Community policing looks to the community for authority and campus policing looks to faculty, staff and students—people who constitute the campus community. Both campus and community police explicitly recognize variation in the norms among communities and campuses; these norms, in turn, provide the legitimization and authority for "individualized" police service (Lanier, 1993). Thus, the source of police authority varies under each model. Under a traditional model, the police operate as an extension of the larger criminal justice system. By contrast, community and campus police are an extension of the community's normative structure.

The police role varies significantly among the three models of policing; such variation is inevitable because of the components discussed above. In general, campus and community police are going to work to solve a variety and a plethora of community problems, while traditional police only work at resolving crime-related problems.

There is also variation found among the models in agency type and the amount and type of community interaction. All three agency types are concerned with having strong and positive relations with the local community. The difference is that with traditional policing, a special liaison office or community relations board is primarily responsible for bridging the gap between the police and community. With campus and community policing, the local community works as equal partners with the police to both establish the police agenda and to select the most appropriate responses to crime and other problems. This latter approach distributes responsibility and should improve police-community relations.

Finally, the political considerations associated with each model need to be examined. The traditional model of policing emphasizes "professionalism," a reform movement that developed partly in response to a close, often detrimental connection between local politicians and the police (Klockars, 1985). On the other hand, community policing efforts often attract considerable political and media attention (Lanier, 1993). Line officers must juggle community-level interests, police responsibilities, and appeasement of local politicians. This "balancing of interests" is a possible source of concern for community police officers in a municipal setting (Lanier, 1993). However, the nature and the structure of university administrations may help reduce political problems commonly associated with community policing efforts in municipalities.

Despite the variety and number of universities using community policing efforts, there are several parts of community policing that have generated controversy and concern. These criticisms are important to those seriously interested in establishing or improving community policing in the university setting.

ADDRESSING THE CRITICISMS

Despite the increased chance of success for community police efforts on campus and its potentially positive effects, there are theoretical and methodological issues associated with community policing which need to be addressed (Bayley, 1988; Greene & Mastrofski, 1988). Some of these criticisms may be intensified for campus-based community policing efforts. These criticisms are discussed below.

One theoretical problem with community policing has been a tradition of difficulty in operationally defining what constitutes a community (Mansour & Sloan, 1992; Meenahan, 1972; Minar & Greer, 1969; Hillery, 1955). However, regardless of the definition of community that is used, a campus community experiences significant turnover among its members. Each year, some of the students leave and new students arrive; faculty members and staff also arrive and leave. If community policing is regarded

TABLE I
A COMPARATIVE ANALYSIS OF CONTEMPORARY POLICE MODELS

	Traditional Law Enforcement	*Community Policing*	*Campus Policing*
Police Mandate	Control of crime: response time, deterrence, apprehension	Crime control as a means to community order, peace and security	Law enforcement and disciplinary action as means of control to insure campus order, peace and security
	Law enforcement Crisis response	Preventive as well as reactive policing	Preventive as well as reactive policing
Police Authority	Authority from law	Authority from society, community granted through law	Authority primarily from faculty, staff and students; granted through regulations and law
	Agency of criminal justice system	Agency of municipal government and and community	Agency of the university Administration and community
Police Role	Legally defined/ limited by law Distinct and separate agencies Law enforcement officers/professional crime fighters Address crime only	Socially defined, expanded role Legal and social agencies One of a number of agencies of order Address crime and social problems that affect crime	Environmentally defined Legal, educational and social agencies Peacekeeping/ educational professionals Address crime and environmental problems that affect crime
Community/Police Relationship	Passive role Supportive, adjunct to police	Active role; policy making Shared responsibility for crime and social order Community as client	Active role; policy making Shared responsibility for crime and social order Community member, community as client

Source: Jackson (1992:64)

as a *philosophy* of policing and not a police *tactic,* the practice and tradition of community policing should persist regardless of changes in the makeup of the community (Lanier, 1993). As an analogy, consider the fact some post-secondary institutions are labeled "party" schools; this label is applied over time, regardless of current students and faculty members. At some campuses, efforts directed at changing this image have resulted in student resistance (e.g., the rowdy "Riverfest" celebration on the campus of Michigan State University). Thus, a campus must *first* develop a strong tradition of community policing if the effort is to be successful.

More important, campus police officers alone will be ineffective in promoting informal social control. Research on domestic assault has indicated "the effectiveness of legal sanctions rests on a foundation of informal control" (Sherman, Smith, Schmidt & Rogan, 1992:688; Berk, Campbell, Klap & Western, 1992). In fact, "formal arrest has no effect on the occurrence of a subsequent assault" (Pate & Hamilton, 1992:691). If these findings can be extrapolated and applied to campus crime, although there is no evidence this extension is currently warranted, then informal control mechanisms may become increasingly important to campus law enforcement agents. However, even if consensus were achieved on a broadening of the police mandate needed for a transition from formal to informal means of social control, it is not clear if they can do so effectively. For example, Greene and Taylor (1988:206) question whether police officers are equipped to broaden their mandate:

> [I]t may also be erroneous to assume that police officers can function as agents of informal social control and even if that were possible, the amount of training required to assure effective community responsiveness has not been demonstrated.

However, community policing requires that police and citizens alike (students, faculty, staff) work jointly as equals to resolve problems. From this perspective, it is possible for those involved in the partnership to promote informal social control mechanisms.[2]

Another theoretical criticism of community policing is that it may encourage potentially discriminatory police practices because the police only may empower people and groups most ideologically and demographically similar to themselves. As Riechers and Roberg (1990) have argued, theoreticians "worry that reliance on nonlegal norms and community definitions of order can quickly become extensions of class and racial bias and thereby introduce more injustice" (Greene, 1987:4). This problem has no obvious solution. American college campuses are increasingly populated by students and employees who are women, or ethnic or racial minorities. This is in direct contrast to the dominant demographic characteristics of campus police officers. For example, Sloan (1992) found that at research universities located in the Midwest and the Southeast, 88 percent of campus police officers working at these institutions were white and 90 percent of the officers were male. The increasing ethnic diversity of students, faculty members, and staff (a reflection of national demographic trends) may exacerbate this problem.

Turning to methodological concerns, more research on community policing needs to be conducted. There is a scarcity of rigorous evaluations of community policing and even fewer evaluations of campus-based community policing efforts (Benson, 1993).

Other methodological criticisms including problems with the level of analysis and problems with research designs (e.g., defining of the treatment and the effect) can be addressed by rigorous application of acknowledged social scientific methodologies which have been shown to be effective. As previously mentioned, such has not been done on college campuses and is a crucial area needing to be studied.

One challenge to the methodological soundness of community policing on campus is the use of a variety of community policing strategies by agencies at diverse campuses (e.g., urban, rural, private, or public). There is a crucial need to define and develop measures of concepts central to community policing. For example, despite increasing trends toward community policing among municipal police departments, Alpert and Moore (1993) have noted that "community policing remains a concept and philosophy in search of a process, without proper ways to document or evaluate its efforts" (p. 109). Furthermore, increased community involvement with police activities demands innovative performance measures. Alpert and Moore (1993) have echoed this concern when they argued, "[A]s society and the police approach a new understanding of how each can contribute to the other, it is [crucial] to develop new measures to determine how well the police perform" (p. 120).

Such an important, yet basic, methodological step was taken by Lanier (1993) when he developed a set of psychometrically sound scales to measure the essential constructs of community policing: fear of crime, disorder, and community cohesion. Further, these core elements should be applicable in all community policing intervention sites, despite wide variation in officer and department styles of community policing and diversity among college campuses (including problems and solutions limited to each location). Therefore, regardless of university characteristics and practices, a baseline set of measures are now available to help measure the effectiveness of community policing efforts. Additional measures, reflecting the diversity of community policing and problems, should be developed for use on college campuses.

Having defined what I mean by "community policing" and arguing for progressive crime control strategies on campuses, I presented a historical basis for the expected success of campus-based community policing programs. Next, I discussed some potential problems that could arise with community policing on campus. Now, I present examples of proactive campus police efforts. While these examples are obviously not all-encompassing, they are typical of campus-based community policing efforts in this country.

EXAMPLES OF CAMPUS-BASED COMMUNITY POLICING VENTURES

Increasingly, university police departments are using community policing, in various forms, on their campuses. One of the largest and the oldest campus community policing programs can be found at Michigan State University (MSU). This effort has enjoyed considerable guidance because the National Center for Community Policing is located in the School of Criminal Justice at MSU (Benson, 1992, 1993; Trojanowicz, Benson & Trojanowicz, 1988).

The MSU campus (located in East Lansing) is geographically large and has over 40,000 students, approximately 4,000 faculty and staff, and many visitors. The pristine campus has extensive nature trails and is intersected by the Red Cedar River. However, this idyllic environment presents safety hazards. Typical problems include assaults of female students while walking the trails after dark, and the activities of drug-wielding inner-city youth from nearby Detroit.

Bruce Benson, current director of Public Safety at MSU, was involved with the first large community policing program in Flint, Michigan. When he became director of Public Safety at MSU, he strongly endorsed community policing for the campus police.

In September of 1987, a community policing program involving all Department of Public Safety (DPS) officers was made fully operational on the MSU campus (Benson, 1993; Trojanowicz, Benson & Trojanowicz, 1988). The campus was divided into three large segments, and "teams" (consisting of command and line officers) were assigned to each district. The teams of officers actively recruited students and staff to assist with the program. They also established offices in the larger dormitories (some 20,000 students at MSU reside in on-campus housing). The teams first conducted surveys and completed a needs-analysis to help determine the most pressing problems in each district. Then, working jointly with students and campus employees, they developed detailed strategies to tackle the problems.

A frequent problem on the MSU campus involved nighttime assaults occurring on the nature trails which link the libraries, museums, the student union, classrooms, and dormitories. Acutely aware of "sworn" personnel limitations, the teams solicited student volunteers to provide an escort service. Each team aggressively worked at increasing the positive interactions students had with police officers and began joint crime prevention efforts.

The University of Washington—another large university—also uses community policing on its campus. Unlike MSU, however, officers at the University of Washington make extensive use of bicycle patrols as part of their community policing strategy. The department has reported success with improving public relations, decreasing response time, patrolling secluded areas, lowering operating expenses and boosting officer morale while, at the same time, improving officers' physical fitness levels (Espinosa & Wittmier, 1991).

Midsize urban universities have also adopted community policing. The most recent example can be found at the University of Cincinnati which instituted community policing in response to increasing problems involving gun-related, drug-related, and possible gang-related activities on its campus (*University Currents,* 1994). Although the university has several branch campuses, community policing is the best strategy for treating the problems facing each branch campus. Similar to community policing efforts on other campuses, a "steering committee" was set up to solicit greater community involvement. According to Eugene Ferrara, Director of Public Safety at UC, "a university is not immune from the problems of society, but as a close-knit community, the university has an advantage in [addressing] them" (*University Currents,* 1994:2). Community policing was selected as the best method for harnessing the university's "advantage."

Other universities have also embraced community policing. For example, Virginia Commonwealth University (VCU) recently began a community policing program (Carlson, 1991). VCU enrolls about 15,000 students on its primary campus and uses 49 sworn campus police officers. To establish community policing, the officers first organized Local Management Groups (LMG) consisting of assorted members of the university community who meet regularly to formulate ways to increase positive interaction of students with the police. A survey was also developed and circulated to help meet this need. Second, police job descriptions and hiring criterion were revised to reflect principles of community policing. Next, a Corps of Preventive Specialists (COPS) was recruited and created a campus watch program that was staffed by student volunteers. Finally, similar to the Michigan State model, the campus was divided into eight sectors and officers were permanently assigned to each area. According to Carlson (1991:23), officers are responsible for "designing, initiating, and maintaining various crime-prevention programs within their assigned sectors."

SUMMARY AND CONCLUSION

Community policing continues to be adopted on increasing numbers of college campuses. Some reasons for the growing popularity of community policing include: increasing concern by the police and the campus community with issues (disorder, fear of crime, and community cohesion) once considered peripheral, the philosophical appeal of specialized police services, and increased acceptance of—and reliance on—volunteers to work with the police.

University police are in an excellent position to take advantage of community policing, partly because of their historical genesis, and partly because of their proximity to concerned and educated people. Miller and Pan (1987:27) have noted that the university policing environment is "characterized by a . . . homogeneous population of young adults . . . generally motivated to succeed." Carlson (1991:22) has suggested the "university environment may be particularly receptive to such an approach" because of "its inherent community cohesiveness." Finally, campus police continue to emphasize service over law enforcement facets of policing.

However, to be successful these programs must be rigorously evaluated and continuously revised to address changing problems on campus.

Equally important, just as the 1990 Crime Awareness and Campus Security Act mandates compilation of national-level campus crime statistics, there needs to be a national forum at which campus-based community policing practices can be shared and comprehensive research programs developed and instituted (with care taken to address the criticisms presented by Greene and Mastrofski, 1988). The National Center for Community Policing or the International Association of Campus Law Enforcement Administrators (ICLEA) are logical venues for such an effort. The Police Foundation is another competent source of research-based services.

Greater attention must also be directed toward the demographic composition of campus police forces. Ethnic sensitivity training should be made part of a regular training schedule, especially when it is not possible to immediately hire female and minority officers. Additionally, hiring older officers may also have benefits. Regardless, hiring practices and training must increasingly reflect community policing principles.

Community policing appears poised to become the dominant police strategy on campus. Therefore, it is very important to examine the issues raised in this chapter if it is to be successful.

NOTES

(1) "Temperamental diversity" refers to the reputations held by some colleges and universities (e.g., "Party U" or "Blue-Blood Academicians").

(2) The efforts at Michigan State University and Virginia Commonwealth University (discussed below) illustrate this situation.

REFERENCES

Alpert, G. and M. Moore (1983) "Measuring Police Performance in the New Paradigm of Policing." In *Performance Measures for the Criminal Justice System.* Washington, DC: U.S. Department of Justice, pp. 109–141.

Bayley, D.H. (1988) "Community Policing: A Report from the Devil's Advocate." In J. Greene and S. Mastrofski (eds.) *Community Policing: Rhetoric or Reality.* New York: Praeger, pp. 235–238.

Benson, B. (1992) "Campus Policing at Michigan State University." *Journal of Security Administration 16*(1):58–66.

Berk, R.A., A. Campbell, A., R. Klap, and B. Western (1992) "The Deterrent Effect of Arrest in Incidents of Domestic Violence: A Bayesian Analysis of Four Field Experiments." *American Sociological Review 57*(5):698–708.

Brown, L.P. and M.A. Wycoff (1987) "Policing Houston: Reducing Fear and Improving Service." *Crime and Delinquency 33*(1):71–89.

Bordner, D.C. and D.M. Petersen (1983) *Campus Policing: The Nature of University Police Work,* Lanham, MD: University Press of America.

Bowers, W.J. and J.H. Hirsch (1987) "The Impact of Foot Patrol Staffing on Crime and Disorder in Boston: An Unmet Promise." *American Journal of Police 6*(1):17–43.

Bromley, M.L. (1992) "Campus and Community Crime Rate Comparisons." *Journal of Security Administration 15*(2):49–64.

Brug, R.C. (1984) "Cal-Poly Maximizes Use of Students." *Campus Law Enforcement Journal 14*(1):45–46.

Carlson, W.R. (1991) "Community Policing at Virginia Commonwealth University: Designing Strategies for a Campus Environment." *ControlCampus Law Enforcement Journal 21*(1):22–25.

Currie, E. (1985) *Confronting Crime.* New York: Pantheon Books.

Eck, J.E. and W. Spelman (1989) "A Problem-Oriented Approach to Police Service Delivery." In D.J. Kenney (ed.) *Police and Policing.* New York: Praeger, pp. 95–111.

Espinosa, G. and R. Wittmier (1991) "Police Bicycle Patrols: An Integral Part of Community Policing." *Campus Law Enforcement Journal 21*(1):10–13.

Esposito, D. and D. Stormer (1989) "The Multiple Roles of Campus Law Enforcement." *Campus Law Enforcement Journal 19*(1):26–30.

Fernandez, A. and A.J. Lizotte (1994). "An Analysis of the Relationship Between Campus Crime and Community Crime: Reciprocal Effects?" In B.S. Fisher and J.J. Sloan, III (eds.) *Campus Crime: Legal, Social and Policy Perspectives.* Springfield, IL: Charles C Thomas.

Friedmann, R.R. (1987) "Citizen's Attitudes Toward the Police: Results from an Experiment in Community Policing in Israel." *American Journal of Police 6*(1):67–93.

Gelber, S. (1972) *The Role of Campus Security in the College Setting.* Washington, DC: U.S. Government Printing Office.

Greenberg, M. (1987) "Harnessing Campus Humanism for the Sake of Public Safety." *Campus Law Enforcement Journal 17*(1):41–42.

Greene, J.R. (1987) "Foot Patrol and Community Policing: Past Practices and Future Prospects." *American Journal of Police 6*(1):1–15.

Greene, J.R. and S.D. Mastrofski (1988) *Community Policing: Rhetoric or Reality.* New York: Praeger.

Greene, J.R. and R.B. Taylor (1988) "Community-Based Policing and Foot Patrol: Issues of Theory and Evaluation." In J.R. Greene, and S.D. Mastrofski (eds.) *Community Policing: Rhetoric or Reality.* New York: Praeger, pp. 195–224.

Hillery, G.A. (1955) "Definitions of Community: Areas of Agreement." *Rural Sociology 20*(1):111–123.

Jackson, E. (1992) "Campus Police Embrace Community Based Approach." *The Police Chief 59*(12):63–64.

Kelling, G.L. and J.K. Stewart (1989) "Neighborhoods and Police: The Maintenance of Civil Authority." *Perspectives on Policing.* Washington, DC: U.S. Department of Justice.

Kelling, G., A. Pate, D. Dieckman, and C. Brown (1974) *The Kansas City Preventive Patrol Experiment: A Summary Report.* Washington, DC: The Police Foundation.

Lanier, M.M. (1993) "Explication and Measurement of the Theoretical Constructs Underlying Community Policing." Unpublished doctoral dissertation, Michigan State University.

Lederman, D. (1993) "Colleges Report 7,500 Violent Crimes on Their Campuses in First Annual Statements Required Under Federal Law." *The Chronicle of Higher Education,* January 20, pp. A32–A43.

Manning, P.K. (1989) "Community Policing." In R.G. Dunham, and G.P. Alpert (eds.) *Critical Issues in Policing.* Prospect Heights, IL: Waveland Press, pp. 395–405.

—— (1988) "Community Policing as a Drama of Control." In J.R. Greene and S.D. Mastrofski (eds.) *Community Policing: Rhetoric or Reality.* New York: Praeger, pp. 27–46.

—— (1984) "Community Policing." *American Journal of Police 3*(2):205–227.

Mansour, N. and J.J. Sloan (1992) "Campus Crime and Campus Communities: Theoretical and Empirical Linkages." Paper presented at the 1992 Annual Meetings of the Academy of Criminal Justice Sciences.

Meenaghan, T.W. (1972) "What Means 'Community'?" *Social Work 19*(1):6–94.

Miller, J.L. and M.J. Pan (1987) "Student Perceptions of Campus Police: The Effects of Personal Characteristics and Police Contacts." *American Journal of Police 6*(1):27–44.

Minar, D.W. and B.S. Greer (1969) *The Concept of Community.* Chicago: Aldine.

Moore, M.H. and R.C. Trojanowicz (1988) "Policing and the Fear of Crime." *Perspectives on Policing.* Washington, DC: U.S. Department of Justice.

Mullendore, P. (1991) "The Federal Campus Crime Reporting Act: Challenges and Opportunities for Campus and Local Law Enforcement." *Journal of California Law Enforcement 24*(2):110–116.

Munro, J.L. (1987) "The Decision for Community Policing: The Cases of Victoria and South Australia." *Police Studies 10*(2):140–153.

Pate, A. and E. Hamilton (1992) "Formal and Informal Deterrents to Domestic Violence: The Dade County Spouse Assault Experiment." *American Sociological Review 57*(5):691–697.

Pate, A. (1986) *Reducing Fear of Crime in Houston and Newark: A Summary Report.* Washington, DC: The Police Foundation.

Police Foundation (1981) *The Newark Foot Patrol Experiment.* Washington, DC: The Police Foundation.

Riechers, L.M. and R.R. Roberg (1990) "Community Policing: A Critical Review of Underlying Assumptions." *Journal of Police Science and Administration 17*(2):105–114.

Schwartz, J. and T. Exter (1989) "All Our Children." *American Demographics 11*(5):34–37.

"Major Crime Varies in Largest U.S. Universities" (1985) *Security Newsletter 15*(1):19.

Seng, M.J. (1995) "The Crime Awareness and Campus Security Act: Some Observations, Critical Comments, and Recommendations." In B.S. Fisher and J.J. Sloan, III (eds.) *Campus Crime: Legal, Social, and Policy Perspectives.* Springfield, IL: Charles C Thomas.

Seng, M. and N. Koehler (1993) "The Crime Awareness and Campus Security Act: A Critical Analysis." *Journal of Crime and Justice 16*(1):97–110.

Sherman, L.W., D.A. Smith, J.D. Schmidt, and D.R. Rogan (1992) "Crime, Punishment, and Stake in Conformity: Legal and Informal Control of Domestic Violence." *American Sociological Review 57:*680–690.

Sloan, J.J. (1994) "The Correlates of Campus Crime: An Analysis of Reported Crimes on College and University Campuses." *Journal of Criminal Justice 22*(1):51–61.

—— (1992) "The Modern Campus Police: An Analysis of Their Evolution, Structure, and Function." *American Journal of Police 11*(1):85–104.

Sparrow, M.K. (1988) "Implementing Community Policing." *Perspectives on Policing.* Washington, DC: U.S. Department of Justice.

Trojanowicz, R.C. and B. Bucqueroux (1990) *Community Policing: A Contemporary Perspective.* Cincinnati, OH: Anderson Publishing.

Trojanowicz, R.C. and D.L. Carter (1990) "The Changing Face of America." *FBI Law Enforcement Bulletin 59*(1):6.

—— (1988) *The Philosophy and Role of Community Policing.* East Lansing, MI: National Neighborhood Foot Patrol Center.

Trojanowicz, R.C., B. Benson, and S. Trojanowicz (1988) *Community Policing: University Input into Campus Police Policy-Making.* East Lansing, MI: National Neighborhood Foot Patrol Center.

"Drug Arrests Bring Police Interest in Tougher Rules." (1994) *University Currents,* March 3, pp. 1,22.

Wilson, J.Q. (1983b) *Thinking About Crime.* New York, NY: Vintage Books.

—— (1983a) *Crime and Public Policy.* San Francisco, CA: Institute for Contemporary Studies.

Wilson, J.Q. and G. Kelling (1982) "The Police and Neighborhood Safety: Broken Windows." *Atlantic Monthly 127:*29–38.

POSTSCRIPT

As campus crime continues to be the focus of the media, the judicial and legislative branches of government, and social scientific inquiry, campus administrators face difficult times. They face lawsuits from campus crime victims, various mandates from government to report and disseminate their crime statistics and crime prevention programs, and demands from students, their parents, and other interested parties to "do something" about the problem. However, their decisions must not be made hastily nor be based on insufficient information.

The collected works in this volume present a current picture of the arena of campus crime research. They address many prominent legal, social, and policy issues associated with campus crime. More important, these works are a foundation on which future research and policy can be based. They have, however, only "scratched the surface."

As many of the contributors point out, much more needs to be done to more fully understand the complex issue of crime on college and university campuses. Campus administrators can no longer ignore, dismiss, or "cover up" crimes occurring on their campuses. Administrators must face the problem, develop new policies to address the problem, or suffer serious financial and public relations consequences.

Yet, much remains unknown about campus crime. Basic questions like "how much crime is there on college campuses?" remain unanswered. Additionally, little is known about the dynamics and causal mechanisms of campus crime. Is campus crime the product of "outsiders" preying on campus community members? What role do institutional characteristics play in shaping the extent and nature of crime on college campuses? How do the "routine activities" of campus community members affect the likelihood of victimization? Researchers and policymakers alike must first answer these basic questions, or else policy decisions about security, policing, and even campus design will be flawed.

For too long, campus policymakers left the problem of crime on their campuses to the police or security departments, or to student affairs.

Campus administrators must realize that addressing the problem of crime on their campuses involves interdepartmental cooperation. Expertise in campus design and planning, security and policing, student life, and research design and program evaluation must be incorporated into policy decisions by administrators. Importantly, this expertise exists on most campuses; administrators need only seek it out. It is no longer enough for administrators to leave the problem *solely* to the police or security experts.

Much remains to be done to address the problem of campus crime. Basic questions about the extent, nature, and causes of campus crime remained unanswered. Legislation intended to assist with the problem is flawed. Decisions on the future of campus policing remain to be made. The collected works in this volume, we believe, provide the impetus for taking the next steps necessary to understand, control, and reduce campus crime, as well as to develop effective policies to address the problem.

AUTHOR INDEX

V

van Dijk, J., 144, 155
Verma, A., 153
Viano, E.C., 173
Vollmer, August, 231

W

Walker, S., 231, 245
Wandersman, A., 184, 207
Ward, S.K., 81, 101, 158, 160, 163, 169, 170, 171, 178
Warr, M., 180, 181, 208
Warshaw, R., 158, 163, 166, 167, 169, 170, 171, 178
Wasilchick, T., 134, 154
Watts, D., 171, 173
Webb, J., 230, 245
Weiner, L., 164, 165, 174
Weis, K., 178
Weitzman, L.M., 160, 161, 164, 168, 174
Western, B., 255, 260

White, G.F., 133, 135, 155, 169, 170, 171
White, S., 102, 158, 160, 163, 178
Wilkins, Deborah L., x, xvi, 78, 179
Williams, J.R., 217, 226
Williams, K., 81, 101, 158, 160, 163, 169, 170, 171, 178
Wilson, J.Q., 129, 155, 183, 208, 246, 247, 263
Wilson, K.R., 81, 102, 178
Wilson, O.W., 231
Wirth, L., 184, 208
Wisniewski, N., 81, 101, 175
Witham, D.C., 245
Wittmier, 258, 261
Wooldredge, John D., x, xv, 43, 50, 77, 103, 104, 106, 111, 113, 120, 121, 122, 185, 190, 191, 209
Wycoff, M.A., 185, 205, 250, 261

Z

Zamble, E., 185, 209
Zellman, G.L., 175
Zimmer, C.G., 171, 177

SUBJECT INDEX